Volume 1   Train the Trainer Guide

Foundations & Delivery

The Basics to Becoming a
Successful Trainer

Info-
line

An Info-line Collection

*Linking People,
Learning & Performance*

Info-line is a series of "how-to" reference tools; each issue is a concisely written, practical guidebook that provides in-depth coverage of a single topic vital to training and HRD job performance. *Info-line* is available by subscription and single copy purchase.

ISBN: 1-56286-278-2
Library of Congress Catalog Card No. 00-110773

Printed in the United States of America.

Volume 1   Train the Trainer Guide

Foundations & Delivery

The Basics to Becoming a Successful Trainer

Editor
Cat Sharpe Russo

Contributing Editor
Ann Bruen

Production
Kathleen Schaner

Introduction

Dear Readers,

Today, workplace learning and performance is experiencing a ground swell of activity. Propelled by emerging technology and ever-increasing demands on productivity and process reengineering, management at all levels in all organizations is calling on the training department to come up with answers. Whether it is called training, performance improvement, workplace learning, or on-the-job education, the way individuals learn and the steps trainers use to put learning into place remain grounded in solid principles of adult learning, presentation skills, curriculum design, evaluation, and technology.

Since its inception in 1984, *Info-line* has provided readers with a quick, useful means of acquiring new information and applying that information on the job. Many people use *Info-line* as a tool for new trainers, to bring them up to speed without spending too much time studying "the books"—*self-directed learning* before the term was ever popular. The fact that the training profession sees new entrants every day is one of the reasons *Info-line* has been so successful. Because practitioners seem to enter, leave, and reenter the field frequently, *Info-line's* founding mission of being "the training reference tool" with a long shelf life has become a self-fulfilling prophecy.

Realizing that many of our issues needed updating, we undertook a four-year project to revise a substantial number of our oldies, but goodies. At the same time, we made a concerted effort to publish new topics that reflected feedback from our reader surveys. Combining more than 75 revised titles with 60 new issues, we have now put together a comprehensive *Train the Trainer Guide*, which is divided into five volumes. Beginning with the foundations for training, each volume focuses on a specific area that not only helps novice practitioners acquire new knowledge but also serves as a handy reference tool for seasoned practitioners.

Here is how we devised the volumes:

Volume 1: Foundations & Delivery. Containing everything you need to get started as a trainer, this collection pays special attention to learning and training styles, good learning environments, facilities set-up, and presentation skills.

Volume 2: Instructional Design & Implementation. After reading this volume, you will have an essential understanding of instructional design and how to develop a training curriculum. As an introduction, you can learn project management and budgeting skills, vital to any curriculum developer.

Volume 3: Training Programs. Here are programs you can implement. Selected from our most popular issues, the contents of this volume will get you started with facilitation and workshop skills. Using this foundation, you then can move on to presenting programs based on these titles: orientation, mentoring, succession planning, change management, and much more.

Volume 4: Measurement & Evaluation. The best way to quantify the results of your training is to measure and evaluate those results. Here is an all-inclusive volume that details how to collect data from numerous sources, including benchmarking, focus groups, paper evaluations, and so forth. Then you will have all the methods available for calculating your return-on-investment as well as special evaluation practices.

Volume 5: Applying Technology to Learning. Emerging technology, especially e-learning, is having a major impact on training and the delivery of training. This collection gives you the best learning technologies and e-learning concepts for training applications.

Whether you are using an individual volume by itself or as part of the complete set, I hope you find these books a useful addition to the *Info-line* series of collections.

Sincerely,

Cat Sharpe Russo
Editor

Basic Training for Trainers

Issue 8808

Basic Training for Trainers

Editorial Staff for 8808

Consultants
Mary Lippitt, Ph.D.
David W. Miller, Ph.D.

Revised 1998

Editor
Cat Sharpe

Contributing Editor
Ann Bruen

ASTD Internal Consultant
Phil Anderson

Basic Training for Trainers

According to a 1996 ASTD study, U.S. corporations currently invest more than $55 billion in formal employee education and retraining. And some experts believe that the need for employee training could double by the end of the century because of:

- the need for the United States to sustain a competitive edge in a global economy

- rapid changes in technology

- an increasing shortage of skilled labor

- continued shortcomings in the U.S. educational system to prepare students for future employment

This means that organizations are looking increasingly within their own ranks as well as to professional trainers for education and retraining. With this growing need, more people are being called upon to train others in management, technical, communication, and technology skills.

But a new trainer faces a situation something like the proverbial mosquito in the nudist colony: Where does one begin? For our purposes, we will begin with the question, "What is a trainer?"

The answer is: "A trainer is anyone who helps people increase their knowledge or skill." This can include, for example:

- showing a new employee how to use the voice mail system

- instructing an individual on how to use a word processing software package

- teaching a person how to make a product

Through instruction and practice, a trainer helps other people:

- gain new awareness
- gain new knowledge, skills, or behaviors
- achieve a defined performance standard

Trainers tend to focus their efforts in one of four areas:

1. Technical skills (on-the-job training in specialized fields such as electronics or health care).

2. Work management skills (management-by-objectives, strategic planning, decision making, problem solving, performance consulting).

3. People management skills (performance, delegating, conducting appraisals, setting skills standards).

4. Personnel management skills (stress, career planning, diversity, workplace).

When is a trainer a facilitator or a teacher? Typically, we think of trainers as people whose primary focus is on relaying content, technical or otherwise, while a facilitator's main focus is on learning through group process. A teacher brings to mind someone whose main teaching method is lecturing and who is responsible for discipline. Many individuals in the human resource development (HRD) and performance fields have strong feelings about these differences.

To many, a good trainer is also a good facilitator and a good teacher. Since a trainer deals in the work environment, he or she works primarily with adults. Therefore, a good trainer uses a variety of appropriate methods to help a broad range of adults acquire new skills and knowledge effectively and efficiently.

Learning How to Train

There are four essential areas of basic knowledge and skills that a trainer needs:

1. Learning theory.

2. Training styles and methods.

3. Presentation and delivery.

4. Evaluation.

For the purposes of this issue, we are assuming that the new trainer will be presenting a packaged training program—one that has been designed on the classic Instructional Systems

ISD: What Is It?

Instructional Systems Development (ISD) is based on the belief that training is most effective when it provides learners with a clear statement of what they must be able to do as a result of training, and how their performance will be evaluated. The program is then designed to teach the skills through hands-on practice, or performance-based instruction.

There are many ISD models, among them the ADDIE model. The name ADDIE represents the first letter contained in each of the five elements of this model: Analysis, Design, Development, Implementation, and Evaluation. Below is a short description of each component.

Analysis—the who, what, where, when, why, and by whom of the design process. It includes analysis of:

- needs
- goals and objectives
- trainees' profiles
- delivery systems
- resources and constraints

Design—the planning stage. It consists of the following:

- developing instructional objectives
- identifying the learning steps required
- developing tests to show mastery of tasks to be trained
- listing entry behaviors required
- developing the sequence and structure of the course

Development—the phase in which training materials and content are selected and developed based on learning objectives. This phase includes development of:

- the instructional management plan

- training materials (instructor guides, agendas, reading material, audiovisual aids)

- training methods

- program evaluation materials (evaluation plan, checklists, tests, questionnaires)

- training documentation (trainees' records and course documentation, such as objectives, course material, and lists of instructors)

Implementation—the phase during which the course is taught and evaluated.

Evaluation—the ongoing process of developing and improving instructional materials based on evaluations conducted during and following implementation.

For more information, see *Info-line* No. 9706, "Basics of Instructional Systems Development."

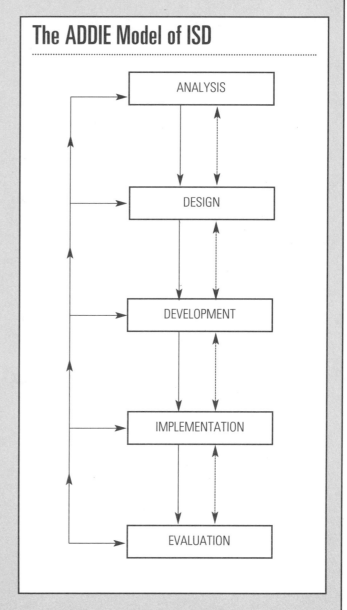

The ADDIE Model of ISD

ANALYSIS → DESIGN → DEVELOPMENT → IMPLEMENTATION → EVALUATION

Development (ISD) model (see the box on the previous page). The trainer needs to remember that within each designed program, there is a lot of flexibility depending on the number, background, and learning styles of the participants; the learning environment; and other variables. In addition, the trainer will need to be familiar with such items as:

- effective ways to present the material
- how to deal with problem participants
- how to keep momentum going
- how to define what participants have learned

Often a line manager or subject matter expert (SME) is called upon to train. Simply having a skill or specialized knowledge does not automatically mean that a person can train others in that skill or convey knowledge. First trainers must master a set of behaviors (knowledge, skills, and attitudes—KSAs) that people need to have in order to train others as effectively and efficiently as possible. This translates to a focus on the learning needed—the information, performance, and perceptions that employees need to acquire.

Successful trainers come, as they say, in all shapes and sizes. But most successful trainers have these two personal qualities:

Presence—the ability to hold people's attention and be taken seriously.

Self-confidence—the ability to handle skepticism or rejection from the inevitable hostile participant who for one reason or another does not want to be there.

This *Info-line* presents the four basic skills and knowledge areas in some detail and features some tips on the art of training gleaned from experienced trainers.

Learning Theory

Malcolm S. Knowles has written extensively about learning styles, particularly the perceived learning styles of children (popularly called pedagogy) and those of adults (andragogy). Knowles and other adult-learning theorists note that since adults have a vast amount and variety of experience from which they have learned, and are responsible for making their own decisions and living with the consequences, they:

- need to see the relevance of the training to their own life experience

- learn best when they have some control over their own learning experience

- have a vast store of knowledge and experience from which to draw and apply to the current learning situation

- regard growth in self-understanding equally as important as growth in learning

- need to take an active part in the learning process

- generally learn best in task- or experience-oriented learning situations

- learn best in cooperative climates that encourage risk taking and experimentation

The *pedagogical* learning style traditionally has been applied to the teacher-in-front-of-the-student situation, where the learners absorb knowledge imparted from the teacher. But Knowles himself acknowledges that the issue is not andragogy vs. pedagogy, since both youth and adult learning situations can and should encompass a variety of learning styles and methods. The fact remains, however, that adult learning styles generally follow the andragogical model.

Adult learning is most effective when the learner can satisfy a personal goal or need. According to Knowles, adults will respond to *extrinsic* factors, such as promotions, job changes, or better working conditions. But more potent motivators are *intrinsic*, such as self-esteem, recognition by peers, better quality of life, greater self-confidence, or the need for achievement and satisfaction.

Although a well-designed training program includes a variety of exercises and training methods, it is important for the trainer to understand adult learning styles and why some techniques may work better in some situations than others.

Basic Trainer Competencies

The following list is selected and adapted from ASTD's *Models for HRD Practice,* which describes the competencies needed by people who are involved in the whole range of activities composing the field of human resource development. This list focuses on the basic competencies required by trainers.

Technical Competencies

Adult Learning Understanding: knowing how adults acquire and use knowledge, skills, attitudes; understanding individual differences in learning.

Competency Identification Skill: identifying the knowledge and skill requirements of jobs, tasks, and roles.

Computer Competence: understanding and or use of computer applications (various software programs, CBT training, multimedia applications, Internet, intranets, World Wide Web).

Electronic Systems Skill: having knowledge of functions, features, and potential applications of electronic systems for the delivery of training and management, such as teleconferencing, video conferencing, satellite/remote conferencing, electronic meeting support, and Electronic Performance Support Systems (EPSS).

Facilities Skill: planning and coordinating logistics in an efficient and cost-effective manner.

Objectives Preparation Skill: preparing clear statements that describe desired outputs.

Performance Observation Skill: tracking and describing behaviors and their effects.

Subject Matter Understanding: knowing the content of a given function or discipline being addressed.

Training Theories/Techniques Understanding: knowing the theories and methods used in training; understanding their appropriate use.

Business Competencies

Business Understanding: knowing how the functions of a business work and relate to one another; knowing the economic impact of business decisions.

Cost-Benefit Analysis Skill: assessing alternatives in terms of their financial, psychological, and strategic advantages and disadvantages.

Organization Behavior Understanding: seeing organizations as dynamic, political, economic, and social systems that have multiple goals; using this larger perspective as a framework for understanding and influencing events and change.

Organization Understanding: knowing the strategy, structure, power networks, financial position, and systems of a specific organization.

Project Management Skill: planning, organizing, and monitoring work.

Interpersonal Competencies

Coaching Skill: helping individuals recognize and understand personal needs, values, problems, alternatives, and goals.

Feedback Skill: communicating information, opinions, observations, and conclusions so that they are understood and can be acted upon.

Group Process Skill: influencing groups so that tasks, relationships, and individual needs are addressed.

Presentation Skill: presenting information orally so that an intended purpose is achieved.

Questioning Skill: gathering information from stimulating insight in individuals and groups through use of interviews, questionnaires, and other probing methods.

Relationship Building Skill: establishing relationships and networks across a broad range of people and groups.

Writing Skill: preparing written material that follows generally accepted rules of style and form, is appropriate for the intended audience, is creative, and accomplishes its purpose.

Intellectual Competencies

Data Reduction Skill: scanning, synthesizing, and drawing conclusions from data.

Information Search Skill: gathering information from printed and other recorded sources; identifying and using information specialists and reference services and aids.

Intellectual Versatility: recognizing, exploring, and using a broad range of ideas and practices; thinking logically and creatively without undue influence from personal biases.

Model Building Skill: conceptualizing and developing theoretical and practical frameworks that describe complex ideas in understandable ways.

Observing Skill: recognizing objectively what is happening in or across situations.

Self-Knowledge: knowing one's personal values, needs, interests, style, and competencies and their effects on others.

Adults, it has been shown, gain information in two ways:

actively, through direct involvement

or

passively, through absorption of information.

Then the information is processed either:

deductively, from the general to the specific

or

inductively, from the specific to the general.

See the chart on the next page for training applications of these learning styles.

The ultimate objective of training is to increase performance through a change in behavior. The adult learner generally goes through the following four levels of learning to reach the level of behavioral change:

1. Awareness: the learner experiences or is introduced to the learning situation or event.

2. Understanding or knowledge: the participant places the learning event in context, connecting causes, components, and consequences associated with the event.

3. Skill: the learner applies the understanding or knowledge learned.

4. Attitude: the learner sees value in the application of the new knowledge and skills.

At the skill level, the learner can perform the new behavior; at the attitude level, he or she wants to perform the new behavior.

Addressing Participant Learning Preferences

As mentioned previously, adults have different ways of learning; some gather information actively, some passively. Some are better at processing information inductively and some learn better through deductive reasoning. The trainer who recognizes these differences will include a variety of training techniques to address these learning preferences. This chart shows how some training methods apply to the different learning preferences.

	Gathering Information		Processing Information	
	Active	Passive	Deductive	Inductive
Lecture/presentation		X	X	
Group discussion	X		X	
Readings	X	X		
Simulation and role play	X			X
Programmed instruction	X			X
Games	X			X
Panels		X	X	
Demonstration		X		X
Case study	X		X	

Created by Mary Lippitt

Training Styles and Methods

The classical style of teaching is based on the instructive or didactic style. It is generally regarded as teacher led and subject centered, suiting the previously mentioned pedagogical learning style. Many now believe, however, that the facilitative or participatory training style—in which the trainer guides the learner to "discover" what is to be learned—is more appropriate for adult learners. It is defined as trainer facilitated and learner centered, better suited in most cases for the andragogical (adult) learning style.

Most adult learning situations are more suited to the facilitative or participatory style, but the instructive or didactic style has its place in certain situations. When the trainer is aware of the differences in learning and teaching styles, then he or she can consciously apply what is most appropriate for the learner and the situation. The scale on the next page will help you assess your training methods and style, from the participatory (1) to the didactic (5).

A trainer knowledgeable in adult learning theory can then apply that knowledge to his or her style and method of training. All predesigned training programs should designate appropriate training methods throughout the course. It is important, however, to know the variety of training or facilitating methods available to use according to learners' needs and the information that has to be learned.

Here are some widely used training methods:

■ *Lecture*
This is probably the most popular training method. Here, the trainer "stands and delivers" the information to be learned. Properly designed lectures can impart a lot of information to varied groups of learners, but they require superior presentation skills and limit audience participation.

Training Styles Scale

Participatory	Didactic	Score				
The trainer elicits examples from others.	The trainer provides examples.	1	2	3	4	5
The goals and objectives are flexible.	The goals and objectives are established.	1	2	3	4	5
Learners influence timing and pace of the program.	The trainer controls program timing or pace of learning.	1	2	3	4	5
Design options are built into the program.	There is a single design.	1	2	3	4	5
The program relies on practice.	The program relies on conceptual understanding.	1	2	3	4	5
Learners are assumed to be experienced or knowledgeable.	Learners are assumed inexperienced or uninformed.	1	2	3	4	5
The program addresses the skill level of training.	The program addresses the awareness or knowledge level.	1	2	3	4	5
The trainer asks questions.	The trainer makes statements.	1	2	3	4	5
The trainer seeks alternatives, creativity, and originality.	The trainer seeks consistency.	1	2	3	4	5
Participants are seen as the primary resource.	The trainer is seen as the primary resource.	1	2	3	4	5
The trainer relies on active training methods.	The trainer relies on passive methods such as lecture.	1	2	3	4	5
The trainer uses ongoing or midcourse evaluation.	The trainer uses end-of-course evaluation.	1	2	3	4	5

SCORING

On a scale of 1 to 5, 1 equaling fully participatory and 5, fully didactic, circle the most appropriate score. Scores of 40 or higher are appropriate for briefings and for orientation events. Training targeted at adult learners is generally more effective when the scores are below 25.

Created by Mary Lippett and David W. Miller

■ *Group Discussion*

This is an informal training method with a leader or moderator to guide the sharing of learners' information and experience. Discussions need to be well organized and limited to small groups. Trainers and participants all benefit from the opportunity to contribute to the learning activity, but this teaching method can be time consuming. (See the box below). Sometimes, a trainer will encounter participants who are unresponsive or disruptive—those who talk too much, or not enough, or who monopolize the discussions. For solutions to such situations, see *Tips for Dealing with Problem Participants* on the next page.

■ *Readings*

In this method, assigned readings contribute to the learners' store of knowledge. The readings can augment information acquired through lecture or discussion. For maximum effectiveness, learners should be encouraged to analyze what they have read.

Facilitating Group Work

Experienced trainers know that facilitating group work does not just happen. They have learned from their own experiences how to foster cooperative learning in a supportive learning environment—a key element in adult learning—by following these principles.

■ *Would You Mind Repeating…?*

Questions are a trainer's most powerful tool. People can avoid thinking during a lecture or a speech, but they cannot avoid it when they are questioned. They may not answer, but the can't *not* think. And when they think, they are bound to learn. Here are some proven questioning tips and techniques:

- Know what questions you want the group to answer. Write them down in your trainer's guide in larger print than your lecture notes.

- Give trainees a chance to share their knowledge and experience from the way you phrase your questions: "Joan, you have expertise in this area. What you do think…?"

- Your key questions may be found in the course objectives. If the objective reads, "Participants will list three ways to arrange a training room and explain the purposes and effects of each," your question becomes, "What different room arrangements have you experienced, and what are the advantages and disadvantages of each?"

- If the group strays from the original question, you can get them back on track most easily simply by restating the question.

■ *Silence Is…*

This sounds obvious, but wait for the answer after you ask a question. Listen to what the participants say so well that you can say it back to them. Paraphrase to let them know they have been heard and to check your own understanding. Roam around the training space just listening to how the participants are handling the task at hand and what they are saying.

■ *When Small Groups Are Working*

During the time that participants are working in groups, you can assess their progress by doing the following things:

- Check each group to see whether the directions and objectives are clear. Ask: "Excuse me—is everyone here clear on the task?"

- Keep the groups on the task—and yourself out of the authority role—by sitting down or kneeling by the table (height is imposing) and saying, "I'm just here to listen in—is that OK with you?" or "What does anyone else in the group think is the answer to Jim's question?"

- Check to see how far each group has gotten on the task and how much more time each feels it needs to complete the task. Then announce a compromise time to the entire group: "We have three more minutes."

Created by David W. Miller

■ *Simulation and Role Play*

This is a technique in which participants are assigned a predetermined "role" to act out a given situation in order to solve a problem or achieve a level of understanding. This method is not appropriate for large groups, or for participants who may feel threatened or are too self-conscious to take part.

■ *Games*

This method uses competitive activities governed by rules that define players' actions and determine outcomes. Games provide high group member involvement, while facilitating meaningful and fun learning. They can also be used as icebreakers or warm-ups for new groups.

■ *Panels*

In this method, a moderated group of three to five experts read prepared statements, then discuss them with one another and respond to audience questions. Panels provide different opinions and thereby provoke better discussions. The frequent change of speaker keeps attention from lagging.

■ *Demonstration*

This is an activity in which a trainer shows learners how to successfully perform a given task through demonstration, description, and explanation. Demonstrations stimulate interest and engage the audience's attention. They should be carefully planned and limited to small groups.

Tips for Dealing with Problem Participants

Most training sessions will have at least one person who is "not with the program." By anticipating possible disruptions, the trainer can plan for effective action to handle any problems. Here are some suggested solutions to situations in which the individual does the following things:

Talks too often. Ask the rest of the group: "What does anyone else think about this point?" or "Who else has some ideas?" or "Let's make sure everyone gets a chance to contribute before any one person speaks twice." Or, talk to the person outside the meeting, describe his or her behavior and its effects in factual terms, and ask the person what the solution might be. For example, you might say: "Jack, you made some helpful points today. However, you tended to add something after each other person made a contribution. Did you notice how few others spoke? Mary and Ted hardly said a thing. What could you do to encourage others to contribute?"

Talks too long. Wait for a pause, however brief, and interrupt, saying: "Could you summarize your idea in a few words so I can write it down?"

Talks to someone else at length. Say: "Pardon me, John. We can't hear what you and Sue are saying. Would you mind sharing it with all of us?" or "John, what are your thoughts on the point Marian just raised?"

Brings up personal or irrelevant issues. Say: "Sue, I'm not clear how that fits the issue we are talking about. Could you help me?"

Talks too little. Simply ask: "Fred, what are your thoughts on this question?" or "Helen, you're new to the group, so I think your views could be especially valuable. What do you think?"

Recycles what's already been decided rather than focusing on the question at hand. Say: "Our purpose is not to go over what's already been decided. It is to identify potential problems coming from those decisions and to work out solutions. Now, what do you see as a way to resolve the problem of..., Fred?"

Challenges your ideas or opinions. Try one of the following:

- Cite the authorities you used as a source and acknowledge that other authorities (name them if possible) think otherwise.

- Acknowledge that the challenger's idea or opinion has merit, and that you will need to think about the effect it has on your own thinking.

- Ask the group what they think about the challenger's idea or opinion.

In general, never put down a problem participant; try to make a positive comment while at the same time asking for a change in behavior. Deal with the problem early before it becomes serious.

■ *Case Study*

In this method, a statement of a problem or "case" is followed by group problem solving to find solutions for complex issues. This method allows students to apply the new knowledge and skills they have acquired through other teaching methods.

Presentation and Delivery

No matter how many participatory exercises are built into a training program, the trainer will frequently need to take the role of lecturer or presenter. Trainers sometimes fail in their objective of changing behavior or attitudes simply because their presentation style failed to "grab" their audience.

Some people simply have "it"—*it* being the ability to capture and hold the audience's attention. But *it* can be learned. Here are some tips on achieving the kind of presence that grabs and holds an audience. For additional information, see *Info-lines* No. 8411, "10 Great Games and How to Use Them"; No. 8911, "Icebreakers"; No. 8606, "Make Every Presentation a Winner"; No. 9106, "More Great Games"; and No. 9409, "Improve Your Communication and Speaking Skills."

Use Effective Openings

The opening sets the tone for the presentation and can make or break it. A good opening will do the following things:

- capture the audience's attention
- reveal the trainer's training style
- raise the comfort level of the audience
- introduce the topic of the presentation

Any number of techniques can be used to warm up the audience, such as the following:

- Share a personal anecdote related to the subject.

- Ask questions relevant to the subject.

- Use creative introductions. Rather than simply going around the room having participants introduce themselves, have them introduce one another, or respond to specific topics, such as "the most important book I have read," or "what I hope to learn from this course."

Set Expectations

Let the participants know what to expect from the beginning. Basic information can be worked into the opening or presented immediately afterward. Participants will need to know:

One another—either directly or through techniques described in the above resources.

Objectives of the session—what they will learn and why it is important.

Instructional techniques—how they will learn: through discussions, films, guest speakers.

Evaluation expectations—how their learning will be evaluated and how they will critique your presentation.

Agenda—times for sessions, plus any assignment schedules.

Structure Your Presentation

A trainer's job often calls for giving a structured presentation. In his book *Secrets of a Successful Trainer,* Clark Lambert lists four elements of structuring an effective oral presentation.

1. Opener.
   This element should get the audience's attention; introduce the key point(s) of the presentation; establish audience rapport; state a benefit to be gained by the listeners; and create anticipation for the rest of the presentation.

2. Bridge.
   This element is the transition to the key points, by way of example or anecdote.

Audiovisual Aids

Training programs often will provide sample flipcharts, audiotapes, overhead projector transparencies, and other training aids. The designed programs also tell the trainer which aids are appropriate and when to use them. But a basic knowledge of training aids increases the trainer's confidence and skill level. Here are some commonly used audiovisual aids, some of their advantages and disadvantages, and tips on their use.

Aids	Advantages	Disadvantages	Tips
Slides	Compact, relatively easy to use, economical, high impact.	Inhibit eye contact, note taking, and discussion.	Preset projector and screen and double-check order and position of slides.
Flipcharts	Flexible, easy to make and use, economical, promote good interaction.	Limited viewing distance, markers often dry out, do not last.	Check sight lines, quantity of paper, and markers. Use dark colors that show up; red reads particularly well from a distance. Do not talk to the chart or stand in front of it when you are not writing on it.
Overhead Projectors	Readily available, easy to use, good with large groups.	Limited sight lines, danger of keystone images (top or bottom of image is larger than the other).	Check order of transparencies. Adjust the projector so that the beam hits the screen straight on, not at an angle.
Films	High interest, lend credibility.	Decreased interaction, high cost, hard to transport, more difficult to use the projector.	Preset the projector and screen. Thread and focus the projector. Check sound levels.
Videotapes	High interest, easily transported, less expensive than movies.	Limited audience size without multiple monitors.	Check unit operation and sound levels. Make sure all participants can see and hear well.
Audiotapes	Portable, set a mood.	Limited attention span since there is no visual stimulation, no interaction.	Rewind and cue up tape. Check machine operation and sound levels. Try to limit segments to two or three minutes.

For more information, see *Info-line* No. 8410, "How to Prepare and Use Effective Visual Aids," which outlines how to make and use overhead transparencies, 35mm slides, and flipcharts.

3. Main Body.
This element provides the heart of the talk, supported by facts, figures, and examples as well as a rationale for the presentation.

4. Close.
This is one of the most important elements of the entire presentation. It should paraphrase key points, restate the most important point, and contain a benefit statement that tells the audience what is in it for them.

Develop a Presence

The quality of speaker "presence" can be developed. A presenter who has it will exhibit many of the following qualities:

- pleasant, appropriate appearance

- effective use of body language—natural, open gestures

- a well-paced delivery style, with effective use of the pause for emphasis and reinforcement

- a well-pitched voice, loud enough to be heard well without being grating or annoying

- genuine enthusiasm and sincerity

- effective eye contact with the audience

- a natural, relaxed style that puts the audience at ease

Evaluation

The information below is designed to complement the evaluation portions incorporated into most training programs. Donald Kirkpatrick developed what is perhaps the best known and most widely used framework for evaluation. His four levels of evaluation are closely related to the four levels of learning (awareness, knowledge, skill, behavior), discussed earlier.

Training is evaluated on each of the four levels to determine the following:

Awareness or reaction. Are the trainees happy with what they are getting? Is the material relevant? Is the training design appropriate? How effective is the trainer's leadership?

Knowledge and skill. Do the materials and methods actually teach the attitudes, concepts, and skills they are supposed to?

Behavior. Have the trainees changed their behavior based on what they have learned? Do they use the newly acquired skills, attitudes, or knowledge back on the job?

Results. Are the new behaviors having a positive effect on the organization?

Generally, evaluation becomes harder moving from the first to the fourth level of evaluation. Evaluation instruments usually will be built into the training design, especially for the second level and above. The trainer, however, will generally administer the evaluation, especially to get reactions (Level 1), and find out how much has been learned (Level 2).

Techniques for Level 1 Evaluation

This issue will discuss only Level 1 (reaction) evaluation, since it is the easiest and is usually an ongoing and spontaneous process. At this level, the trainer will probably use some kind of predesigned questionnaire that asks for feedback related to various aspects of the program, such as length, content, lectures, audiovisuals, training methods, handouts, organization, facilities, and trainer facilitation.

Here are the some steps to follow when performing a Level 1 evaluation:

1. Ask the trainees to state three things they have liked about the program. Then ask for three things they would like to see changed for the next training group.

2. Paraphrase what each person says and list it on a flipchart or a board. If you need clarification, simply ask for more detail; do not defend or argue. Be sure to thank the group for their input.

3. As an alternative to Step 1, you can do the following:

- Hand out sheets with the questions and spaces for three "likes" and three "things I'd like changed."

- Ask the trainees in small groups to discuss their answers and have one member of each group report to the rest of the participants.

- Put the responses on a flipchart or board (you can collect the sheets afterward).

Steps 1 and 2 will take about five minutes. Step 3 takes an additional five minutes or so.

This technique is used for midcourse evaluation and for building trainer credibility with the group. Try it just before a lunch break, or at the end of each day. But do not use it unless you genuinely want to hear what people have to say, even if it is negative, about the program or the trainer.

Managers as Trainers

A great deal of all training is done on the job by supervisors and managers. Those who do training from within the company range from executives teaching management skills to line managers showing workers how to perform technical jobs.

According to consultant Geoffrey Bellman, training conducted by line managers will differ from that conducted by professional trainers in the following ways:

- Trainees will have a different reaction to the training and are more likely to take it seriously.

- The program design will have more emphasis on structured activities.

- Trainees will be evaluated from the learner's viewpoint, not the trainer's.

Managers make good trainers if they:

- are properly prepared

- are respected by and have good rapport with follow workers

Do's and Don'ts for the New Trainer

Here are some suggestions for you to follow in order to be a successful trainer:

Do
- Prepare, prepare, prepare.
- Make the objective clear.
- Make the session participatory.
- Review and stick to the agenda.
- Encourage questions.
- Have an opening and closing.
- Gear sessions toward learners' needs.
- Promote networking among participants.
- Use visuals or varied learning techniques.
- Survey the facility in advance.
- Dress professionally.
- Market the training program internally.
- Use transfer of training techniques.
- Evaluate.

Don't
- Start late.
- Criticize or embarrass a participant.
- Hesitate to say "I don't know."
- Hide behind the podium; circulate around the room.
- Permit discussions to stray from the subject.
- Indulge in bad presentation habits.
- Overload learners; divide information into modules.
- Let your delivery overshadow the content.
- Limit yourself to one method of delivery.
- Get stale; vary your routine.
- Pigeonhole yourself; stretch your talents.
- Go it alone; ask experts for help.
- Worry about new challenges.

Adapted from Info-line No. 9608, *"Do's and Don'ts for the New Trainer."*

- can master the skills and knowledge needed to be effective trainers

- are motivated to train

- know their subject

- have good communication skills

There are several advantages to using managers as trainers because they:

- communicate corporate culture—"the company line"

- provide positive role models and motivation for trainees

- lend credibility because of their knowledge of the subject

- understand the connections between training and on-the-job behavior and see that workers are actually learning all the time

- understand the subject content in relation to the job to be done

- increase their own career development through the communication skills they learn by training

"Companies need to pay special attention to their managers' potential to train and motivate," Bellman says. But he adds a caveat: "Training must be something the managers want to do. If they see training as a burden, it will be reflected in their training style and attitude." Companies can get around that problem, he says, by seeing that the managers are trained well in areas such as problem solving and presentation skills, and contracting with them to do the training as part of their own career development.

ASTD recommends the following strategies for preparing managers to train:

- Keep the groups small.

- Videotape managers' practice presentations to help them polish their skills before facing an audience.

- Provide follow-up and refresher training.

In addition, Bellman advises team teaching for line managers when feasible. That way, individual trainers can have manageable portions to teach, help one another, and add more variety to the content.

Four-Step Skills Training Method

The Four-Step Skills Training Method of job instruction was first developed during the 1920s and was used extensively during World War II as the most efficient and effective way to teach skills. It is still an effective method and an excellent way to introduce first-time trainers to the basic training process.

Before beginning the training, however, the trainer needs to do the following things:

Identify the best procedure for performing the job. The best method minimizes costs, learning difficulty, errors, and safety hazards. Look at how the best performers do the job, then compare the various methods and pick the best features of each.

Analyze the job to identify the tasks involved; determine the key points and any areas of difficulty to be emphasized; and define the performance standards for each step, so that both the trainer and the learner will know when the job has been done right.

Prepare the workplace. Be sure that all needed equipment, materials, and supplies are available in the training area, and that the area is properly arranged.

Case Study: ODS, Inc.

Preparing trainers to teach courses takes time and requires a carefully designed plan of action. Donald L. German, of Organizational Development Systems, Inc. (ODS), in Houston, Texas, has described the "integrated intervention" training model that his company offers. The participants are professionals with little or no training experience who have inherited their training assignments, or experienced trainers who need to learn how to teach a particular workshop, seminar, or course. ODS introduces and applies the basic concepts of teaching by focusing on the four phases of adult learning: preparation, instruction, integration, and application.

■ Preparation

During this phase, trainers focus on needs assessment, audience analysis, course design, learning objectives, and delivery style. Customizing materials to meet the exact needs of the target audience is a pervasive theme of the program.

■ Instruction

The workshop presents a variety of instructional methods for communicating information, concepts, and skills. This includes manuals and lectures as well as interactive methods, such as role play, simulations, peer group instruction, and discussion groups. During this phase, participants receive immediate feedback on their progress via videotaped presentations and one-on-one critiques of their teaching styles.

■ Integration

In this phase, trainers learn how to link the skills they are learning to their jobs or personal goals. They acquire a full range of tools that they will use in their future training assignments by experiencing and analyzing adult learning techniques and activities used in teaching.

■ Application

During the workshop, trainers use their own course materials and apply the skills they are learning to workshop assignments. In this manner, they are learning to think within the integrated intervention model.

Specifically, the ODS three-day workshop prepares instructors and instructor candidates to conduct training successfully by addressing these areas.

Content. The workshop introduces the basic skills and techniques of teaching seminars by covering the following topics:

- understanding adult learners
- using effecting learning tools and activities
- planning a seminar or workshop
- understanding group dynamics
- using effective speaking techniques

Design and Format. The participants experience and analyze the following adult learning techniques and activities used in teaching:

- role play
- group synergy techniques
- self-analysis
- videotaped presentations and critiques
- simulation
- case studies
- group discussions
- short interactive lectures
- one-on-one instruction
- use of audiovisuals
- use of tests and performance demonstrations

Participants receive immediate feedback and coaching throughout the workshop.

Results. Participants leave the workshop with specific tools, techniques, and skills to apply in future training assignments. These skills include the following:

- incorporating adult learning principles into course design

- writing learning objectives

- using interpersonal skills to create a positive learning experience

- developing group synergy

- creating and using audiovisual aids to enhance a workshop

- handling participants' questions

- handling problem participants

- using proved techniques to create instructor's notes

- spotting and diagnosing problems

Adapted from "On Target: Training the Trainer," Technical Skills & Training, April 1994. Used with permission.

Now that you are ready to train, here are the four steps you must follow:

1. Prepare the worker by putting the learner at ease. State the job to be learned, find out what the learner already knows about the job, and then position the learner so that he or she can see the operation clearly.

2. Demonstrate and explain the operation in the following manner (if it is complicated, break it into smaller instructional units):

   - Give a general overview of the task, its purposes, and steps involved.

   - Demonstrate the procedure in order, step by step, explaining what, how, and how well you want the job done as you go along.

   - Instruct at a rate that allows the learner to comprehend the task.

   - Stress key points.

   - Instruct clearly, completely, and patiently.

   - Demonstrate the task a second time, summarizing as you go.

   - Ask for questions from the learner.

3. Give the learner practice by following these steps:

   - Have the learner do the job.

   - Give frequent, specific, and accurate feedback on the learner's performance.

   - Give corrections in a calm and friendly way.

   - Praise specific successes.

   - Ask questions that test understanding, such as: "Why did you…?" or "What would happen if…?" or "What else do you…?" or "What do you do if…?"

   - Have the learner continue to practice until the task is finished according to standards discussed at the beginning.

4. Follow up by doing these things:

   - Encourage further questions.

   - Designate someone to give the learner further assistance if needed.

   - Put the learner on his or her own.

   - Check the learner's procedure and results periodically, tapering off over time.

The Four-Step Skills Training Method is simple and effective if all the steps and substeps are followed. It can be adapted to many tasks, from a simple physical procedure to more complex jobs, by dealing with an employee problem in a systematic and calm way. For a step-by-step overview of this training method, see the job aid on the last page of this issue.

Case Study: Malawi Institute

The Malawi Institute of Management in east central Africa developed the following 12-step method for training subject matter experts (SMEs) to train. This approach entails a high level of trainee involvement, blending theory and practice, that equips trainers with theoretical knowledge as well as the confidence and skills they need to be successful trainers.

1. Agenda building—what participants want to learn and how they prefer to learn it; course directors take notes and incorporate participant views into course content.

2. Theory-based coverage of training concepts—question-and-answer periods cover education, training and development, role of trainers, principles of adult learning.

3. Introduction to front-end analysis—using case studies, participants identify solutions to a given performance problem.

4. Identification of performance problems and solutions—practical sessions, participants interview line managers to pinpoint performance problems, report back to class.

5. Analysis of training activities—participants learn to select tasks for training, determine training population, and write training objectives.

6. Case study analysis—participants work in small groups to analyze job duties and tasks, examine actual performance, and write training objectives to fill performance needs.

7. Theory of training design—lecture and discussion cover performance objectives, standards and conditions, training objectives, enabling objectives, teaching points, and design of evaluation checks.

8. Practice in training design—using previously developed analyses, participants clarify performance objectives and design appropriate training objectives.

9. Theory of classroom instruction—covers lesson plans, training objectives, enabling objectives, and teaching points; session introduction; main body of instruction; evaluation; and conclusion.

10. Practice in classroom instruction—hands-on session; groups complete lesson plan and make 30-minute presentations.

11. Individual presentations—participants identify topic, develop training objectives and a lesson plan, and give 30-minute presentations, which are videotaped.

12. Feedback on individual presentation—trainees see videotaped presentations and get feedback from other trainers.

Adapted from "Training Nontrainers to Train," Training & Development, *August 1995. Used with permission.*

References & Resources

Articles

Bellman, Geoffrey M. "The Whats, Whys, and Hows of Teaching Managers to Be Trainers." *Trainer's Workshop,* June 1978, pp. 31-32.

Broadwell, Martin M., and Carol B. Dietrich. "How to Get Trainees into the Action." *Training,* February 1996, pp. 52-56.

Dervarics, Charles. "T3: Training the Trainer at Saturn." *Technical & Skills Training,* January 1993, pp. 20-24.

Dzimbiri, Lewis B. "Trainer Training—the Malawi Case." *Training & Development,* August 1995, pp. 17-18.

Eline, Leanne. "Choose the Right Tools to Reach Your Training Goals." *Technical & Skills Training,* April 1997, p. 4.

Hequet, Marc. "Instructive Moments." *Training,* January 1996, pp. 68-74.

Luke, Robert A. Jr. "Never Run Over into Lunch." *Training & Development,* August 1995, pp. 15-17.

Marsh, P.J. "Training Trainers." *Technical & Skills Training,* October 1995, pp. 10-13.

Minton-Eversole, Theresa. "Make Your Training Presentation 'Click.'" *Technical & Skills Training,* October 1996, p. 8.

Oppelt, Janis K. "On Target: Training the Trainer." *Technical & Skills Training,* April 1994, pp. 11-14.

Reynolds, Angus. "The Basics: Overhead Transparencies." *Technical & Skills Training,* August/September 1995, pp. 9-10.

Swanson, Richard A., and Sandra K. Falkman. "Training Delivery Problems and Solutions." *Human Resource Development Quarterly,* Winter 1997, pp. 305-314.

Wircenski, Michelle D., and Jerry L. Wircenski. "Greek to Me: Training Effectively with Unfamiliar Content." *Technical & Skills Training,* February/March 1997, pp. 28-30.

Zahn, David. "Lessons from the Front, Back, and Sides of the Room." *Training & Development,* January 1998, pp. 12-13.

Books

Bullard, Rebecca, et al. *The Occasional Trainer's Handbook.* Englewood Cliffs, NJ: Educational Technology Publications, 1994.

Carnevale, Anthony P., et al. *Workplace Basics.* San Francisco: Jossey-Bass, 1990.

Denham, Wendy, and Elizabeth Sansom. *Presentation Skills Training.* New York: McGraw-Hill, 1997.

Eitington, Julius E. *The Winning Trainer.* Houston: Gulf Publishing, 1996.

Figueroa, Joseph D. *Training for Non-Trainers.* Amherst, MA: HRD Press, 1994.

Goad, Tom W. *The First-time Trainer.* New York: AMACOM, 1997.

Kirkpatrick, Donald L. *Evaluating Training Programs: The Four Levels.* San Francisco: Berrett-Koehler, 1994.

Knowles, Malcolm. *The Adult Learner: A Neglected Species.* 4th edition. Houston: Gulf Publishing, 1996.

———. *Designs for Adult Learning.* Alexandria, VA: ASTD, 1995.

Lambert, Clark. *Secrets of a Successful Trainer.* New York: Wiley, 1986 (out of print).

McLagan, Patricia A. *Models for HRD Practice: The Models.* Alexandria, VA: ASTD, 1989.

———. *Models for HRD Practice: The Practitioner's Guide.* Alexandria, VA: ASTD, 1989.

Merriam, Sharan B., and Ralph G. Brockett. *The Profession and Practice of Adult Education.* San Francisco: Jossey-Bass, 1997.

Milne, Derek, and Steve Noone. *Teaching and Training for Non-Teachers.* Leicester, United Kingdom: BPS Books, 1996.

Mitchell, Garry. *The Trainer's Handbook: The AMA Guide to Effective Training.* 3rd edition. New York: AMACOM, 1998.

Vella, Jane. *Training Through Dialogue.* San Francisco: Jossey-Bass, 1995.

Wilson, Joe B. *Applying Successful Training Techniques.* Irvine, CA: Richard Chang Associates, 1994.

Info-lines

Callahan, Madelyn R., ed. "10 Great Games and How to Use Them." No. 8411 (revised 1999).

Eline, Leanne. "How to Prepare and Use Effective Visual Aids." No. 8410 (revised 1997).

Garavaglia, P. "Transfer of Training." No. 9512 (revised 2000).

Hodell, Chuck. "Basics of Instructional Systems Development." No. 9706.

Novak, Clare. "High Performance Training Manuals." No. 9707.

O'Neill, Mary. "Do's and Don'ts for the New Trainer." No. 9608 (revised 1998).

Plattner, Francis. "Improve Your Communication and Speaking Skills." No. 9409 (revised 1997).

Preziosi, Robert. "Icebreakers." No. 8911 (revised 1999).

Sharpe, Cat, ed. "How to Create a Good Learning Environment." No. 8506 (revised 1997).

Sullivan, Rick. "Transfer of Skills Training." No. 9804.

"Training and Learning Styles." No. 8804 (revised 1998).

Waagan, Alice. "Essentials for Evaluation." No. 9705.

Wircenski, Jerry L., and Richard L. Sullivan. "Make Every Presentation a Winner." No. 8606 (revised 1998).

Job Aid

Training Trainers with the Four-Step Skills Training Method

Use this job aid to introduce the Four-Step Skills Training Method to new trainers. First, hand out the checklist below to the trainees for use in observing and evaluating train-the-trainer sessions. Then demonstrate the technique for the trainees and provide them with enough materials to practice until they have established the skill.

Directions for trainees.

1. Review the checklist.

2. As you watch the facilitator demonstrate the Four-Step Skills Training Method, use the checklist to evaluate what happens.

3. Identify some relatively simple task you can train someone to do (such as tying a necktie, reloading a mechanical pencil, starting up a computer) and use the "Preparing to Train" part of the checklist to get ready to train.

4. In groups assigned by the facilitator, each trainee in turn trains one other person while the rest evaluate, using the checklist. Which steps are well done, and how did you know it (what did you observe)? Which steps were missing and what was the effect?

5. When you are finished, share your likes and concerns, then discuss what you have learned or re-learned about training.

Checklist for the Four-Step Skills Training Method

Preparing to Train. Did the trainer:

☐ Identify the best procedure?
☐ Analyze the tasks involved?
☐ Make sure all necessary material, equipment, and supplies were on hand?

Step 1: Preparing the Worker. Did the trainer:

☐ Put the learner at ease?
☐ State the job?
☐ Find out what the worker already knows about the job?
☐ Make sure he or she can see the operation?

Step 2. Demonstrating and Explaining the Operation. Did the trainer:

☐ Give an overview of the task?
☐ Demonstrate the procedure step by step?
☐ Instruct at a comfortable rate?
☐ Stress key points?
☐ Instruct clearly, completely, and patiently?
☐ Demonstrate a second time and summarize?
☐ Ask for questions?

Step 3: Giving the Learner Practice. Did the trainer:

☐ Have the learner do the job?
☐ Give feedback?
☐ Correct in a friendly and calm manner?
☐ Praise specific successes?
☐ Ask questions that test understanding?
☐ Have the learner practice until the task was done to standard?

Step 4: Following Up. Did the trainer:

☐ Encourage further questions?
☐ Designate someone to give further help?
☐ Put the learner on his or her own?
☐ Check on the learner's progress periodically?

Training and Learning Styles

CONSULTING AUTHOR

Susan Russell
Micros Systems, Inc.
1200 Baltimore Avenue
Beltsville, MD 20705
Tel. 302.210.8000 ext. 2701
Fax 301.210.3427
Email susanrussell@micros.com

Susan Russell is a practitioner in the training and development field specializing in analysis and evaluation of trainer interventions. She holds a master's degree in business from Johns Hopkins University and is completing a second master's degree in instructional systems development through the University of Maryland Baltimore County.

Editorial staff for 8804

Editor
Diane E. Kirrane

ASTD Internal Consultant
Greta Kotler

Revised 1998

Editor
Cat Sharpe

Contributing Editor
Ann Bruen

Training and Learning Styles

Training and Learning Styles

"How can you *say* that? How can you even *think* like that?"

"You mean you study with the TV on? That would *never* work for me."

"Can you *believe* it? That guy didn't get our point at all!"

How often have you heard people question the ways in which other people perceive and process information? Whether with frustration, amusement, or acceptance, adults realize that working with people means dealing with their distinct information-handling styles. Our different habits and points of view shape our learning styles, which as psychologist David Kolb has pointed out, are closely tied to our problem-tackling and problem-solving styles for getting along in life. It is true: Adults "live and learn" how to cope.

If you are a trainer, you may sometimes have a chance, through administration of learning style assessment instruments, to predetermine learners' styles, and perhaps to group training participants according to results. But this usually is not possible. Yet just by being aware of the strengths and weaknesses of different training and learning styles and methods you can do the following:

- take an important step toward improved communication with learners who don't share your style tendencies and preferences

- build on the strengths of your training style

- do a better job of designing, developing, and delivering training that accommodates learners' individual needs

This issue of *Info-line* presents examples of typical training styles, their strengths and weaknesses; and training and learning style factors that influence the choice of appropriate training activities. It also contains descriptions of educational and psychological assessment instruments related to training and learning styles.

Background Influences

People in a training setting—trainers and learners—inevitably have differences in several areas.

■ *Cultural Legacies/Childhood Experiences*
Have you ever visited a hospital nursery? At first the newborns' behavior may have looked much alike to you. But on closer observation, you probably noticed that some infants seemed more watchful; some more startled by noise; and some, calmer or more agitated than the rest. From birth, we vary in our responses to the world's "blooming, buzzing confusion."

As we grow up in our homes, communities, and nations, we get and react to expressed and tacit signals about how to process information. For example, when we were children, we may have had the following experiences:

- Adults may have encouraged us to touch and manipulate things, to ask questions, and to express our opinions. Or they may have told us to be quiet and leave everything alone.

- We may or may not have seen neighborhood adults—at work or for pleasure—often reading or working with their hands. We may or may not have seen women or minority group members in positions of authority.

- We may have enjoyed school activities and the approval of our classmates and teachers. Or we may have felt confused or left out.

■ *Adult Experiences and Learning*
Adult learners have various histories of formal education and training. An adult may also say "I learned my lesson" through a life experience. What is interesting is that the same "life lesson" may lead different people to different conclusions. A "failure" causes one person to give up, a second to redouble efforts, and a third to reflect, change in some way, then try again. And, as individuals, each may be making a rational, valid choice or may be reacting to the emotional aftermath of an earlier, perceived failure.

Your Perception or Mine?

Ask a group of people how to spell a difficult word. Watch what they do: Some close their eyes and whisper to themselves; some appear to be writing with an invisible pen; some hunt around for paper so they can write with a real pen or pencil. In trying to retrieve the word's spelling from their memories, they reveal something about the "sensory intake" or "perceptual" style with which they originally learned the word's spelling. In this case, some people hear the spelling; some feel it; some see it.

According to W.B. James and M.W. Galbraith, a learner's primary "perceptual modality," and the attendant preferred mode of learning, may be one of the following:

Print: the reader or writer who learns well from traditional texts and pencil-and-paper exercises.

Visual: the observer who likes to look at slides, films, videos, exhibits, demonstrations, charts, and graphs.

Aural: the listener who enjoys lectures and learns well from audiotapes and records.

Interactive: the talker who learns best from discussions and question-and-answer sessions.

Tactile (manipulative/haptic): the toucher/handler who likes hands-on activities, model building, and sketching.

Kinesthetic (enactive/psychomotor): the mover who likes role plays, physical games, and activities.

Olfactory: the smeller/taster who associates learning with smells and tastes.

Many learners are unaware of their perceptual styles. What they *do* know is which learning activities they usually like or dislike. Some people are "dyadic learners" who learn better as a partner in a pair than they do alone or in a group. Some people learn better if they play music while they read, view slides, or write; but others find it distracting.

James's and Galbraith's research indicates that more adults are visual learners than any other perception style. But whatever our preference, we also learn—just not as efficiently—through all our senses. So when a trainer varies activities to create multisensory training, it increases the likelihood of appealing to each learner's style and also helps each learner reinforce skills or knowledge acquired through the preferred modality.

■ Perceptions and Skills

Sensory perceptions and psychomotor (physical), attitudinal (behavioral/affective), and cognitive (thinking/knowing) skills differ from person to person. Our bodies and brains—and their interrelated workings—differ. We may be left-handed, right-handed, or ambidextrous; we may be fundamentally left-brain (linear), right-brain (holistic), or integrated thinkers; we may be morning people, afternoon people, or born to work the night shift. Some of us score well on IQ tests, and some of us don't; some of us who don't are still considered "smart" by our peers. Psychologist Howard Gardner's theory of intelligence posits that there are the following kinds of smart:

● logical-mathematical—awareness of groupings, patterns, and sequences

● linguistic—awareness of shades of difference in word meanings

● spatial—awareness of shapes or forms and spaces

● bodily-kinesthetic—awareness of bodily control and relationship to physical surroundings

● musical—awareness of sounds and rhythms

● interpersonal—awareness of the feelings and intentions of others

● intrapersonal—awareness of one's own feelings and interests

■ Individual Differences

We all differ in our personalities, feelings, values, biases, preferences, and expectations. We "walk with personality, talk with personality," and may "have a great big smile." These characteristics too affect our ways of learning and motivation to learn. For instance, after a minor training setback, we might say: "There must be something wrong with this test (simulator, equipment); I know I can do it." Or "I think I should study some more (practice, read the directions again); then I'll get it." Or "I knew I wouldn't be any good at this; I'll never catch on." Or "Not bad for a first try, huh?" (See *Feelings, Nothing Less Than Feelings* on the following page.)

Who's In Charge?

Training styles relate to social and managerial styles. Without a doubt, trainers need to command respect from training participants. But needing to "command" participants themselves is something else.

To begin with, who should set program or lesson goals and objectives? There is no right or wrong answer. Trainers may not always be in control of selecting the subject matter or the method of instruction. Employers may request in-house or vendor-supplied training because its advertised goals and objectives match their own. If top management insists that a group of employees acquire certain new skills or knowledge, an instructional designer will work to convert managerial goals into measurable learning objectives. In doing so, he or she may solicit information on learner opinions and styles so these can be woven into the training design.

Several factors influence trainer versus learner control *within* a training session, such as those detailed below.

Resource Constraints

Like it or not, there is not always time to allow learners to explore and discover knowledge for themselves. And cramped meeting facilities may crush plans for learner-centered activities such as role play. On occasion, a solitary subject matter expert (SME), text, or multimedia resource may be the only available source of information on a topic. When that is true, the question of trainer versus learner control takes a backseat, and information content drives the training event.

Feelings, Nothing Less Than Feelings

Adults usually manage to look calm and rational, especially at their places of employment. But the prospect of training can stir deep feelings. Each training session's group dynamics are different. Not being a mind reader, you will not always know what is going in people's thoughts. But sometimes their actions or words will tell you. And, sooner or later, you will face training participants with obvious or invisible emotional baggage marked with one of the following tags:

Anger: Why am I in this class? Don't they think my work is good enough? Don't they realize I'm too busy to make time for this?

Fear: I hope I don't make a fool of myself. What if I don't get it? Will I be fired? Will I have to pay if I foul up and break something? How dangerous is that machine over there? Who are all these people? Who will let me sit at their table? Will anyone talk to me during the breaks? Will they like me?

Confusion: Am I in the right room? Why did I sign up for this? Maybe I should just stick to the way I have been working. How does this have to do with that stuff I'm supposed to take care of back at work?

Bravado: I'll bet I could teach a thing or two to this character who is supposed to be such an expert. And these other guys don't look so smart either. I'll show them.

Sorrow: I'm going to miss my old job. After this training, our gang will be split up; I'll miss them.

Confidence: Let me at it. This is going to be interesting. And, I guess learning about it will help me do a better job. That ought to help my chances for promotion.

Helping ease training participants' anxieties is an important part of preparing for and beginning a training session. Many "petty" administrative details, when done right, help hold participants' negative feelings to a minimum. For example, you might try the following:

- clear maps, directions, and signs pointing the way to the training site

- icebreaker activities to introduce participants to one another as well as to the training topic

- short, matter-of-fact statements regarding your qualifications; the advantages of learning the material; the means by which participants' learning will be assessed; the location of nearby telephones and rest rooms; the frequency of breaks

Learning Tasks and Materials

What is to be learned? Some tasks (such as learning how to repair machinery) require hands-on experience. Sometimes safety considerations demand tight trainer control. Much training information is suitable for translation into packets of self-paced instructional material (workbooks, tapes, computer-based instruction guides).

Group and Individual Learner Needs

How many participants will there be? How many trainers? What education, past training, learning tasks, and so forth do participants have in common? How alike are their learning needs? That is, how similar are they in their preparation for this training, and are all of them to be held to the same standard of evaluation? To what extent are they prepared to be independent learners? Do they have the necessary level of maturity and training or experience in managing their own learning?

Individuals may lack the maturity needed for independent learning. What trainer hasn't met with typical problem learners such as:

- the nonparticipant who declares resistance to the very idea of being trained

- the clinger who, dissatisfied with a fair share of individual attention, tries to monopolize the trainer

- the show-off who competes with both topic and trainer for the group's attention

Most adult learners *are* mature enough to recognize and accept their individual responsibility for learning. But they are likely to be accustomed to having training "presented" to them—and, if they are not training professionals, probably won't know how to find learning resources efficiently. It is often appropriate for a trainer to develop alternative materials and activities from which participants may choose. In some cases, it may be worthwhile to create a training course in "self-managed learning," and to give its graduates access to training materials and meeting space.

Trainer Philosophy, Knowledge, and Skills

What does the session's trainer think about the nature of people? That they are basically industrious or basically lazy? That they are usually self-propelled or that they usually need a push? What does the trainer think motivates people—money, status, sense of mastery, fear, or other internal or external factors? How confident is the trainer of his or her expertise in the training topic.

The ability to field individuals' questions and to answer in a context that is valuable to a group is grounded in in-depth knowledge. Does the trainer have the maturity, experience, and skill to be a facilitator? A trainer may be sufficiently mature and objective to step back and let learners lead. But if, by learners' own standards, they go astray, a trainer needs practiced skills to resist the expediency of taking over, but still help them find their way back on track.

Authors Frederic H. Margolis and Chip R. Bell warn trainers not to say things like "I want you to read section C"—because such remarks invite a learner to think, "Who cares what you want? I *don't* want to do that." A better approach is to tell learners what they will get out of the effort of reading section C (or doing whatever else you ask of them): "In section C you will find a description and several illustrations of the kind of computer you will be working on next week."

And Margolis and Bell cite the flawed thinking behind the following negative trainer stereotypes:

The professor who dispenses knowledge and approval, but does not expect classes to value learning for its own merits.

The comedian who keeps classes laughing, but seems less concerned about what they learn.

The projectionist who is an audio-visual/CBT wizard, but apart from getting the tape, film, or computer program running, does not feel obligated to offer learners help.

The inspirer who gets classes all worked up, but offers no substance to work on.

The drill instructor who thinks class members are dull and lazy, and concentrates on repetition, repetition, and more repetition.

Each stereotype derives from an unbalanced over-concentration on one of the following desirable trainer traits: knowledge of subject; sense of humor; technical skill; awareness of others; and willingness to lead when necessary.

How can you discover *your* training style, your strengths and weaknesses? Comments from training participants' end-of-course evaluations, or "smile sheets," can be a starting point. If you are surprised by the comments, you are getting a reflected view of your "blind spot." Psychologist Joseph Luft and psychiatrist Harry Ingram developed a model called a Johari Window (note the

Learner Styles and Needs; Trainer Roles

Several years ago, Ronne Toker Jacobs and Barbara Schneider-Fuhrmann developed companion learner-trainer style inventories. One result of their studies and analyses is this chart.

Learner Style	Learner Needs	Trainer Role	Trainer Behavior
Dependent: May occur in introductory courses, new work situations, languages, and some sciences when the learner has little or no information when entering the course.	Structure Director External reinforcement Encouragement Esteem from authority	Director Expert Authority	Lecturing Demonstrating Assigning Checking Encouraging Testing Reinforcing Transmitting content Grading Designing materials
Collaborative: May occur when the learner has some knowledge, information, or ideas and would like to share them or try them out.	Interaction Practice Probe of self and others Observations Participation Peer challenge Peer esteem Experimentation	Collaborator Co-learner Environment setter	Interacting Questioning Providing resources Modeling Providing feedback Coordinating Evaluating Managing Observing process Grading
Independent: May occur when the learner has much knowledge or skill on entering the course and wants to continue to search on his or her own or has had successful experiences in working through new situations alone. The learner may feel that the instructor cannot offer as much as he or she would like.	Internal awareness Experimentation Time Nonjudgmental support	Delegator Facilitator	Allowing Providing requested feedback Providing resources Consulting Listening Negotiating Evaluating Delegating

Reprinted by permission

exotic spelling of Joe-Harry). Their model has four "panes:"

1. **Arena**—aspects of personality known to self and others.

2. **Facade**—aspects known to self, but not known to others.

3. **Blind spot**—aspects known to others, but not known to self.

4. **Unknown**—aspects not known to conscious self, not known to others.

You can also compare yourself to descriptions of training style types to see whether you recognize yourself in any of the models. Or you can fill out and score a learning or training styles inventory such as the one described in the job aid at the end of this issue.

Testing

In its broader definitions, learning style encompasses many aspects of the human body, mind, and spirit. Alexander Pope's poetic assertion that "a little learning is a dangerous thing" surely applies to a trainer's involvement in testing to discover the psychological components of learners' styles. There are numerous psychological tests and instruments designed to disclose the following information about learners:

● acculturation
● anxieties
● aptitudes
● interests, particularly vocational interests
● personality/temperament type
● reading ability or style
● self-esteem
● self-efficacy (expectations of success)

Using Assessment Instruments

Among the many educational and psychological instruments that relate to training and learning styles, training and learning style inventories (TSIs and LSIs) are of particular interest to trainers. As a rule, these assessment instruments are self-administered and scored.

Several inventories have "normative" versions; that is, researchers administered the instrument to large groups of people and then compiled and analyzed their scores so that subsequent participants can compare scores to standards (norms) set by those groups. Most inventories are "ipsative"; that is, a score stands on its own, falling as a point on a spectrum or into one or more categories, all of which are considered normal. Because there are no right or wrong answers, most inventory developers prefer not to call TSIs or LSIs "tests." In *Learning How to Learn: Applied Theory for Adults,* Robert M. Smith lists the following guidelines for using these inventories.

■ *Use or Devise One or More of Them*
A person may score differently on different inventories—or differently on the same inventory at different times. This variance is partly explained by the subjective nature of these instruments; our preferences may fluctuate, or our self-awareness may be heightened by having worked through one inventory—which influences the outcome of a second. An inventory's vocabulary may affect scores: People who agree that the word *spontaneous* fits their style may not associate themselves with an item that is designed to assess the same training, but uses the word *impulsive.*

■ *Supplement Inventory Information*
This means observing and asking questions. As mentioned earlier, people have "blind spots." Watch what people do and, if it seems appropriate, comment on what you have observed. But be diplomatic. Describe a person's actions rather than announce that you know what he or she "is." It is often better to make these observations privately to individuals instead of turning a person's behavior into a "case" for group commentary. If people may be subjected to group scrutiny and comment, they should be alerted to that possibility in course advertisements or notices—and your professional background should include training in how to handle such a session. One-to-one comments are usually less sensitive. Say something like "I noticed that you stood near the doorway for a while, then waited by the tables for a time before you joined a table. I wondered whether that hesitation meant anything." You may be expecting to hear someone confess to feeling uneasy about joining groups, but hear instead how it took a few minutes to adjust to the lighting in the room—which leads to the next point.

■ *Avoid Overly Simplistic Conclusions*

Realize that to some extent any training or learning styles inventory will simplify human complexity. That is valuable because it helps us isolate and manage part of our infinite complexity. Acknowledge to learners both the inherent advantage and limitation of simplification.

■ *Share Scores/Conclusions with Learners*

If the instrument(s) you choose are not self-scoring, tell each learner the results. After all, the main reason for assessing someone's style is to build on its strengths. A person may want to moderate his or her style by shoring up weak spots, but it is not desirable to try to change styles and risk diminishing strengths.

Training Style Inventories

Among the training style inventories frequently used and spoken of in training circles are the following:

■ *Training Style Inventory*

Developed by Richard Brostrom, this instrument categorizes trainers' styles according to the trainers' basic assumptions and their alignment with major training-learning theories (see sidebar on the next page). Increasingly, Brostrom says, he sees trainers taking an eclectic "field approach." For a given training content, a trainer starts with a theoretical focus and concentrates on its corresponding ways of delivering training, but also puts the "content in context" by bringing in training methodologies associated with other theories. Suppose a basically behaviorist trainer designs a computer-delivered programmed-instruction course on an aspect of automation. The trainer might supplement that with a learners' walkthrough of an automated facility, research and writing assignment, and support group.

■ *Trainer Type Inventory*

Developed by Mardy Wheeler and Jeanie Marshall, this instrument draws on the work of Malcolm Knowles, Richard Brostrom, and David Kolb. It describes trainers as falling into the following basic categories:

Listeners, who create an affective learning environment that encourages learners to express personal needs.

Directors, who create a perceptual learning environment that provides learners different perspectives.

Interpreters, who create a symbolic learning environment that encourages learners to memorize and understand terms and rules.

Coaches, who create a behavioral learning environment that allows learners to experiment and evaluate their own progress.

Learning Style Inventories

There are many widely used learning style inventories that address personality differences, information processing styles, social interaction differences, and instructional preferences. The results can yield useful learner profiles. But it is at least unethical—and sometimes dangerous or illegal—to use these instruments unless you are adequately trained in their proper administration, scoring, interpretation, and application.

Personality Testing Instruments

The Myers-Briggs Type Indicator (MBTI) is one of the most widely used personality assessment instruments. Katherine Briggs and her daughter Isabel Briggs Myers based their work on that of Swiss psychologist Carl Jung. The instrument they developed has a person "self-report" on indications of individual preferences for the following:

■ *Extroversion (E) or Introversion (I)*

An extrovert is aware of and relies on the environment for stimulation, is action oriented, and frank. An introvert is stimulated by the inner world or concepts and ideas—is thoughtful. In the MBTI, "introverted" does not necessarily mean "shy," but it does imply enjoyment of solitude.

■ *Perception by Sensing (S) or Intuition (N)*

Sensing means being aware of what is observed through the senses. This preference is associated with a "now" orientation, realism, memory for detail, and practicality. Intuition means having insight that may take a person into the realm of future possibilities. This preference is associated with interest in meanings and relationships, and with abstraction and creativity.

Training Styles Theory and Practice

Richard Brostrom developed this chart that shows how a trainer's philosophy ties into learning theories and practices:

	Behaviorist	Structuralist	Functionalist	
Orientation to Teaching-Learning	New behavior can be caused and "shaped" with well-designed structures around the learner.	The mind is like a computer; the teacher is the programmer.	People learn best by doing, and they will do best what *they* want to do. People will learn what is practical.	
Basic Assumptions	Training designers select the desired end behaviors and proceed to engineer a reinforcement schedule that systematically encourages learners' progress toward those goals. Imaginative new machinery has made learning fun and thinking unnecessary. Learners often control the speed.	Content properly organized and fed bit by bit to learners will be retained in memory. Criterion tests will verify the effectiveness of teaching. The teacher "keeps people awake" while simultaneously entering data—a much-envied skill.	The learner must be willing (or motivated) by the process or the product; otherwise it is useless to try teaching. Performance on the job is the true test. Opportunity, self-direction, thinking, achieving results, and recognition are important.	
Interpersonal Style	*Supportive:* emphasis on controlling and predicting the learner and learning outcomes—cooperative, stimulus-response mentalities are valued. Process is product centered.	*Directive:* planning, organization, presentation, and evaluation are featured. Process is teacher centered.	*Assertive:* a problem-focused, conditional, confrontational climate—striving, stretching, achieving. Process is task oriented and learner centered.	
Strengths	*The Doctor:* clear, precise, and deliberate; low risk; careful preparation; emotionally attentive; complete security for learners; a trust builder; everything "arranged"; protective; patient; in control.	*The Expert:* informative, thorough; certain; systematic; stimulating; good audio-visual techniques; well rehearsed; strong leader; powerful; expressive; dramatic; entertaining.	*The Coach:* emphasizes purpose; challenges learners; realistic; lets people perform and make mistakes; takes risks; gives feedback; builds confidence; persuasive; gives opportunity and recognition.	
Limitations	*The Manipulator:* fosters dependence; overprotective; controlling; manipulative; "for their own good"; sugar-coating; hypocritical agreeing; deceptive assurances; withholds data.	*The Elitist:* preoccupied with means, image, or structure rather than results; ignores affective variables; inflexible (must follow lesson plan); dichotomous (black or white) thinking; superior.	*Sink or Swim:* ends justify means; loses patience with slow learners; intimidating; insensitive; competitive; overly task oriented; opportunistic; return-on-investment mentality.	
Major Theorist	B.F. Skinner	Robert Mager	David McClelland	
Key Words and Processes	stimulus-response; practice; shaping; prompting; behavior modification; pinpointing; habit formation; reward and punishment; teaching machines; environmental design; successive approximation; sensitizing; training; extinction; token economy; mastery	task analysis; lesson planning; information mapping; chaining; sequencing; memory; audio-visual media; presentation techniques; standards; association; evaluations; measuring instruments; objectives; recitation	problem solving; simulation; "hands-on"; reasoning; learner involvement; reality-based consequences; achievement; failure; confidence; thinking; motivation; competence; discipline; recognitions; feedback; working	

Humanist

Learning is self-directed discovery. People are natural and unfold (like a flower) if others do not inhibit the process.

"Anything that can be taught to another is relatively inconsequential" (Rogers). Significant learning leads to insight and understanding of self and others. Being a better human being is considered a valid learning goal. Can be a very inefficient, time-consuming process.

Reflective: authenticity, equality, and acceptance mark relationship. Process is relationship centered.

The Counselor: sensitive; empathic; open; spontaneous; creative; a "mirror"; nonevaluative; accepting; responsive to learners; facilitative; interactive; helpful.

The Fuzzy Thinker: vague directions; abstract, esoteric, or personal content; lacks performance criteria; unconcerned with clock time; poor control of group; resists "teaching"; appears unprepared.

C.R. Rogers

freedom; individuality; ambiguity; uncertainty; awareness; spontaneity; mutuality; equality; openness; interaction; experiential congruence; authenticity; listening; cooperation; feelings

Reprinted by permission

■ *Judgment by Thinking (T) or Feeling (F)*
People with a "thinking" orientation tend to be analytical, objective, interested in cause-and-effect and fairness, and to see connections through the passage of time. People with a "feeling" orientation can surely "think" in the lay person's idea of the term, but are more concerned with personal and group values. Feelers are, in other words, more involved with the "people" side of problems rather than the technical aspects. They are affiliative and may wish to preserve values of the past.

■ *Attitude of Judgment (J) or Perception (P)*
A judging person plans, organizes, decides, and typically seeks "closure." A perceiving person tends to be more spontaneous and adaptable— seeking more information.

The MBTI was *not* designed to assess level of maturity, degree of motivation, state of mental health, or level of intelligence. But ill-informed people may speak as if it were a measure of those things. The publishers of MBTI and other psychological tests and measures normally require that would-be purchasers be properly accredited for using their products so that their material is not misused. Psychological instruments are not parlor games, and inexpert trifling with psyches could lead to serious, even tragic, consequences.

Information Processing Inventories

There are a number of instruments that address the various ways learners process and organize information. Some of the most widely used of them are as follows:

■ *Kolb Learning Style Inventory*
Developed by David Kolb, these are part of his work in "experiential learning"—which he describes as an "integrative perspective. . .that combines experience, perception, cognition, and behavior." His impressive body of research relates learning styles to the following:

• Jung's personality types
• educational specialization
• careers and jobs
• adaptive consequences

Kolb's Learning Styles

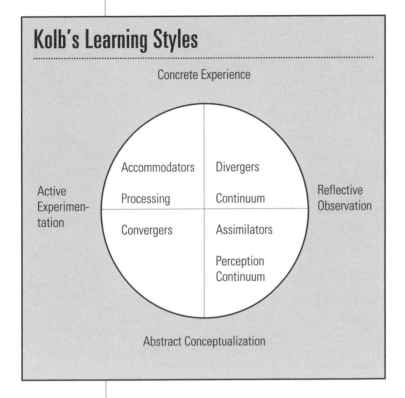

3. **Abstract conceptualization.** This orientation concentrates on "thinking as opposed to feeling." People with this orientation like to take a scientific, systematic approach and like working with symbols and analyzing information to formulate general theories. Their trainers should serve as coaches, providing guided practice and feedback.

4. **Active experimentation.** This orientation "focuses on actively influencing people and changing situations. . .(and) emphasizes practical applications." People with this orientation like to get things done. Instructors of these people should stay out of the way, providing them maximum opportunities to discover for themselves.

Kolb asserts that the key to effective learning is being competent in each mode when it is appropriate. Kolb's LSI identifies a person's learning style according to quadrants between pairs of modes—and Kolb's LSI is scored and plotted to indicate where *within* a quadrant a person's responses fall. Kolb categorizes learners and their respective "adaptive competencies," as follows:

Convergers. These people do best with "one right answer" tests and situations. They are strong in resolving technical problems, but do not fare as well in interpersonal dealings. They are decisive, experiment with new possibilities, and set goals.

Divergers. These people are imaginative and sensitive to meanings, values, and feelings. They keep an open mind, gather information, and can envision the implications of situations and choices.

Assimilators. These people are good at creating abstract models. They organize information, test theories, design tests and experiments, analyze quantitative information, and can construct conceptual models.

Accommodators. These people take risks, adapt to circumstances, and take action. They often work by trial and error, depend on other people for analysis of information, and may be viewed as impatient by the more contemplative types. They look for and use opportunities, are involved and committed, and can work well with, or lead, people.

Kolb has written about learners' orientation to four learning modes: concrete experience, reflective observation, abstract conceptualization, and active experimentation (see figure above). Each orientation is explained more fully below, along with the training style that is most appropriate for working with these learners.

1. **Concrete experience.** This orientation "emphasizes feeling as opposed to thinking." People with this orientation take an "artistic" approach. They are intuitive, open-minded, and do well in the absence of structure. Trainers of people with this orientation should function as motivators.

2. **Reflective observation.** This orientation involves "understanding the meaning of ideas and situations by carefully observing and impartially describing them." People with this orientation can see the implications of different approaches and are good at understanding different points of view. Instructors of people with this orientation should function as experts.

■ *4MAT Survey Battery*

Developed by Bernice McCarthy, this instrument draws on her experience and the work of researchers in learning styles, right-left brain dominance, and creativity. She recommends that instruction should do the following, in sequence:

- create an experience for learners

- encourage learners to reflect on or analyze that experience

- help them integrate the experience into defined concepts and "givens"

- provide materials and activities to help learners develop understanding and practice use of defined concepts and givens, thereby "adding something of oneself"

- provide learners an opportunity to analyze application(s) of learning for "relevance and usefulness"

- lead to application of learning, sharing it with others, and using it as a stepping stone to new learning

McCarthy's model categorizes learners as (a) *innovative learners,* who need the trainer to "give them a reason" that answers the question "why" or "why not;" (b) *analytic learners,* who need the trainer to "teach it to them," answering the question "what;" (c) *common sense learners,* who need the trainers to let them try things for themselves so they can answer the question "how does this work;" and (d) *dynamic learners,* who need the trainer to let them teach themselves (and possibly others) to discover answers to the questions "what can I make of this" and "what can become of this?"

■ *Gregorc's Style Delineator*

Anthony Gregorc based his research on different functions performed by the left and right hemispheres of the brain. His premise was that people make sense of their world through specific mental qualities that enable them to perceive and order the world around them. The Gregorc style instrument groups learners into four categories:

1. Abstract random (nonlinear) learners who are attentive to ambiance and who learn well through group discussion followed by personal reflection.

2. Abstract sequential learners who learn well from symbols and who like well-organized, substantial material—but dislike distractions.

3. Concrete sequential learners who learn well from hands-on experience and like step-by-step directions.

4. Concrete random learners who learn well through trial and error, like a stimulating environment, and dislike structure that may impede "intuitive leaps."

■ *Herrmann Brain Dominance Instrument*

Developed by Ned Herrmann, this method classifies learners in terms of the preferences for thinking in four different modes based on brain function:

1. Left brain, cerebral—logical, analytical, quantitative, factual, critical.

2. Left brain, limbric—sequential, organized, planned, detailed, structured.

3. Right brain, limbic—emotional, interpersonal, sensory, kinesthetic, symbolic.

4. Right brain, cerebral—visual, holistic, creative.

Social Interaction Inventories

These instruments address how learners interact in the classroom. The Grasha-Riechmann Learning Style Inventory, developed by Anthony F. Grasha and Sheryl Riechmann-Hruska, classifies learners as independent, dependent, collaborative, competitive, participant, and avoidant. It focuses on how learners interact with teachers and colleagues with respect to the learning process, and is suitable for use with college-age employees.

Instructional Preference Inventories

These instruments address the individual's preferred environment for learning. Among them are the following:

■ *PEPS*

The Productivity Environmental Preference Survey, commonly known as PEPS, was developed by Rita Dunn, in collaboration with Kenneth Dunn and Gary Price. It identifies the following individual adults' preferences for conditions in a working and learning environment:

- preferred physical environment (sound, light, temperature)

- emotionality (taking responsibility for task, persistence)

- sociological needs (self or group orientation)

- physical needs for learning (perceptual preference, biorhythms, need to move around)

■ *Canfield Learning Style Inventory*

Developed by Albert Canfield, this inventory assesses learning influences such as the following:

- conditions (a preference for an affiliation or competition)

- content (a preference for inanimate help such as computer-based training versus help from people)

- mode of learning (preference for listening, reading, direct experience, and so forth)

- expectation of success

■ *Learning Style Questionnaire*

Developed in England by Peter Honey and Alan Mumford, this instrument categorizes a learner as primarily one of the following:

- an activist who likes doing things, if only for the sake of doing

- a reflector who stands back to think

- a theorist who wants things tidy and rational

- a pragmatist who prefers to get on with whatever works

Honey and Mumford have correlated their work to Kolb's experiential learning cycle. They suggest that once you become aware of your learning style, you can accept it, building on your strengths and recognizing your limitations; or work to develop skills in your style's weak spots.

Matching Learner and Trainer Styles

Although it is tempting to try to tailor training to the learning styles of learners, it is not very practical. Training in the workplace must be designed to meet the requirements of the performance task, rather than to accommodate any particular learning style.

Awareness of style differences, both your own and those of your training participants, is useful in several ways. First, it captures the cognitive and affective differences among the trainees. Second, it should encourage the trainer to use a wider variety of teaching techniques. Third, it helps learners understand their own styles and preferences better. Finally, it enables trainers and learners alike to be more accepting of the differences among people. In this manner, new means of communication are established in the diverse audiences that most trainers face in today's workplace. Whatever their own styles, today's trainers and developers have much to think about and do in the continuing discussion, application, and research of training and learning styles.

References & Resources

Articles

Armstrong, J.L., and S.L. Yarbrough. "Group Learning: The Role of Environment." *New Directions for Adult and Continuing Education*, Fall 1996, pp. 33-39.

Cadwell, Charles. "Train the Trainer: How People Learn." *Trainer's Workshop*, January/February 1993, pp. 3-62.

Caudron, Shari. "Can Generation Xers Be Trained?" *Training & Development*, March 1997, pp. 20-24.

Cranton, Patricia. "Types of Group Learning." *New Directions for Adult and Continuing Education*, Fall 1996, pp. 25-32.

Dastoor, Barbara, and John Reed. "Training 101: The Psychology of Learning." *Training & Development*, June 1993, pp. 17-22.

Devarics, Charles. "On Target: Styles of Learning." *Technical & Skills Training*, November/December 1995, pp. 6-7.

DiResta, Diane. "Grace Under Pressure: Managing the Q & A." *Training & Development*, May 1996, pp. 21-22.

Eastman, Valerie, and Rebecca Smith. "Linking Culture and Instruction." *Performance & Instruction*, January 1991, pp. 21-28.

Eline, Leanne. "Choose the Right Tools to Reach Your Training Goals." *Technical & Skills Training*, April 1997, p. 4.

Eshelman, C.K., and Craig Woodacre. "Reviving Your Regulatory Training." *Technical & Skills Training*, April 1996, pp. 18-21.

Fauley, Franz E. "Learning Styles Have an Impact on Computer-based Training." *Computing Canada*, September 2, 1991, p. 34.

Fauley, Franz E. "Training Management." *Technical & Skills Training*, January 1992, pp. 34-35.

Filipczak, Bob. "Different Strokes: Learning Styles in the Classroom." *Training*, March 1995, pp. 43-48.

———. "Dog Day Afternoon." *Training*, February 1997, pp. 60-66.

Finley, Michael. "What's Your Techno Type—and Why Should You Care?" *Personnel Journal*, January 1996, pp. 107-109.

Flannery, D.D. "Global and Analytical Ways of Processing Information." *New Directions for Adult and Continuing Education*, Fall 1993, pp. 15-24.

Harp, Candice, et al. "Many Paths to Learning Software." *Training & Development*, May 1997, pp. 81-84.

Hill, Tom. "Make Your Program Responsive to the Learner." *Multimedia & Internet Training Newsletter*, October 1997, p. 8.

James, W.B., and W.E. Blank. "Review and Critique of Available Learning Style Instruments for Adults." *New Directions for Adult and Continuing Education*, Fall 1993, pp. 47-57.

James, W.B., and M.W. Galbraith. "Perceptual Learning Styles: Implications and Techniques for the Practitioner." *Lifelong Learning*, January 1985, pp. 20-23.

James, W.B., and D.L. Gardner. "Learning Styles: Implications for Distance Learning." *New Directions for Adult and Continuing Education*, Fall 1995, pp. 19-31.

Lowy, S.H. "From Chalk to Click: Multimedia Comes to the Classroom." *CBT Solutions*, March/April 1996, pp. 12-18.

Miller, Dusty. "Computer-skills Training 101." *Technical & Skills Training*, February/March 1996, pp. 12-16.

Porter, Gayle, and Judith Tansky. "Learning Orientation of Employees: Moving Toward Organization-based Assessment." *Human Resource Development Quarterly*, Summer 1996, pp. 165-178.

Rakes, G.C. "Visuals in Instructional Design." *Performance & Instruction*, March 1996, pp. 30-32.

Rao, S.S. "Putting Fun Back into Learning." *Training*, August 1995, pp. 44-48.

Repman, Judi, and Suzanne Logan. "Interactions at a Distance: Possible Barriers and Collaborative Solutions." *Techtrends*, November/December 1996, pp. 35-38.

Sims, R.R. "The Enhancement of Learning in Public Sector Training Programs." *Public Personnel Management*, Summer 1993, pp. 243-254.

Steffey, Marda. "Managing Diversity in the Classroom." *Training & Development*, April 1993, pp. 22-24.

Stuart, Peggy. "New Directions in Training Individuals." *Personnel Journal*, September 1992, pp. 86-94.

Ullius, Diane. "ART: Acronyms Reinforce Training." *Training & Development*, February 1997, pp. 9-10.

Wircenski, J.L. "Improving Your Questioning Skills." *Technical & Training Skills*, May/June 1996, pp. 25-27.

Wircenski, M.D., and J.L. Wircenski. "Greek to Me: Training Effectively with Unfamiliar Content." *Technical & Skills Training*, February/March 1997, pp. 28-30.

References & Resources

Books

Bell, Chris, et al. *Implementing Flexible Learning.* London: Kogan Page, 1997.

Briggs, K.C., and I.B. Myers, *Myers-Briggs Type Indicator.* Palo Alto, CA: Consulting Psychologists Press, 1977.

Brostrom, R. "Training Style Inventory." In *The 1979 Annual Handbook for Group Facilitators,* edited by J.E. Jones and J.W. Pfeiffer. San Diego: University Associates, 1979.

Canfield, A.A. *Canfield Learning Styles Inventory (LSI).* Los Angeles: Western Psychological Services, 1988.

Corder, Colin. *Teaching Hard, Teaching Soft: A Structured Approach to Planning and Running Effective Training Courses.* Brookfield, VT: Gower, 1990.

Denham, Wendy, and Elizabeth Sansom. *Presentation Skills Training: 30 High-involvement Training Designs.* New York: McGraw-Hill, 1997.

Dunn, R., et al. *Productivity Environmental Preference Survey.* Lawrence, KS: Price Systems, 1982.

Eitington, J.E. *The Winning Trainer: Winning Ways to Involve People in Learning.* Houston: Gulf Publishing, 1996.

Garratt, Ted. *The Effective Delivery of Training Using NLP.* London: Kogan Page, 1997.

Goleman, Daniel. *Emotional Intelligence.* New York: Bantam Books, 1995.

Gregorc, A.G. *An Adult's Guide to Style.* Maynard, MS: Gabriel Systems, 1982.

Herrmann, N. *The Creative Brain.* Lake Luree, NC: Brain Books, 1990.

Honey, P., and A. Mumford. *Learning Styles Questionnaire.* King of Prussia, PA: Organization Design and Development, 1989.

House, R.S. "Classroom Instruction." In *The ASTD Training and Development Handbook,* edited by Robert L. Craig. New York: McGraw-Hill, 1996.

Jacobs, R.T., and B. Fuhrmann. "The Concept of Learning Style." In *The 1984 Annual: Developing Human Resources,* edited by J.W. Pfeiffer and L.D. Goodstein. San Diego: University Associates, 1984.

Kolb, D. A. *Experiential Learning: Experience as the Source of Learning and Development.* Englewood Cliffs, NJ: Prentice-Hall, 1984.

———. *Learning Style Inventory.* Boston: McBer, 1985.

Kolb, D.A., et al. *Organizational Psychology: An Experiential Approach to Organizational Behavior.* 4th edition. Englewood Cliffs, NJ: Prentice-Hall, 1984.

Margolis, F., and C. Bell. *Instructing for Results.* Minneapolis: Lakewood Publications, 1986.

———. *Managing the Learning Process.* Minneapolis: Lakewood Publications, 1984.

McCarthy, B. *The 4MAT System: Teaching to Learning Styles with Right/Left Mode Techniques.* Barrington, IL: Excel, 1980.

Merriam, S.B., and R.G. Brockett. *The Profession and Practice of Adult Education: An Introduction.* San Francisco: Jossey-Bass, 1997.

Myers, I.B., and M.H. McCaulley. *Manual: A Guide to the Development of the Myers-Briggs Type Indicator.* Palo Alto, CA: Consulting Psychologists Press, 1985.

Silberman, Mel, and Karen Lawson. *101 Ways to Make Training Active.* San Francisco: Pfeiffer, 1995.

Smith, R.M. *Learning How to Learn.* Chicago: Follett Publishing, 1982.

Wheeler, M., and J. Marshall. "The Trainer Type Inventory: Identifying Training Style Preferences." In *The 1986 Annual: Developing Human Resources,* edited by J.W. Pfeiffer and L.D. Goodstein. San Diego: University Associates, 1986.

A Training Styles Inventory

Use Richard Brostrom's inventory to check how your training style ties in to various training theories and practices.

For each of the following 15 phrases, rank in the order to your best satisfaction the four statements given to complete the phrase. Give your *most* favored statement a rank of 4; your next favored, 3; your next, 2; and your *least* favored statement, a rank of 1. Place your ranking for each statement in the check box provided.

1. In planning to conduct training, I am most likely to:
   c ☐ survey the problem and develop valid exercises based on my findings.
   b ☐ begin with a lesson plan—specify what I want to teach, when, and how.
   a ☐ pinpoint the results I want and construct a program that will almost run itself.
   d ☐ consider the areas of greatest concern to the participants—and plan to deal with them regardless of what they may be.

2. People learn best:
   h ☐ when they are free to explore—without the constraints of a "system."
   g ☐ when it is in their selfish interest to do so.
   f ☐ from someone who knows what he or she is talking about.
   e ☐ when conditions are right—and they have an opportunity for practice and repetition.

3. The purpose of training should be to:
   a ☐ develop the participants' competency and mastery of specific skills.
   b ☐ transfer needed information to the learner in the most efficient way.
   c ☐ establish the learner's capacity to solve his or her own problems.
   d ☐ facilitate certain insights on the part of the participants.

4. Most of what people know:
   f ☐ they have acquired through a systematic educational process.
   e ☐ they have gained through a natural progression of self-discovery rather than some "teaching" process.
   h ☐ they have learned by experience in trial-and-error fashion.
   g ☐ is a result of consciously pursuing their goals—solving problems as they go.

5. Decisions on what is to be covered in a training event:
   a ☐ must be based on careful analysis of the task beforehand.
   d ☐ should be made as the learning process goes along and the learners show their innate interests and abilities.
   c ☐ should be mutually derived by the learner and teacher.
   b ☐ are based on what learners now know and must know at the conclusion of the event.

6. Good trainers start by:
   f ☐ gaining proficiency in the methods and process of training—how to teach—and then bringing in the content.
   g ☐ recognizing that learners are highly motivated and capable of directing their own learning—if they have the opportunity.
   h ☐ mastering the field themselves and becoming effective models for the learners.
   e ☐ considering the end behaviors they are looking for and the most efficient ways of producing them in learners.

7. As a trainer, I am least successful in situations:
   d ☐ where learners are passive, untalkative, and expect the trainer to do all the work.
   a ☐ that are unstructured, with learning objectives that are unclear.
   b ☐ where there is no right answer.
   c ☐ when I am teaching abstractions, rather than concrete, specific ideas.

8. In a training event, I try to create:
   g ☐ the real world—problems and all—and develop capacities for dealing with it.
   h ☐ a learning climate that facilitates self-discovery, expression, and interaction.
   e ☐ a stimulating environment that attracts and holds the learners and moves them systematically toward the objective.
   f ☐ an interesting array of resources of all kinds—books, materials, and so forth—directed at the learners' needs.

9. Emotions in the learning process:
   a ☐ are utilized by the skillful trainer to accomplish the learning objective.
   b ☐ have potential if the trainer can capture the learners' attention.
   d ☐ will propel the learner in many directions, which the trainer may follow and support.
   c ☐ provide energy that must be focused on problems or questions.

10. Teaching methods:
    g ☐ should be relatively flexible but present real challenges to the learner.
    f ☐ should be determined by the subject.
    e ☐ must emphasize trial and feedback.
    h ☐ must allow freedom for the individual learner.

11. When learners are uninterested in a subject, it is probably because:
    c ☐ they do not see the benefit.
    d ☐ they are not ready to learn it.
    b ☐ the instructor has not adequately prepared the lesson.
    a ☐ the instructor planned poorly.

12. Learners are all different; therefore:
    h ☐ some will learn, but others may be better suited for another activity.
    g ☐ the best approach is to teach the basics well and put learners on their own after that.
    e ☐ with an effective training design, most tasks can be mastered by the majority of learners.
    f ☐ an experienced teacher, properly organized, can overcome most difficulties.

(Job Aid continued on page 40)

Job Aid

13. Evaluation of instruction:

d ☐ is done by learners regardless of the instructor; the instructor; the instructor should be a sounding board.

a ☐ should be built into the system, so that learners continually receive feedback and adjust their performance accordingly.

c ☐ is ultimately decided when the student encounters a problem and successfully resolves it.

b ☐ should be based on preestablished learning objectives and one at the end of instruction to determine the learning gains.

14. Learners seem to have the most regard for a trainer who:

g ☐ taught them something, regardless of how painful.

e ☐ guided them through experiences, with well-directed feedback.

f ☐ systematically led them step by step.

h ☐ inspired them and indirectly influenced their lives.

15. In the end, if learners have not learned:

b ☐ the trainer has not taught.

a ☐ they should repeat the experience.

c ☐ maybe it was not worth learning.

d ☐ it may be unfortunate, but not everyone can succeed at all tasks.

Scoring and Interpretation

Add all the numbers that you placed in the "a" and "e" boxes. Place this total in the "a + e" box in the figure below. This is your behaviorist score. Do the same for "b + f," "c + g," and "d + h." The figure diagrams your degree of orientation toward major training-learning theories. For more information, see the sidebar and read about Brostrom's views described previously.

People deal with wholes, not parts—intuitive, emotionally, physically. They move spontaneously, "unpredictably," instinctively, unconsciously, nonlineally (right-brain activity).

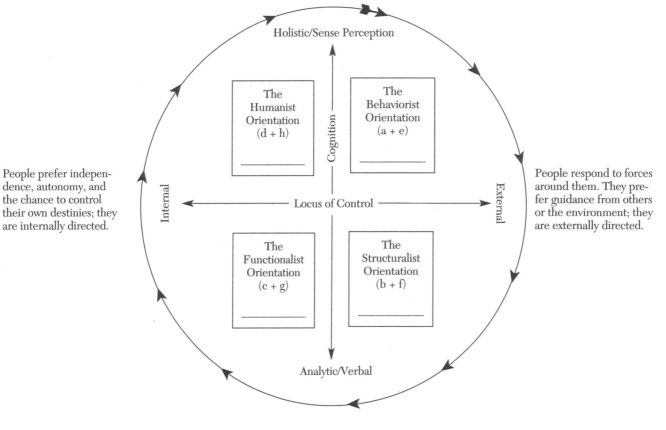

People prefer independence, autonomy, and the chance to control their own destinies; they are internally directed.

People respond to forces around them. They prefer guidance from others or the environment; they are externally directed.

People's minds work "rationally," intellectually, scientifically. Information is processed systematically, sequentially, for storage (memory) and retrieval (language) (left-brain activity).

Transfer of Training

Issue 9512

AUTHOR

Paul L. Garavaglia
The ADDIE Group, Inc.
57 Dennison Street
Oxford, MI 48371-4812
Tel: 248.969.4920
Fax: 248.969.2342
Email: ADDIEGroup@aol.com

Paul Garavaglia is a principle consultant at The ADDIE Group. He is the author of numerous articles on training transfer and is a two-time winner of the ASTD Instructional Technology Blue Ribbon Award.

Editorial Staff of 9512

Editor
Barbara Darraugh

Assistant Editor
Warren Shaver Jr.

Revised 2000

Editor
Cat Sharpe Russo

Contributing Editor
Ann Bruen

Production Design
Leah Cohen

Transfer of Training

Transfer of Training

You have trained a group of workers. They all passed the course's final skill evaluation and every last one of them delivered glowing smile sheets. Yet 12 months later, few of them are using these new skills on the job. Performance has not improved. Upper management wants to know what the problem is.

This is the classic transfer of training conundrum. Why does a room full of trainees, who seem to have learned the material and are genuinely enthusiastic about it, stop using their new skills and knowledge back on the job?

Our training efforts will do little good if they do not improve organization, group, or individual performance. While training can equip individuals or groups with new information, insights, and skills, it does not guarantee that these efforts will eventually improve job, work group, or organization performance. This means all training should be designed and implemented with such improvement in mind.

Although researchers may disagree on specifics, one thing seems certain: We cannot focus on just a single piece of the training puzzle. Clearly, trainers and developers need a holistic strategy to improve the transfer of training and, thus, performance on the job. We need to look at what happens before, during, and after the training program.

Consider this issue of *Info-line* a transfer of training primer. You will learn what the experts think transfer means, a few activities that can help improve transfer, and the whys and hows of measuring the transfer of training.

Other issues of *Info-line* that you might find helpful to learning about training transfer are these: No. 8906, "Lesson Design and Development"; No. 8907, "Testing for Learning Outcomes"; No. 9110, "Measuring Affective and Behavioral Change"; No. 9605, "How to Focus a Training Evaluation"; No. 9711, "Create Effective Job Aids"; No. 9804, "The Transfer of Skills Training"; No. 9911, "Teaching SMEs to Train"; and No. 9909, "Technical Training."

Making the Transfer Process Work

Even when needs analysis suggests training is appropriate, too often the performance problem does not go away after training. An examination of the training field shows that the amount of training delivered is not slowing, yet the application of skills gained in training is not growing. So we must conclude that training and increased productivity do not necessarily go hand in hand. Becoming familiar with transfer of training can shed some light on this dilemma. We must begin making the transfer process work in order to increase organization performance.

What Is Transfer of Training?

Transfer of training is the effective and continued application to trainees' jobs of the knowledge and skills gained in training. In theory, transfer of training is a relatively simple concept, but in practice it is difficult to obtain. The reasons are numerous, and the solutions are only now becoming apparent. To help put parameters around the transfer problem, you should understand the most common types of transfer.

Near and far transfer are two terms commonly used by human resource development (HRD) practitioners. Near transfer occurs when trainees apply skills in contexts that are the same as those encountered in training. Examples of near transfer include logging on to a computer, filling out a shipping request, or baking a pie.

Far transfer occurs when trainees apply skills in contexts that are different from those encountered in training. Examples of far transfer include handling an employee with personal problems, negotiating a contract, and making a sale.

Transfer Design Model

Use this model to analyze the transfer process in your organization and then choose appropriate interventions to solve any problems that are uncovered.

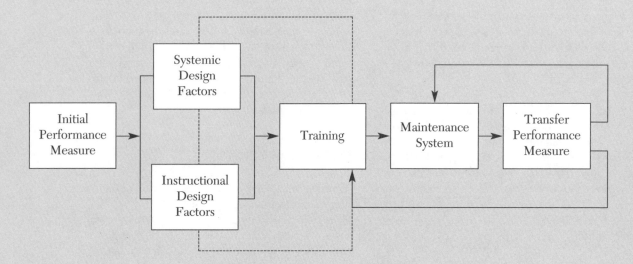

Stage	Description
Initial Performance Measure	A measure of baseline performance that the organization wants to improve with training.
Systemic Design Factors	Characteristics of the trainee or organization that may be barriers to transfer of learning.
Instructional Design Factors	Methods of presenting information, helping trainees practice skills, and assessing performance.
Training	The actual training program.
Maintenance System	The environment to which the trainee returns that should promote the use of the trainee's newly acquired skills.
Transfer Performance Measure	A measurement of the effect training had on correcting the original performance problem.

The Transfer Design Model

To ensure transfer, both training materials and organization systems should have transfer techniques designed into them. The *Transfer Design Model* at left provides a comprehensive process for doing just that. It is used to organize thoughts, ideas, and data and serves as a stimulus for understanding the transfer process. The model can help you analyze and understand transfer problems in your organization, and provide insight into selecting appropriate interventions for solving those problems.

Stage 1: Initial Performance Measure

The *Transfer Design Model* is represented in stages of a process and begins with an initial performance measure—the baseline performance measure—that we are trying to improve with training. Without an initial performance measure, we will be trying to hit a target that may not exist. You can obtain the initial performance measure from needs analysis data, which has been quantified and tied to business needs, problems, or opportunities.

Stage 2: Systemic Design Factors

The next two stages can be both concurrent and iterative. Systemic design factors expand the instructional management system in the areas of trainee and organization characteristics that were previously barriers to transfer.

Trainee Characteristics

Trainee characteristics consist of the affective attributes of trainees and the effect they have on learning. They can be divided into three categories: motivation, training, and the trainee.

■ *Motivation*
A critical aspect of motivation consists of trainee emotions and attitudes. Those that are detrimental to learning and affect motivation should be identified, challenged, and changed.

■ *Training*
The training category includes goal-setting versus self-management approaches. People trained in setting goals and what makes goals effective have lower transfer and performance levels than people trained in self-management techniques that focus on goals and how to obtain them, according to training researchers Anna Bavetta, Marilyn Gist, and Cynthia Kay Stevens.

In addition, further research by Katherine Karl and Duangkaew Ungsrithong has shown that the training overview at the beginning of the training session is vital. An optimistic overview stating what trainees are going to learn and be able to do at the end of training has a more positive impact on transfer than a realistic overview in which both positive and negative information is relayed. The realistic overview can be discouraging for trainees. Furthermore, belief in the value of the training—the "what's in it for me" syndrome—is important. If trainees find the content invalid, they may transfer knowledge and skills that are inappropriate for effective job performance.

■ *The Trainee*
This category describes how the ability level of trainees affects transfer, as does self-efficacy (one's belief that one can execute a given task in a given setting) and outcome expectancies (one's belief that the given outcome will occur if one engages in the behavior). The experiential background of trainees can at times help or hinder transfer. In her book *Designing Instruction for the Adult Learner*, instructional technology professor Rita Richey states that the more education and training experience the trainee has, the greater the knowledge retention after training.

Organization Characteristics

Organization characteristics that affect transfer include a trainee's perception of reality regarding the organization climate. These perceptions, formed from interactions with supervisors and peers, can affect transfer. For example, if supervisors are unfamiliar with the training content and perceive it as having no value, they will be reluctant to allow their employees to attend training programs. This eliminates any chance for new skills to be applied on the job.

The supervisor's perception of the trainees' skills and abilities also affects the trainees' opportunity to perform new skills. Supervisors with little confidence in their trainees will not assign them challenging tasks in which new skills can be applied. But sometimes supervisors do not have a choice in assigning challenging tasks, so they *must* prepare their employees for the challenges that re-skilling efforts and increasing complexity of work will bring.

Interestingly, employees tend to model their supervisor's behavior to gain rewards and recognition. And, if a supervisor behaves in ways congruent with training objectives, trainees will model that behavior and transfer will increase. Support from peers also can increase the likelihood of transfer, as can the pace of the work flow. If the work flow is fast, trainees may react in one of two ways—they may think they are too busy to try new skills, or they may think that using the new skills is the only way to achieve their goals. In either case, transfer is affected. If the pace of the work flow is too slow, trainees may forget how to use their new skills.

Stage 3: Instructional Design Factors

While instructional designers are building training materials that take into account systemic design factors, they must also incorporate instructional design factors that will increase the likelihood of transfer. As with systemic design factors, instructional design factors in the *Transfer Design Model* have been expanded to include a greater number of factors than other instructional design models offer—specifically, presenting information, practicing skills, and assessing performance.

Presenting Information

Trainers have a variety of presentation methods to choose from. Following is a discussion of some of them:

■ *Examples*
Use examples to facilitate transfer. Multiple, varied examples allow the trainee to see guidelines applied in different settings or circumstances. For clarification purposes, pair an example with a nonexample, that is, one that is often considered the same as, or easily confused with, the example.

■ *Analogies*
Use analogies to show how important concepts and principles apply in various situations. Analogies describe structural, functional, or causal similarities. They also can point out differences between two things. Properly used analogies create an anchor for the trainee to tie new concepts and principles to old ones.

■ *Principles*
Principles are statements of cause-and-effect relationships that provide for action. Explaining the principles behind what the trainee is learning allows the trainee to become more like an expert than a novice in the attempt to use new skills on the job. For example, if you teach trainees the principles of electricity, such as alternating and direct current, they will be able to connect a three-way electrical switch right the first time. Otherwise, they may find that when they plug in and turn on the hair dryer, the lights will come on instead.

■ *Advance Organizers*
Use advance organizers to provide relevance for the upcoming training material, thus making trainees feel the training they receive is pertinent. Advance organizers often link what trainees already know to what they are about to learn, provide a preview of what is to be learned, or provide both a link and a preview.

■ *Mnemonics*
Use mnemonics to create mental images that make instruction meaningful. For example, to remember the stages or phases of a generic instructional design model, use ADDIE, for Analysis, Design, Development, Implementation, and Evaluation. You can also use catchy phrases with special meaning and specific numbering patterns as mnemonics.

■ *Information Displays*
Understanding the impact of information displays is important in order to bring creativity to training design. Use information displays to draw attention and create perception. Consider that effective training is seen as mediating optimally between trainees and the subject matter, taking into account the characteristics of both. Therefore, the better the information displays, the better the trainees will learn the subject matter.

■ *Advance Distribution of Training Materials*
Allowing trainees the opportunity to explore training materials prior to attending the session has many benefits. These benefits include allaying fears, arousing interest, and engendering positive feelings about the upcoming training. Training materials can be sent to trainees in many formats, such as videotapes, audiocassettes, training manuals, tips for getting the most out of the training, and so forth.

Practicing Skills

Simulations make learning faster and safer by providing hands-on experience in controlled environments. A simulation is a model of a process or activity that generates test conditions approximating actual or operational conditions. Depending on what trainees need to learn, use the following methods:

● psychomotor-task simulations for psychomotor and perceptual aspects of a task

● cognitive-task simulations to teach the concepts and abstractions that underlie rules and principles

● verbal-task simulations to teach communication and coordination skills

● virtual reality when you want trainees to experience, interact, and manipulate three-dimensional images

Drill and practice are useful also. Knowing when to drill or practice is important because the proper practice technique can go a long way toward streamlining training and facilitating transfer. It is best to communicate by repetition (drill) when critical stimulus elements do not vary. Allow for practice when they do vary.

Assessing Performance

It is not enough to present information and practice skills; you must also assess performance. When assessing performance, consider learner-driven or problem-centered techniques, such as action learning. These techniques are popular because trainees are coming to the classroom—or the classroom is coming to them—with the goal of acquiring increased productivity on the job. Learner-driven or problem-centered techniques enable trainees to produce real outcomes in the work environment.

According to author Paul Froiland, action learning occurs when work groups—usually between six and 30 employees (sometimes including vendors and customers)—take an actual problem to the training and are responsible for solving the problem. Action learning has trainees commit to an action plan and holds them accountable for carrying out the plan. Action learning works well with trainees who have "do it," "jump on it" personalities. (For more information, see *Info-line* No. 9704, "Action Learning.")

Learning outlines, a form of self-assessment, may be the most effective type of assessment for some trainees. Learning outlines define what behaviors the trainees will start, stop, and keep doing as a result of training, and how they will measure the success of each action.

Stage 4: Training

After assembly of the training materials, the next stage of the model is the actual training. This is the stage in which we begin to sense what effect the training will have on the original performance problem. In the *Transfer Design Model*, some training factors (goal setting versus self-management, and realistic overview versus optimistic overview) were included in the systemic design factors because they need to be incorporated into the design of training.

The timing of the actual training can affect the trainees' transfer of skills. For best results, consider the following issues when scheduling employee training:

● Will the organization climate support the use of new skills?

● Will the work flow allow for the use of new skills?

● Will follow-up training or support be available when the "training high" wears off?

● Are personal or family stresses at an acceptable level to facilitate teaching?

Training Transfer Pitfalls

Managers can establish a transfer process whose benefits will come back tenfold by focusing on what it takes to make sure the right content and personnel get into the training; eliminating work distractions for trainees while they are in training; and providing ongoing reinforcement for trainees back on the job. It sounds easy, but seldom is. You may encounter some pitfalls along the way, such as these that are adapted from *On-the-Level: Performance Communication That Works* by Patricia McLagen and Peter Krembs:

- Employees may be afraid to admit they need to develop and learn. They may feel development is for the incompetent.

- Development plans and actions are not sufficiently compelling and relevant. The development plan does not relate to real needs and produce specific results.

- Programs are only offered as special benefits or limited to a special few.

- Development is given up because the payoffs lose their allure or get lost in the day-to-day shuffle.

- Development activities that should result in changed performance and capabilities (output) in order to be meaningful become a conglomeration of competing activities.

- Development plans that are not tailored to each person based on their learning style result in training failure.

- Resources that are not available when needed increase the length of the development process, resulting in less focused development plans.

- Employees do not recognize and appreciate the ongoing, widespread nature of learning and development.

Training Results

According to management professors Timothy Baldwin and J. Kevin Ford, there are basically five outcomes that can be obtained in regard to transfer:

1. Trainees transfer skills initially and then taper off, slowly approaching the pretraining level.

2. Trainees fail to transfer skills, as the posttraining level drops immediately upon returning to the work site.

3. Trainees attempt to use the new skill on the job, but after a period of time, there is a sharp decline in the use of the skill, quickly approaching the pretraining level.

4. Trainees learn and retain minimal information; therefore, there is little chance for transfer.

5. Over time, trainees increase their skill level once back on the job.

Both systemic and instructional design factors can determine whether skills are learned (see No. 4). The maintenance system (see Nos. 1, 2, 3, and 5) can affect how skills are used or not used on the job. Rita Richey suggests that 20 percent to 45 percent of the variance in posttraining behavior is the result of design (systemic and instructional) factors. Can we conclude from this that 55 percent to 80 percent is caused by maintenance system factors?

Stage 5: Maintenance System

After training, the employee goes back to the job and into a maintenance system that should promote the use of the newly acquired skills. Maintenance of behavior occurs after training, but decisions on what will maintain behavior should be made before training begins. Successful transfer of training requires a concerted effort on the part of both the trainee and the supervisor. A robust maintenance system takes into account motivation, the organization, the work environment, and teamwork.

Managers as Transfer Agents

Asking managers to change poses quite a dilemma. We all hate change and love it at the same time. What we want is for things to remain the same, but somehow get better. To make that happen in today's business climate, managers need to examine their behavior. They can begin by answering these questions: What did you do to facilitate transfer before, during, and after the last time you sent an employee to training? Did you just approve the budget expense for training, or did you go beyond that?

A manager who is committed to being a transfer agent will take these actions:

● Help develop individual action plans for on-the-job application of skills and knowledge.

● Develop plans and programs for supporting transfer of learning to the work environment.

● Participate in constructing materials to support training efforts.

● Help modify the work environment to support the application of learning.

Research has determined that the three greatest barriers to transfer are a nonsupportive organization climate, lack of reinforcement on the job, and interference from the immediate (work) environment. These, for the most part, are in a manager's control. To establish a transfer climate, here are the factors most in need of improvement:

● Trainee discussion of anticipated objectives with their manager prior to attending training.

● Trainee discussion of progress toward achieving objectives with their manager after training.

● Identification and removal of obstacles to transfer.

● Allowing trainees to meet with the trainer to discuss posttraining performance.

● Pairing of trainees together to reinforce posttraining performance.

Becoming a transfer agent—one who helps employees apply formal and informal learning experiences on the job, and serves as a mentor or coach to team or organization members—is worth the effort in order to see a return on the training investment.

Managers must put a process in place that will evaluate training and trainees, identify obstacles to transfer, provide feedback to upper management, and allow changes in the system to be made. Becoming a transfer agent is an ongoing process. This is a result of ever-changing trainee needs, organizations realigning and reorganizing for strategic advantage, and the nature of work changing rapidly.

The transfer climate of today may not look anything like the transfer climate of tomorrow. The problem in the immediate future will not be the lack of opportunities for managers to become transfer agents—training budgets are on the rise—but a lack of informed managers ready and able to take advantage of opportunities to become transfer agents. John F. Kennedy expressed it best when he said: "There are risks and costs to a program of action. But they are far less than the long-range risks and costs of comfortable inaction."

Motivation

Rewards and incentives can encourage the application of skills and knowledge gained in training, but make sure that rewards and incentives are just that. Giving trainees more to do because they did a good job will not work. Sending a trainee out of town to the main office to work on a "highly visible" project is not a perk if that employee does not enjoy travel, or being away from his or her family. Know your employees (what makes them tick), and reward them in a timely, fair, and appropriate manner.

Positive reinforcement is a way of maintaining new skills and knowledge gained in training. It consists of words of encouragement or acknowledgement of a job well done. Positive reinforcement can be given "in process," while trainees are working on a project—for example, telling them to keep up the good work; or "post process," when trainees have completed a project—telling them they did a great job or that the customer was delighted.

If a feedback loop is not established between trainees and their supervisor or manager, the transfer process can come to a halt. Trainees need feedback to correct or improve unacceptable behavior (active/formative feedback) as well as to acknowledge and maintain satisfactory performance (active/maintaining feedback). Passive feedback—feedback that identifies performance as unacceptable—is not enough, because it does not give trainees any insight into how to correct their performance. To get the most out of feedback, discuss the anticipated objectives and outcomes with trainees prior to training. Remember to give feedback in a timely manner and not wait until something goes wrong.

The Organization

When obstacles are identified through the trainee-supervisor feedback loop or other evaluation efforts, remove them. It is not enough to identify obstacles, jot them down, and file them away until some magical later date. It would be a shame to waste the valuable feedback obtained from discussions with trainees, and the richness of data gathered in evaluation efforts, just because removing obstacles might mean changing the status quo. Obstacles are anything (or anyone) that prevents skills and knowledge gained in training from being applied on the job, and their elimination will help facilitate transfer.

At times, removing obstacles to transfer necessitates changes in the system. These changes can be made to the organization structure, that is, the functions of an organization and their reporting relationships; or to the organization system, that is, how the work gets done.

Organization structure changes focus on the following areas:

Span of control—the number of functions or people reporting to managers.

Organization depth—the layers between top and bottom management as well as management and the workers.

Organization system changes focus on work processes. A well-defined work process can make the transition from the training program to the job much smoother by:

- defining and structuring roles and responsibilities for workers

- empowering employees

- aligning work processes with organization values and culture

The Work Environment

The work environment should be conducive to the use of new skills on the job. Having the correct computers, tools, and materials to do the job is a must for streamlining the way work gets done and increasing productivity.

Incorporate ergonomics into the effort to establish a work environment that promotes efficiency and avoids expensive mistakes. For example: Have you ever gotten a sore back or wrist from working on a computer? Have you ever not been able to reach some controls because of their placement on the control panel? It is not necessary to become an expert in ergonomics to improve the workplace—just a willingness to identify and then make the needed changes.

Job aids act as on-the-job cues for guiding performance. (For more information, see *Info-line* No. 9711, "Effective Job Aids.") They reduce the amount of information trainees need to memorize.

Moreover, job aids can be accessed in real time, provide sufficient direction on how to perform a task, and tell the employee when to perform the task. Use job aids when there is limited—or no—time available for training. They are also helpful when the task is: performed rarely, very critical, highly complex, or changes frequently.

Providing job aids may not always be appropriate, however. Proceed with caution if:

- a worker's hands and eyes are engaged in other activities

- employees may lose credibility by using a job aid

- workers do not have the skills for using the job aid

- being able to recall the information is a matter of life and death

Teamwork

The likelihood of transfer increases with the use of booster sessions (meetings with the trainee and trainer to discuss the use of new skills on the job) and buddy systems (the pairing of trainees together to reinforce each other and maintain learning). The goals of these strategies are to provide guidance for using new knowledge and skills; maintain and encourage trainee learning; and avoid relapse to pretraining levels of performance by keeping trainees motivated.

Stage 6: Transfer Performance Measure

Ultimately, the transfer performance measure determines how successful training was at correcting the original performance problem. (See the section "Measuring Transfer" that follows for a more complete discussion of this topic.) The *Transfer Design Model* uses the transfer performance measure as the pivot point for making decisions. By comparing the transfer performance measure with the initial performance measure and finding insufficient transfer, you can determine whether the problem lies in the maintenance system or in the training. If the problem is the training, the systemic design or instructional design

factors may be at fault. Some of the reasons for obtaining a transfer performance measure include the following:

- ensuring job security by providing data that training is effective

- showing how training leads to organization improvement

- verifying the soundness of the curriculum and maintenance system

Rationale

The transfer performance measure can determine how the training needs to change, what assistance trainees need after they return to the job, and what prevents trainees from applying what they learned in training on the job. It also can measure the longevity of a new skill by comparing performance at follow-up time with performance at the end of training. It is estimated that 40 percent of the skills learned transfer immediately, 25 percent remain six months later, and 15 percent remain one year later. These measurements are based on the most common time frame for measuring transfer—six months—and the most common intervals—six-month or one-year intervals. Before taking a transfer performance measure, ensure that the trainee has had enough time to use the new skills on the job.

The Players

To establish a method, system, or individual(s) for making sure transfer gets measured, you must determine the most likely candidates to measure the transfer. Cost, bias, and time are the main criteria that affect a transfer performance measure, and the interplay of these criteria may be different for each organization.

Numerous candidates for measurement exist. For example, to evaluate training programs, you could use your own training staff or professional evaluators, depending upon the available resources and the need to avoid bias. You could also ask for feedback from instructors, trainees, line managers, supervisors, or external contractors.

The Techniques

Measuring transfer is important to show management the value of the training program. To measure transfer, determine these four things:

1. Cost of developing the method or instrument.

2. Type of skill and knowledge to be measured.

3. An acceptable response rate.

4. If measurement is necessary, and how long it will take to train interviewers, observers, data collectors, and so forth.

Some commonly used methods for measuring transfer are as follows:

- line manager or supervisor reports
- surveys or questionnaires
- action plans
- interviews
- observation
- trainee self-reports
- qualification sessions
- job simulation
- performance appraisal data

Focusing a transfer performance measure can help determine which method to use. If the goal is to prove something, then present evidence that explains how skills and knowledge are applied on the job. If you wish to illuminate, then discover facts that determine what helps and hinders transfer. To establish merit, justify the worth of the training program by validating the utility of the training and the maintenance system. If you expect to improve performance, then focus on the change from the initial performance measure to the transfer performance measure. Remember that there may not be one "right" method for measuring transfer.

Once you know what you want to measure, and the appropriate method, determine where you will get your information. The optimum goal is to obtain information from the total group. But time, cost, or other constraints often make this unlikely, and you will have to use a sample of the total group.

Measuring Transfer

You know what it is, and you know ways to improve it. Now, how can you tell if the training transfer worked? The obvious answer is measurement, but measuring the transfer of training is neither always intuitive nor easy.

Why Measure?

Training departments and outside consultants are running into the organization bottom line every day. We need to show that we can help improve workers' performance and, in the process, the organization's profits. Measuring the transfer of training—that is, showing how training has led to performance improvements on the job—is one of the best ways to prove the value of training. Other reasons to measure the transfer of training include the following:

Verifying the curriculum. Is the training program sound? Does it address the right performance problems in the right way? Does the program need to be upgraded or redesigned?

Evaluating the maintenance system. Does the training program have a maintenance system? Does it work? This data can illuminate any organization barriers to transfer of training.

Benchmarking longevity. How long will a worker continue to use a particular skill or knowledge? This data can identify changes in the program or organization that might affect transfer in the future.

When to Measure

Researchers disagree on how long to wait before measuring the transfer of training. Some recommend measuring immediately after the training program ends. Others say to wait one, three, or six months. As mentioned earlier, trainers commonly wait six months to take the first measurements, with follow-up measurements taken at six-month or one-year intervals. When determining when to measure the transfer of training in your organization, consider the following:

The amount of skill and knowledge transferred. The more trainees need to know, the longer it will take them to get up to speed on the job. Wait to measure transfer.

The skill difficulty. The more difficult the job task, the longer trainees will need to practice the skill on the job. Wait to measure transfer.

The skill criticality. The more critical the skill, the less time trainees have to make mistakes. Measure transfer right away.

Staffing or resource levels. If resources are low or if no staff is available, delay measuring transfer.

Who Should Measure?

When deciding who should measure the transfer of training, weigh the pros and cons of cost, bias, and time.

The human resources (HR) staff. This approach can be cost-effective, but the HR department may be biased toward the training if they developed or delivered it. Also, the HR staff may lack the skills to properly develop or administer measurement instruments.

The trainers. This can be inexpensive, depending on whether the trainers are internal or external workers. They too may be biased, however, and assume that skill mastery in a training program equals skill mastery on the job.

The trainees. Trainees can create self-reports of their own progress. These reports, though, may not accurately reflect their true degree of training transfer and performance improvement.

The line manager. Using the line manager to measure for transfer of training is another inexpensive technique. Past performance, however, may bias the manager's observations. Also he or she may simply be too busy to do the measuring.

An external contractor. Outside consultants and professional evaluators—such as industrial psychologists—can usually provide an unbiased opinion, but they tend to be more expensive than in-house staff.

Building a Transfer Climate

To build a climate that fosters the transfer of training, follow these guidelines:

- Provide rewards and incentives to trainees for using the skills gained in training.

- Give positive reinforcement and encouragement to trainees in their efforts to use new skills on the job.

- Provide timely feedback on performance.

- Remove obstacles to transfer that are identified in discussions with trainees and other evaluation efforts.

- Make necessary changes in the system to facilitate transfer.

- Furnish a well-defined work process.

- Provide the necessary equipment, tools, and materials.

- Improve the conditions in which work gets done.

- Provide job aids to guide performance and act as on-the-job cues.

- Establish meetings with the trainee and trainer to discuss the use of new knowledge and skill on the job.

- Pair together trainees to reinforce each other in order to maintain learning.

A combination. Another possibility is to mix expertise. Use in-house staff to evaluate existing programs, and hire professional evaluators for new training programs. Once the professional evaluators have built a foundation for evaluating these new programs, the in-house staff can then take over.

How to Measure

You can use several different techniques to perform a transfer performance measurement effectively. Measuring transfer does not always have to be difficult. In fact, the most problematic issue is probably time. Everyone is busy. But once a person or system is chosen to run the evaluation and time is set aside to do it, any one of these techniques should make the evaluation easy.

Manager's reports. Supervisors are in a position to observe changes in the trainee's duties and tasks and to report data about the trainee's strengths and weaknesses.

Surveys. Send surveys and questionnaires to trainees, managers, and even the trainees' peers, if appropriate. This evaluation method is fast and inexpensive.

Action Plans. Trainees fill out action—or implementation—plans before leaving the training session, and a copy is sent to the trainee's supervisor. Later, the trainee and the manager or trainer can meet to see what items on the plan the trainee has, or has not, done. If transfer fell off, further discussions can help determine why and how to fix it.

Interviews. Trainees, their supervisors, or their peers can be interviewed in any number of formats—one-on-one, in groups, face-to-face, over the telephone, or electronically. Interviews are easy to adapt to different jobs and departments and have low implementation costs.

Observation. Observation techniques are best used for repetitive tasks. Instruments must be carefully constructed to avoid observer bias. This technique also can be expensive and time-consuming. Alternatives to observation include a qualification session, in which the trainee performs each job task in an easily scheduled test environment; or a job simulation that accurately represents the job situation.

Other Techniques

Other less-used techniques for measuring transfer include the following:

Self-reports by trainees. These can be effective if the report format is clear, concise, and easy to complete. Self-reports can also be inaccurate, however.

Performance appraisal data. This may provide a good baseline from which to identify and record changes in on-the-job performance, but only if the data is specific, accurate, and up-to-date.

Control groups. Regardless of the method used, evaluating a control group that did not receive training will help isolate variables in the environment. This approach, however, may not be possible in many organizations.

Choosing the Method

Consider each method and situation individually, and review their pros and cons. Follow these guidelines:

Cost. Determine the cost of developing the method or instrument, both in terms of time and money.

Type of learning. Determine the types of skills and knowledge to be measured and select the most appropriate evaluation method.

Response rates. Determine an acceptable response rate. Evaluation methods will deliver different response rates.

Training. Determine how long it will take to train any necessary interviewers, observers, or data collectors.

Putting It All Together

Successful training involves two phases: the acquisition of skills or knowledge, and maintenance of behavior when the trainee returns to the job site. The *Transfer Design Model* attempts to facilitate successful training by meeting the transfer problem head on. The model recognizes that to be successful, not only must training take into account a greater number of variables, but organization systems need to be put in place that support trainees after they return to the job site. Perhaps this will change the look and feel of training, or radically change the organization structure. Either way, it is an exciting time to be an HRD practitioner as we accept the challenge of showing how training can affect the bottom line.

References & Resources

Articles

Baldwin, T.T, and J.K. Ford. "Transfer of Training: A Review and Directions for Future Research." *Personnel Psychology,* January 1988, pp. 63-105.

Bavetta, A.G., et al. "Transfer Training Method: Its Influence on Skill Generalization, Skill Repetition, and Performance Level." *Personnel Psychology,* March 1990, pp. 501-523.

Bennett, J.B., et al. "Change, Transfer Climate, and Customer Orientation: A Contextual Model and Analysis of Change-Driven Training." *Group & Organization Management,* June 1999, pp. 188-216.

Boyd, S. "Making Computer Training Stick." *Technical Training,* August-September 1997, pp. 31-35.

Brinkerhoff, R.O., and M.U. Montesino. "Partnerships for Training Transfer: Lessons from a Corporate Study." *Human Resource Development Quarterly,* volume 6, number 3 (1995), pp. 263-274.

Broad, M.L. "Overview of Transfer of Training: From Learning to Performance." *Performance Improvement Quarterly,* volume 10, number 2 (1997), pp. 7-21.

Burke, L.A., and T.T. Baldwin. "Workforce Training Transfer: A Study of the Effect of Relapse Prevention Training and Transfer Climate." *Human Resource Management,* Fall 1999, pp. 227-242.

Cruz, B.J. "Measuring the Transfer of Training." *Performance Improvement Quarterly,* volume 10, number 2 (1997), pp. 83-97.

Esque. T.J., and J. McCausland. "Taking Ownership for Transfer: A Management Development Case Study." *Performance Improvement Quarterly,* volume 10, number 2 (1997), pp. 116-133.

Flynn, K. "We Trained and Trained, Why Didn't It Stick?" *Journal for Quality and Participation,* June 1997, pp. 28-32.

Ford, J.K., and D.A. Weissbein. "Transfer of Training: An Updated Review and Analysis." *Performance Improvement Quarterly,* volume 10, number 2 (1997), pp. 22-41.

Foxon, M.J. "The Influence of Motivation to Transfer, Action Planning, and Manager Support on the Transfer Process." *Performance Improvement Quarterly,* volume 10, number 2 (1997), pp. 42-63.

Froiland, P. "Action Learning: Taming Real Problems in Real Time." *Training,* January 1994, pp. 27-34.

Garavaglia, P.L. "Applying a Transfer Model to Training." *Performance & Instruction,* April 1996, pp. 4-8.

———. "How to Ensure Transfer of Training." *Training & Development,* October 1993, pp. 63-68.

———. "The Ins and Outs of Transfer." *Performance & Instruction,* May 1995, pp. 24-27.

———. "Study: Why Training Doesn't Transfer." *Corporate University Review,* volume 5, number 1 (1997), p. 12.

———. "The Transfer of Training: A Comprehensive Process Model." *Educational Technology,* March-April 1996, pp. 61-63.

Inman, P.L., and S. Vernon. "Assessing Workplace Learning: New Trends and Possibilities." *New Directions for Adult and Continuing Education,* Fall 1997, pp. 75-85.

Joinson, C. "Make Your Training Stick." *HRMagazine,* May 1995, pp. 55-60.

Karl, K.A., and D. Ungsrithong. "Effects of Optimistic Versus Realistic Previews of Training Programs on Self-Reported Transfer of Training." *Human Resource Development Quarterly,* volume 3, number 4 (1992), pp. 373-384.

King, M. "Strategies for Transferring Training." *Performance Improvement,* September 1996, pp. 30-32.

Lee, K., and D.J. Pucel. "The Perceived Impacts of Supervisor Reinforcement and Learning Objective Importance on Transfer of Training." *Performance Improvement Quarterly,* volume 11, number 4 (1998), pp. 51-61.

Machin, M.A., and G.J. Fogarty. "The Effects of Self-Efficacy, Motivation to Transfer, and Situational Constraints on Transfer Intentions and Transfer of Training." *Performance Improvement Quarterly,* volume 10, number 2 (1997), pp. 98-115.

Milheim, W.D. "A Comprehensive Model for the Transfer of Training." *Performance Improvement Quarterly,* volume 7, number 2 (1994), pp. 95-104.

Olivero, G., et al. "Executive Coaching As a Training Tool." *Public Personnel Management,* Winter 1997, pp. 461-469.

Ottoson, J.M. "After the Applause: Exploring Multiple Influences on Application Following an Adult Education Program." *Adult Education Quarterly,* Winter 1997, pp. 92-107.

References & Resources

Books

Parry, S.B. "Ideas for Improving Transfer of Training." *Adult Learning,* May 1990, pp. 19-23.

———. "10 Ways to Get Management Buy-In." *Training & Development,* September 1997, pp. 20-22.

Reed, J. "How to Evaluate Training in Order to Increase Skill Transfer to the Job." *Multimedia & Internet Training Newsletter,* August 1998, pp. 6-7.

Rossett, A. "That Was a Great Class, But..." *Training & Development,* July 1997, pp. 18-24.

Rouiller, J.Z., and I.L. Goldstein. "The Relationship Between Organizational Transfer Climate and Positive Transfer of Training." *Human Resource Development Quarterly,* volume 4, number 4 (1993), pp. 377-390.

Yelon, S.L., and J.K. Ford. "Pursuing a Multidimensional View of Transfer." *Performance Improvement Quarterly,* volume 12, number 3 (1999), pp. 58-78.

Yorks, L., et al. "Transfer of Learning from an Action Reflection Learning Program." *Performance Improvement Quarterly,* volume 11, number 1 (1998), pp. 59-73.

Broad, M.L., and J.W. Newstrom. *Transfer of Training: Action-Packed Strategies to Ensure High Payoff from Training Investments.* Reading, MA: Addison-Wesley, 1992.

Haskell, R.E. *Reengineering Corporate Training: Intellectual Capital and Transfer of Learning.* Westport, CT: Quorum Books, 1998.

McArdle, G.E. *Training Design and Delivery: A Single-Source Guide for Every Trainer, Training Manager, and Occasional Trainer.* Alexandria, VA: ASTD, 1999.

McLagan, P.A., and P. Krembs. *On the Level: Performance Communication That Works.* 2nd edition. San Francisco: Berrett-Koehler, 1995.

Nelson, B. *1001 Ways to Reward Employees.* New York: Workman Publishing, 1994.

Phillips, J.J., and M.L. Broad, eds. *In Action: Transferring Learning to the Workplace.* Alexandria, VA: ASTD, 1997.

Richey, R.C. *Designing Instruction for the Adult Learner.* London: Kogan Page, 1992.

Info-lines

Butruille, S., ed. "Lesson Design and Development." No. 8906 (revised 1999).

Dent, Janice. "Technical Training." No. 9909.

Hacker, Deborah Grafinger. "Testing for Learning Outcomes." No. 8907 (revised 1998).

O'Neill, M. "How to Focus a Training Evaluation." No. 9605.

Robinson, D.G., and J.G. Robinson. "Measuring Affective and Behavioral Change." No. 9110 (revised 1997).

Russell, Susan. "Create Effective Job Aids." No. 9711.

Russo, Cat Sharpe. "Teaching SMEs to Train." No. 9911.

Sullivan, R.L. "The Transfer of Skills Training." No. 9804.

Other

Garavaglia, P.L. "Transfer of Training...Guaranteed!" Proceedings of the 1994 World Productivity Assembly and Human Resource Development Asia Conference. Singapore: World Productivity Assembly on Human Resource Development Asia, 1994.

Gradous, B.D. "The Development and Validation of a Transfer-of-Training System." Report. St. Paul, MN: University of Minnesota, May 1991.

Job Aid

Transfer Climate Assessment

The barriers to transfer can be found in a nonsupportive organization climate. Using a scale from 1-5 (1=rarely and 5=consistently), assess your organization by rating how frequently the following factors are practiced:

Organization: _____

		Rarely				Consistently
1.	Trainee performance of new skills is more rewarding than nonperformance.	1	2	3	4	5
2.	Trainees are encouraged in their efforts to use new skills on the job.	1	2	3	4	5
3.	Trainees discuss anticipated objectives with their managers prior to attending training.	1	2	3	4	5
4.	Trainees discuss progress toward achieving objectives with their managers after training.	1	2	3	4	5
5.	Obstacles to transfer are identified and removed.	1	2	3	4	5
6.	Changes in the system are made in order to facilitate transfer.	1	2	3	4	5
7.	Trainees work within a work process that defines and structures roles and responsibilities.	1	2	3	4	5
8.	Trainees work within a work process that empowers employees.	1	2	3	4	5
9.	Trainees work within a work process that is aligned with organizational values and culture.	1	2	3	4	5
10.	Trainees have the necessary equipment, tools, and materials to perform their work.	1	2	3	4	5
11.	Trainees work in an ergonomically "correct" environment.	1	2	3	4	5
12.	If necessary, job/performance aids are provided.	1	2	3	4	5
13.	Trainees meet with trainers to discuss posttraining performance.	1	2	3	4	5
14.	Trainees are paired together to reinforce posttraining performance.	1	2	3	4	5

Total: _____

Score	Description
1-14	Climate needs improvement.
15-28	Climate still needs improvement.
29-42	Climate has potential.
43-56	With a little more effort, a transfer climate will exist.
57-70	Transfer climate exists. (Keep up the good work.)

The material appearing on this page is not covered by copyright and may be reproduced at will.

How to Create a Good Learning Environment

Issue 8506

How to Create a Good Learning Environment

Editorial Staff for 8506

Managing Editor
Madelyn R. Callahan

ASTD Internal Consultant
Eileen West

Revised 1997

Editor
Cat Sharpe

Copy Editor
Kay Larson

Designer
Steven M. Blackwood

Learning Environments

Sometimes it's just as important to know why Johnny can read—especially when Johnny is on your payroll. Nationwide, employers spend $55.3 billion a year on training. Nearly half of that is spent on direct training costs while the other half is attributable to indirect costs, including wages, salaries, and fringe benefits. So, it is hardly surprising that employers and in-house training departments are trying to discover the most effective, cost-efficient ways of improving their workforce. As a result, it is no longer enough to know why training fails; the question is why and how does it succeed?

Some major corporations and industrial pioneers have built their own multimillion dollar training facilities and designed programs to prepare employees for technological changes and increased competition from foreign markets. Xerox, Aetna, IBM, General Motors, and Motorola are among several innovators concerned with where and, more important, how employees learn.

As training costs and new market demands increase, trainers and instructors are expected to handle various roles that include technique, design, planning, and presentation. But the greatest emphasis is on matching the instruction to the trainee's actual work requirements.

Current trends indicate that effective learning environments closely duplicate the day-to-day job or workplace. Trainers are building the job environment into training designs and facilities. In Consolidated Edison's New York facility, groups of trainees learn how to use new technologies and equipment to work on high-voltage cable and gas main problems they may encounter on the job.

Motorola, the Chicago-based manufacturer of industrial and electronic equipment, assigns each employee 40 hours of technical instruction in such areas as computers and robotics. Not only is this training valuable for employees who can transfer it directly to the job, but the hands-on experience also gives sales and advertising personnel additional information to promote the products accurately.

More simplified ways of duplicating the work environment include exercises in role play or case studies. These methods allow learners to apply new knowledge and practice new skills under realistic conditions—situations that include employee error and barriers to productivity. One type of role play is in the "in-basket" exercise: a participant is asked to sit at a simulated work station and process all the information and assignments stacked in an in-basket. Trainers build into the exercise stumbling blocks such as unexpected appointments, emergency typing, and surprise phone calls. For additional information see *Info-line* No. 8412, "Simulation and Role Play."

Combined strategies, relevant course materials, suitable facilities, and reliable instructional instruments all contribute to the success of the learning experience. Independently, these features may not ensure success, but without their relevance to the work environment, it would be difficult to guarantee success under any circumstances. In other words, the product of training—improved or effective job performance—determines the value of an instructional medium.

This issue of *Info-line* will help you to understand the learning phenomenon, the environment, and the assumptions both learners and trainers bring to the experience. It emphasizes how to select techniques and methods according to learners' needs; how to motivate adult learners by supporting their concerns and engaging their interests; and how to provide the necessary resources directly related to their learning goals. The architect of a good learning environment takes cues from trainees and proceeds accordingly.

Adult Learners

The dynamics of a learning environment involve a wide range of training and learning styles; instructional methods and techniques for different kinds of learners; motivations of both learners and trainers; and the personal, intellectual, and job-related needs of learners. Following are several generalizations about adult learning that can help guide you when developing programs:

■ Adults Are Motivated to Learn
Adults' motives to learn play a major role in determining learning outcomes. The degree and quality of their participation in learning activities depend on whether their expectations are being met by the program. If there are obvious shortcomings at the beginning, the adult will quickly withdraw from the program. Motivation can be influenced by instructional goals themselves—the learner who has clear, specific goals that are in line with the training objectives will be a strong participant.

Encouragement and support by trainers, instructors, and managers is equally potent source of motivation. Obstacles or barriers to learning are negative influences and if not recognized and corrected immediately will block the learner's ability to acquire new skills. One kind of obstacle you can encounter is a participant's overly intense motivation—this can easily develop into anxiety for the learner—creating a barrier to learning.

Recommendation:
Give learners the freedom to explore and interpret within reasonable limits. Encourage them to seek beyond their immediate needs and help them set objectives that are individually useful and realistic.

■ Wants to Apply New Skills Immediately
Adults choose training and instruction when they intend to use what they will be learning immediately after the program ends. They seek additional knowledge and skills to improve job performance and are interested in developing attitudes to support and enhance their work.

Recommendation:
Organize and conduct learning activities by offering the most useful mix of improvements in knowledge, skills, and behaviors for your planned outcomes or objectives. Some learning activities, for example, emphasize acquiring an understanding of stress-related problems experienced by line workers. Other activities require developing skills in order to perform the line workers' tasks.

■ Background Influences Learning
Background and experience are strong influences on the adult's approach to learning. Individual differences increase with age and the ability to "unlearn" or be disassociated from a particular skill or method of performing becomes increasingly more difficult. A lapse of several years in learning can result in reduced effectiveness of study and education skills. There is usually marked improvement shortly after instruction is resumed.

Recommendation:
Design effective programs with attention to individual backgrounds and establishing connections between the new learning and relevant previous experience.

■ Ability Impacts Instructional Environment
Learning ability is an important factor in establishing an environment for instruction. Between the ages of 20 and 50 learning ability remains relatively stable but thereafter sometimes declines. High levels of learning ability usually indicate an aptitude for grasping complex material and tasks quickly. In later years, a factor such as poor health can seriously diminish learning ability. Poor physical and mental health substantially reduce learning ability. Whether these conditions occur over time as with the gradual loss of vision or hearing from aging, or they are short-term illnesses such as a cold or flu, the training environment, schedule, and assignments should be modified to help reduce the effect of these problems on learners.

Recommendation:
Carefully estimate individuals' learning abilities and use these estimates in planning training and setting objectives. The decline in sensory faculties can be treated with sound amplification, hearing aids, glasses, and improved lighting. Anxiety and stress interfere with concentration and the use of memory, but can be alleviated with counseling, discussion, and stress reducing exercises.

Minimize the effects of health problems on the learning environment by providing such amenities as adequate low-glare lighting, sound amplification, large and neatly printed visuals, and ramps for wheelchairs. Arrange seating so that visually impaired learners can sit close to lecturers and presenter, and hearing-impaired persons can be close to loud-speakers and presenters (if they prefer to read lips).

■ *Adults Learn Best at Their Own Pace*

Learning effectiveness may decline if the adult is forced to learn faster or slower than his or her normal speed. Though learning power does not diminish with age, older learners proceed at reduced speeds while concentrating more on accuracy. Learning speeds suitable to effective learning vary widely among adults.

Recommendation:

Plan learning activities to help individuals find their best and most effective speed and follow that pace.

■ *Varying Levels Challenge Adults*

The best learning takes place when learning activities and tasks are sufficiently challenging to be engaging but not so excessively difficult or complex that they overwhelm learners. Some learners do not catch on to the more complex tasks as quickly and thoroughly as others; superfluous or irrelevant information tends to make these learners very anxious, especially when they must manage and organize the information.

Recommendation:

Start with simple tasks and gradually build more complex ones onto them as your learners become more confident of their skills and abilities. Simplify difficult tasks by using diagrams, charts, visuals, written instructions, and models.

■ *Teaching Styles Impact Learning Ability*

Effective learning and teaching styles vary with the particular instructional task or material: Mastering skills requires practice and rehearsal; learning effective communication and interpersonal relations is best accomplished in a group; becoming familiar with new analytical or review procedures may entail application and use of the procedures in self-directed, laboratory situation.

Recommendation:

Consider the content and nature of the instruction as you plan and apply the most appropriate techniques for presenting the particular subject matter or conducting the learning activity. Pay attention to the individual learning dynamics applicable to each task or assignment; this will be your best guide for designing and delivering training.

■ *Consistent Feedback*

Learners of any age accomplish more when they receive regular feedback on their progress. Having a standard of excellence helps learners establish goals and knowing where learners are in relation to their goals enables them to plan and direct their efforts.

Recommendation:

If feedback is discouraging, consider modifying the task so that the learner may experience some level of accomplishment and satisfaction. Negative reinforcement or punishment is not as effective as positive reinforcement or reward. Immediate recognition encourages and reinforces new learning. For more information, see *Info-line* No. 9006, "Coaching and Feedback."

■ *Interpersonal Skills Affect Learning*

Serious personal or social maladjustment reduces the effectiveness of learning. Anxiety and defensiveness regarding unsatisfactory performance or failure are the usual causes of poor adjustment. If adults are confident in their abilities, then they perceive complex problems as challenges; conversely, if they lack confidence, then the problems will appear as threats. Those adults most afraid of failure and lacking confidence tend to have limited recent educational experience, while those able to confront and handle failure, usually have many successes that balance out their experiences.

Recommendation:

Provide guidance and support, prevent maladjustment at the beginning and emphasize learners' successes. Strong confidence and a positive outlook on the learning efforts are valuable qualities. These and faith in the trainer or facilitator as a reliable, concerned resource person may be all most learners need to be successful.

■ *Sustained Interest in Continuing Education*

Interest in educational activities develops from encouraging influences. Potential learners pursue education to achieve personal and professional goals, to participate in a group endeavor, to acquire skills and information that will help them meet formal requirements, and to gain understanding of a subject or satisfy curiosity about it. Many times, the appeal of an educational experience begins with the learner's own interest in reading, ideas, and school. Additional support may come from friends, managers, a close correlation between personal goals and available training, and a strong desire to have a better job that requires additional training and education.

Recommendation:

Inform employees of training and educational opportunities: Tell them how the particular programs are relevant to their situations (anyone who uses a computer would want to know how to fully use a software program to achieve the highest level of efficiency on the job); and how the instruction will change their approach to the job (new information or skills regarding computer operations make a significant difference in job performance).

■ *Initial Fears*

Many adult learners enter educational experiences with apprehensions about the unknown and about possible failure. They cannot reconcile their role as student with their idea of the "responsible adult." They also mistakenly believe that learning ability diminishes with age. To maintain and enhance their self-image, adults must have initial successes; positive experiences offset the problems and difficulties that attend change. Learners who have achieved some success and gained recognition tend to seek more challenging educational objectives.

Recommendation:

In the early stages of the program, help learners feel that they are part of the group, that they are welcome and they belong. Participants will begin to concentrate on learning once they have passed the "inclusion" phase. It is best to introduce important input later in the program when learners feel comfortable with themselves and their environment.

Assist learners in accomplishing one of their objectives early in the program. This will boost their confidence and sense of being effective. Talk about past and future learning activities with individuals; show them how the teaching process involves them and helps them learn. When learners understand their needs and feel secure, they will be ready to make changes.

■ *Adults Need to Feel Involved*

Group and organizational tasks at the beginning of a program may not run as smoothly as you would like. As mentioned earlier, the need for inclusion and security are priority concerns for individuals new to the learning environment. Learners' behavior in the early stages of the program will be inwardly or self-directed.

Recommendation:

Include a good icebreaker at the beginning of training so that the learners become acquainted and feel comfortable with one another. Conduct group or organizational activities after the "comfort zone" is established.

■ *Learners Need Support*

Throughout the learning experience, participants require support and encouragement. Group support and emotional encouragement can give assurance and confidence.

Recommendation:

To increase the incidence of positive learning experiences, help learners set realistic, achievable goals and plan multiple outcomes if a chance exists that one or more may not develop. Attend to needs expressed by individuals, small and large groups of participants.

Help participants put negative experiences or failures into perspective by showing them how to learn from and how to reduce the incidence of these experiences. Some ways to decrease the chances of failing include working through problems or mistakes with learners, giving them the freedom to work at their own speed, evaluating the program by using the learner's previous performance as a reference point, and relaxing learners with gentle, nonoffensive humor.

■ *Freedom to Select Their Own Training*

In some ways it is better to have had no contact with trainees than have them drop out of a program after only a few sessions. If former attendees are disappointed or upset about failing, you may not be able to persuade them to take any instruction voluntarily and, as studies have shown, training is more effective when learners are free to choose and pursue it at will.

A high retention rate of participants is determined by various factors such as the match of learners' personal goals and program objectives, the background and education of learners, and the level of their emotional and financial investment in the training. Retention rates decline under the influences of discouraging friends, general disinterest, family conflicts, and job-related problems. As many as half of all withdrawals are unrelated to the instruction, showing that family and work have higher priorities than the training.

Recommendation:
Accommodate conflicting demands by developing a flexible schedule. Participants will feel comfortable about remaining in training and contributing to their potential if they know they will have sufficient time for family, friends, work, and community. Further increase retention rates by sending polite reminders to participants who have missed some sessions. In cases where the retention rate is extremely low, use program evaluations to find out what the program lacks and make the necessary adjustments. Survey dropouts for additional suggestions on how to improve the retention rate.

Characteristics of Adult Learners

Adult learners are motivated to learn when they have a need to do so. They want to know how the training will help them. Before undertaking any instruction, learners need to understand why they must learn the material or skill. Studies show that part of an adult's preparation for learning is to determine the benefits of the learning as well as the disadvantages of not learning.

Adults learn from activity. Practice and continued use increase learning and retention more than other passive (though standard) approaches, such as lectures. Participants respond better when the material is presented through a variety of teaching methods and understood on different sensory levels.

As a group, adult learners vary greatly in their areas of education, background, experience, intelligence, emotional stability, and motivation for achievement. Instructors and trainers must allow for these differences as they plan and present the instruction. An additional consideration is that

---

Tips for a Good Learning Environment

1. Match your training design to your training population. A group of machinists, for example, would not learn well from eight hours of lecture.

2. Vary your style and method of presentation. Use visuals, narratives, guest speakers, and group participation as alternatives to the standard lecture or discussion but remember to make changes on a regular basis; too much of even a good thing can get tiring.

3. Encourage interaction. Adults learn more effectively when they have opportunities to interact and, when appropriate, to contribute input to the training outcome.

4. Eliminate the podium—unless you have a very good reason not to. A podium can be intimidating to many adult learners and may inhibit interaction.

5. Simulate the work environment. Skills and knowledge that are gained in a simulated work environment are more likely to transfer to the job.

6. Provide examples from the "real world" as opposed to trite ones that are unrealistic and difficult to relate to.

7. Design your training setup to facilitate your presentation.

8. Do not impose artificial barriers to learning. When possible, provide restroom and refreshment breaks throughout the session, not just during designated times.

9. Keep the session moving. Do not allow yourself to be drawn away from the subject and the training goals.

10. Learn to read your audience. Recognize when it's time to move or take a break. Look for signs—gestures, facial expressions, body language—that indicate whether participants are tired, hungry, bored, anxious, and so on. Respond promptly by announcing a break or by asking them to initiate discussions on the topic of their choice.

---

adults must have the desire to learn. Following are some adult learning characteristics that you should familiarize yourself with to help you attain better results:

■ *Life Experience*

This is the source from which adults learn, so their structured learning should be based on real-life experiences rather than topics or subjects chosen exclusively by the instructor. Trainees relate the learning to previous knowledge. This is helpful when they are able to make connections between new knowledge and background information they may already have acquired. It is, however, a hindrance if the new knowledge has no relation to what they currently know; in such situations, they may choose to dismiss or reject the new knowledge.

■ *Preference for Informal Environments*

Adults learn well in environments that are more informal than the traditional classroom. A U-shaped seating arrangement, for example, and refreshments add to a more relaxed atmosphere.

Environmental Influences

A variety of factors affect training and instruction in positive ways. Learners should be told how to recognize and use the major influences in the instructional setting to improve performance and personal growth. There are three major influences on training and instruction.

1. Evaluation Criteria.
Standards used to assess the effectiveness of the training are valuable to learners as means of ascertaining progress and as points of reference for short-term goals. Such standards include improved quality, greater productivity, improved performance, increased interpersonal effectiveness, and reduced job time.

2. Encouragement.
Trainers and program sponsors can motivate participants by offering a positive image of the training, being supportive and enthusiastic about the program, and by providing challenging and useful instructional resources.

3. Negative Influences.
Certain factors can be barriers to learning and participation. A hostile competitive atmosphere, exorbitant costs, and anxieties about failure or poor performance are some examples of negative influences on education. If learners are shown how to recognize these influences, they can prepare themselves to offset and deal with them.

■ *Personal Directives*

The adult learner needs to be free to direct himself or herself. This is why trainers and instructors should participate in a dialogue with learners rather than simply disseminate information and assess learners' retention of the material. They need to know if they are progressing. Guidance and deserved praise from instructors are more valuable than grades or letter evaluations.

■ *Getting to the Heart of Motivation*

For the most part, adult learners are mature. Once motivated, these learners will attempt to gain the most out of their training for the purpose of improving their job performance. During training, learners focus on solving job-related problems rather than gathering new information that may or not may have some relation to their work. They take a practical approach to the training. If you offer theory and new knowledge, they will try to apply and relate the information to their backgrounds, jobs, career paths, and so forth.

■ *Underlying Interpretation*

Adult learners are interested in what is below the surface of the learning activities you assign. They will ask about the motivations and purposes, the "whys" and "hows" of an instructional exercise or activity. Don't expect a room full of passive observers; adult learners want to be involved in whatever will improve the quality of their jobs and their skills.

■ *Expectations*

These participants expect to be taught by conscientious instructors who care about their learners, are always well prepared and knowledgeable in the subject area, and can present the instructional material effectively.

■ *Diversity Among Learners*

As a group, learners vary greatly in the areas of education, background, experience, intelligence, emotional stability, and motivation for achievement. Instructors and trainers must allow for these differences as they plan and present the instruction.

■ *Desire to Learn*

Finally, adults must have the desire to learn. Unlike children, they will not learn simply because someone thinks that they should have certain skills or knowledge.

Effective Trainers and Instructors

Successful trainers and instructors share a number of common characteristics. First and foremost, they must have a thorough and comprehensive knowledge of the subject they are teaching. Material should be presented in a clear and straight forward manner using language and written materials geared to the trainees' comprehension level.

Competent trainers will demonstrate a sincere concern for and interest in their students' progress and well-being. They will also show an interest in finding out more about learners' abilities while encouraging them to strengthen and develop their strong points.

To help individual learners progress and overcome problems, effective trainers often will work on a one-to-one basis with students. In addition to providing practical applications of the training, instructors can show learners how to use their new knowledge or skills on the job. Last, top-notch trainers should be comfortable enough to approach the learning environment with a sense of humor, using laughter to lighten rather than create tension.

Tips for Trainers

Find out what your learners need. Conduct comprehensive needs and task analyses to discover what skills and information your group should have in order to perform their jobs successfully.

Be sufficiently prepared. There's no substitute for information and a solid background in the field you are teaching. If you need a refresher or if you have not been keeping up with new developments, take time to get yourself educated. Trainees can spot an ill-prepared trainer in a flash. Being poorly prepared may cause you to spend the rest of the course trying to recover learners' cooperation and confidence in you.

Show concern and interest in your learners. Demonstrate that you understand and at times share trainees' points of view, that you can experience their perspective and present it in an objective and articulate fashion.

Show commitment to your profession. Through your gestures and activity, express your commitment to your work, profession, or field,

---

Participants' Expectations

Learners need to know what you expect of them. For some people, this new training environment will seem strange, especially if they have been away from school and in the workplace for a number of years. Give your learners a solid base from which to start their learning program and consider these suggestions:

- Put the learners at ease by explaining rules and guidelines for behavior in the training environment, whether, for example, they will be participating or quietly listening, actively involved in or passively receiving the instruction.

- Explain their role as learners and tell them how you plan to conduct the class. Describe the course content: role plays, discussion, assignment, and learning exercises.

- Do not jeopardize the learning with surprises. If learners should be aware of an unusual guideline or requirement, let them know early in the course.

- Tell learners what they are going to learn. Give them the course objectives, whether narrow, specific, or general. Regardless of the scope, it is important that they know the course topics and content—what they will learn and how they will be able to use it on the job.

- Deal with learners' fears, anxieties, doubts, questions, and insecurities early in the course. Learners may want to know if they will receive a grade for the course, if their bosses will be apprised of the grade, whether or not the course or grade will affect their jobs and if so, how.

- Do not assume that group members know each other. Help them become acquainted through icebreaker activities involving introductions and teams of participants.

- Treat everyone as an adult. Let your audience know that they—not you—are responsible for their learning and that your responsibility is to provide a quality learning environment.

---

and your enthusiasm for the training and course materials. The best way to motivate your group is to be genuinely motivated yourself.

Be flexible. Maintain your flexibility about both subject matter and participants. Be open and adaptable when conceptualizing topics and themes for presentation. And always be willing to listen and learn from your group.

Encourage trainees to contribute. It is fundamental to learning that participants contribute to the instructional process. Trainees learn best when the educational environment involves everyone. Allow learners to feel free to make contributions, but provide guidance and direction—learners need both independence and a flexible structure.

Define expectations and course structure. During your first meeting with a group, define the structure of the learning environment in clear and simple terms. Discuss your expectations of them and theirs of you so that everyone has a clear idea of what is expected. Include here, how the evaluation process will be handled and throughout the course, adhere to it in an impartial manner.

Have clear course objectives. Begin the training by clearly presenting the course objectives. Select the text materials, learning activities, and style of teaching that best suits the objectives. Keep assignments and learning activities in line with the overall course or training program objectives. This will require you to preplan the instruction and allocate approximate time frames to cover the materials.

Keep your ambitions modest. Don't be overly ambitious at first. Design a short course on a critical topic that consists of no more than four sessions and gradually build from there. Remember that some topics, for example, may be far more difficult to teach than you had imagined; skills that are second nature to you may be a real challenge to newcomers.

Provide necessary course information. Distribute course descriptions, outlines, and schedules. Carefully explain each of these and answer all questions participants may have. Learners' understanding of the material increases in proportion to the amount of information they receive about the course. One way to accomplish this is to use a comprehensive course outline to format this information. The outline should contain the following:

- course title
- instructor's phone and fax number
- instructor's email address
- class time and location
- course objectives, in proper sequence
- participation and class attendance
- prerequisite and course requirements
- examination schedule
- evaluation policy
- list of required reading materials
- list of assignments and due dates
- other available references

Make presentations simple. Use a simple formula for your presentations: State what you are going to tell participants, tell them, and then state what you have told them. Some studies show that learners prefer having instructors control the direction of the training, select emphases, and draw the major conclusions.

Treat learners with respect. Always treat trainees with respect and consideration. Do not try to behave as though your are infallible—everyone makes mistakes occasionally. If you don't know the answer to a question, say so, but you may want to see if anyone in the audience knows the answer. Failing that, research the question and come back with an answer after the next break, or if it takes longer, after the next session. If you try to bluff your way through a question or mistake, your credibility will be lost.

Maintain a calm, rational demeanor. If you disagree with a learner in your group, never try to fight his or her position with personal criticism. Challenge their reasoning, premise, or logic of the opinion on its own terms but never take the individual to task. Respond to all comments and inquiries, however ill-tempered, with a consistently straightforward approach. Sarcasm or a defensive attitude will do more harm than good.

Keep sections focused. Use questions or topic statements to focus lessons and assignments on major points of the instruction. Your learners' responses to these questions and comments can tell you how they are handling the material, as well as how well you are presenting the material.

Reinforce classroom instruction. Field trips, small group discussion, creative projects, role plays, and simulations are some methods you can use to make the training stick.

Keep feedback cycle going. Try to elicit an immediate and continuous flow of feedback from your group. Only they can tell you if they are learning the material, or if it is too simple or too sophisticated for participants to keep up with you.

Checklist for Creating a Good Learning Environment

As trainers and instructors, you know that learning does not rely on superficialities, gimmicks, and devices. If you are organized, well prepared, well versed in the subject matter and conscientious about matching the right training techniques to your audience, you have covered all the basic recommendations. To find out whether or not you are ready to begin training, think through the following checklist:

☐ What is the size of your group? Is it diverse or homogeneous? What are the ages, job titles, educational levels, experience, and expectations of your participants?

☐ What are the training goals and objectives? Are they shared by all the members of your group? Are they realistic in view of group members' capabilities and previous learning?

☐ Do you have the required resources, equipment, instructional materials, guides, and so on to implement the training? Are the meeting space and facilities suitable for your program and your group? Do you have, for example, the necessary amount of break-out room if you decide to divide learners into small groups for icebreaker activities, experiential learning, or role plays?

☐ Are any members of your training population physically, visually, or hearing impaired? Are your materials, facilities, and presentations designed for these participants' use? Do you have, for example, large screens for the visually impaired and seating close to speakers for those who have difficulty hearing or seeing presentations?

☐ What are your time restrictions? Do you have sufficient time to accomplish the training? If you run out of time, will you be able to set necessary priorities to make sure participants receive critical instruction?

☐ Do you have the presentation and facilitation skills to give lectures, mediate discussions, perform demonstrations, conduct role plays and simulations, handle case studies, or employ any techniques you have chosen for the program?

☐ What are your group's barriers to learning and productivity? Do they need more information, basic skills training, rewards, reasonable deadlines, or incentives? How can you cure such deficiencies before training is scheduled to begin?

☐ Have you chosen the best approach to your subject? Do your program devices, techniques, and strategies suit your particular trainee population? Do they clearly match your trainees' instructional needs and closely simulate the actual work environment?

Have tests mirror the course objectives. When constructing a test, keep the overall course objectives in mind and write questions and directions clearly so learners don't have to guess at your meaning. Your reviews and test instructions should clearly explain your intentions.

Time tests accurately. During test construction, schedule time carefully. Don't make the test too long for your time constraints and allow sufficient time for grading. Essay question tests may be less difficult to write than objective or multiple-choice tests, but they take more time to grade.

Have fun. Have fun with your teaching or training project. If you look forward to a rewarding and satisfying experience, your learners will also.

You will also want to experiment with different teaching methods and techniques. Don't be afraid to try something new. A change of pace often enlivens sessions that have begun to drag a bit, and they can reveal new aspects of a subject that may appear over-analyzed to the point of diminishing interest. Be assured that your group will let you know if your innovation is or is not effective.

A good resource for you is to share information or ask advice from colleagues. You can learn a great deal from observing other instructors' classes, from their observations of yours, and by discussing your teaching problems with them. Share training experiences with your colleagues as well—often this is the most effective way to become aware of possible pitfalls and successful approaches.

Training Methods and Strategies

It is up to the trainer to build a rich learning environment where shy and bold participants alike will benefit. Only the trainer is charged with the task of making learning flourish in a designated space with a chosen set of resources and a group of individuals who may be pleased, but many times, not overly excited, about being trained.

Whatever the circumstances, the best preparation for providing as effective a learning environment as you can is to know, understand, and practice a variety of training methods and strategies. The following should be part of every trainer's repertoire; you will not know how valuable they are until you are caught without the one, the only, perfect solution to your problem.

Lecture

The most frequently used method of disseminating knowledge, lectures are often described as speeches or presentations. But what is common to all lecture forms is the fact that each lacks the dynamic of interaction between audience and speaker—stated simply, dialogue. Occasionally, questions are permitted after, but rarely during lectures.

Lecture Characteristics

Lecture delivery may involve reading directly from a script or elaborating on detailed notes or prompts with the bulk of the work having been completed during planning and preparation. Visual displays often accompany lectures to enhance messages. Slides, overheads, flipcharts, computer screens, video, and film add interest and help participants learn because of their appeal to the different senses.

Remote location lectures, which include video-conferencing, Internet, intranet, and satellite transmissions are innovations that provide a cost-, time-, and travel-savings to many organizations. Presentations can be transmitted from specially equipped rooms where participants can listen and respond to questions.

Most lectures are presentations of information and knowledge. They typically describe a subject: office equipment, the history of the company, personnel or job restructuring, new standards, finan-cial status, and so on. Because information lectures involve narrative treatment of a topic, preparation and delivery are not difficult. The lecturer presents various points in sequence that contribute to a final conclusion.

Some lectures start with a particular problem or solution. For example, "How can we find out which products our clients prefer?" The lecturer offers a few solutions (perhaps a marketing survey, test products, or sampling) and then analyzes the advantages and disadvantages of each to determine the best or most viable solution.

Another type of lecture expresses a viewpoint or argument useful in goalsetting or strategic planning sessions. The lecturer proposes a goal or objective, presents supporting information, reviews possible problems, and develops a strategy or position.

Advantages of Lecture Presentations

- If lectures are properly designed and students sufficiently motivated, they can be effective for groups of mixed fast and slow learners.

- Vast amounts of information can be handled quickly in a lecture.

- Any size audience is acceptable for lectures if everyone is able to see and hear the speaker.

- Throughout their presentations, lecturers virtually control what they say and when they say it because they restrict interruptions from the audience.

Disadvantages of Lecture Presentations

- Lecturing is a demanding skill; individuals must be able to sustain concentration and attention, sometimes for several hours.

- Audience participation and contribution is minimal; lectures are designed for passive learning.

- Because lecture involves simply telling or talking to the audience, it does not indicate whether anyone has actually learned anything.

- Lectures by themselves cannot facilitate skills training or any training topic involving practical applications.

Lecture Tips

Beware of long lectures. After a certain point it is difficult to maintain both your energy as a lecturer and the audience's attention. Lectures under one hour are likely to bring success to new, inexperienced lecturers.

Establish credibility with your audience. Let them know your credentials right from the start—that you have an adequate background, experience, and knowledge of your subject.

Take time to introduce yourself. This is the point at which you make your very first impression so use the time wisely. Explain your qualifications slowly, your employment history, your particular interests, pet peeves, and goals. Answer all questions and then ask about the learners' expectations of you as their trainer or instructor.

For additional information on lecturing techniques, refer to *Info-line*s No. 9102, "How to Make a Large Group Presentation"; No. 9409, "Improve Your Communication and Speaking Skills"; and No. 9411, "Theater-Based Training."

Discussion

This is a participative method that relies on interaction and involvement of learners for its success. In discussions, the group explores a specific topic or issue by analyzing, evaluating, or reviewing subject matter. Learners enjoy the flexibility, informality, and opportunity to contribute that characterize most discussion groups.

Characteristics of Discussion Groups

Discussion is a valuable method for problem solving, decision making, and brainstorming issues that occur in committees and staff meetings. It helps learners change their affective behaviors. The group—including the trainer—points out the inaccuracies or problems with other participants' ideas, statements, or descriptions of actions. For example, the group can offer corrective alternatives to someone who won't confront an uncooperative co-worker, but instead always asks a supervisor to intervene on his or her behalf. Other topics may include discussing ways of improving processes such as mail collection, handling accounts payable, and strategic planning.

Discussion in small group training programs is valuable for trainers as well as participants. While the group is working on a particular task or assignment, the trainer observes and listens to the dialogue, noting strengths and weaknesses of individual interactions.

Formal discussion groups are debates. They are characterized by strict rules (designated response time and restricted length of response) and are often directed by group facilitators. Informal discussion groups are not controlled by rules or leaders and discussion may flow without any structured direction or planning.

Another kind of discussion situation is the seminar arrangement or "group tutorial." This involves more structured discussion than informal groups and poses questions about procedures and approaches newly proposed or currently in place. This kind of discussion is a good follow-up to a lecture, videotape, or written assignment and enables learners to critically analyze their own and others' positions on topics.

Advantages of Discussion Groups

- Discussion can be motivating and stimulating for everyone—all participants can contribute and become involved with the learning activity.

- Discussions involving real-life problems and situations give participants opportunities to practice skills and responses. The learning environment simulates participants' actual work places.

- Group input, analysis, and choices in solving problems and making decisions are more effective than individual contributions.

- The group members bring together and share their individual backgrounds, capabilities, knowledge, and experience for collective accomplishments.

Disadvantages of Discussion Groups

● Discussions must be well prepared; if they are not organized they may become completely directionless and accomplish nothing, wasting a great deal of time and energy.

● If more than 10 to 25 participants engage in discussion, it becomes very difficult to make progress.

● Group leaders and other highly visible individuals can dominate the discussion and inhibit others from speaking.

● Discussions take a great deal of time, particularly when the group is varied and requires long introductions, explanations of individuals' backgrounds or past experience, and time to become familiar with any unusual references or jargon.

Discussion Tips

Plan and prepare sufficiently for discussions. Establish a focal point and try not to deviate from it. Leaders can give the group direction and keep it on track, but they should understand that their purpose is to facilitate, not dominate discussion.

Maintain a clear objective. Keep the objective in mind throughout the discussion. This is the best way to ensure that the arguments and explorations will be relevant.

Arrange the seating in a convenient fashion so participants can easily see and hear each other. U-shaped or round table configurations are optimal for discussion groups.

Structure discussions. Set up discussions so that they include an introduction, a middle, and a conclusion. The environment for a discussion should be relaxed and non-threatening, yet organized and methodic.

Ask thought-provoking questions if the discussion lags at points, or take a challenging or even unpopular position. Throw a dazzler into the conversation to get learners' energy and ideas flowing.

Act as catalyst and moderator throughout the discussion. Guide the group by asking new questions and by rephrasing comments or responses.

Never let a discussion fade out. Conclude the group discussion with summaries or other closing statements.

For additional information on discussion groups, see *Info-line*s No. 9406, "How to Facilitate"; No. 9401, "Needs Assessment by Focus Group"; and No. 9407, "Group Process Tools."

Demonstration

This strategy illustrates functions, processes, ideas, relationships, and activities. Like lectures, demonstrations involve telling; learners observe rather than participate though they are sometimes able to practice the skills demonstrated and receive immediate feedback. Unlike lectures, demonstrations emphasize visual more than oral qualities.

Characteristics of Demonstration

Demonstrations typically present skills and techniques in action. They can be used to show how machinery and equipment operate. They also combine information, judgment, and physical coordination.

The demonstration method appeals to the five senses, increasing the impact of the training. Learners often are given the opportunity to test new knowledge and skills in controlled situations. This method is one that stimulates interest and engages an audience's attention.

Advantages of Demonstration Techniques

● Transfer benefits are high because actual on-the-job skills are applied during demonstrations.

● The method is flexible and can be adjusted to accommodate learners' needs without difficulty.

- If learners are given the opportunity to demonstrate skills, the trainer can correct errors before they become habitual on the job.

- A successful demonstration can be inexpensive.

Disadvantages of Demonstrations

- Since learners to not participate directly in the demonstrations, they may lose interest after a short period of time.

- Without careful preparation, the demonstration may fail. For example, inadequate attention to seating arrangements can result in learners not being able to see or hear presenters.

- Demonstrations are limited to small groups of 25 or fewer unless closed circuit TV or video equipment is available.

Demonstration Tips

Plan the demonstration by organizing it. Divide the skill into steps or procedures and put them in logical sequence. Become thoroughly familiar with the steps by practicing them.

Schedule time for practice phases following the actual demonstration. This is the most important learning activity and requires sharp observation and feedback on the part of the trainer.

Pause at key points in the demonstration and emphasize how the particular step or phase relates to the rest of the sequence. It is important to portray the total picture of the skill, rather than a segmented image of different aspects or procedures.

Offer two demonstrations if your subject matter is complex. Perform the skill slowly, so that learners can follow every step, and then repeat it at the average speed.

Reinforce the new knowledge and skills after the demonstration by restating the key points and main ideas. Instruct learners to copy these ideas into their notes along with their observations of the sequence of operations or procedures.

Carefully observe learners' practice performances of the new skills. Take this early opportunity to point out errors and prescribe ways of avoiding mistakes. If the particular skill requires high levels of speed and accuracy, emphasize this as soon as the practice begins.

Make sure groups do not exceed 25 people. If you must work with groups larger than 25, divide them into smaller groups for the practice sessions and appoint a responsible leader for each group.

For more information on demonstration, refer to *Info-line* No. 9804, "The Transfer of Skills Training."

References & Resources

Articles

Abdel-Malek, Talaat. "Assessing Requirements for Developing Your Training Capacity." *International Trade Forum,* October-December 1993, pp. 22-27.

Bahaniuk, Mark. "The Adult Learner: Handle with Care." *Office Administration and Automation,* August 1983, p. 79.

Bittner, Robert. "Five Tips for Training New Staff." *Hotels,* February 1996, p. 22.

Broadwell, Martin M. "7 Steps to Building Better Training." *Training,* October 1993, pp. 75-81.

Chaudron, David. "Avoid the Training Hammer." *Focus,* July 1995, pp. 12-13.

Delamontagne, R.P. "Games that Simulate: A Fun Way to Serious Learning?" *Training: The Magazine of Human Resources Development,* February 1982, pp. 18-19.

Dellafiora, Mary Lou. "Shades of Training." *Training & Development Journal,* November 1989, pp. 33-38.

"Education and Training." *International Journal of Manpower,* May 1992, pp. 45-50.

Filipzcak, Bob. "Frick Teaches Frack." *Training,* June 1993, pp. 30-35.

Filipzcak, Bob, and Jack Gordon. "What Employers Teach." *Training,* October 1992, pp. 43-56.

Fotheringhame, June. "Transfer of Training: A Field Study of Some Training Methods." *Journal of Occupational Psychology,* March 1986, pp. 59-72.

Fowler, Alan. "How to Decide on Training Methods." *People Management,* December 21, 1995, pp. 36-38.

Garavaglia, Paul L. "How to Ensure Transfer of Training." *Training & Development,* October 1993, pp. 63-70.

Ghitelman, David. "Getting Through to Grown-ups: Avoid Information Overload." *Meetings & Conventions,* June 1989, pp. 65-71.

Gordon, Ian. "Wobbling One's Way Along in Words." *New Scientist,* May 1, 1993, pp. 47-78.

Graham, Sandy. "Debunk the Myths About Older Workers." *Safety & Health,* January 1996, pp. 38-42.

Gunsch, Dawn. "Games Augment Diversity Training." *Personnel Journal,* June 1993, pp. 78-84.

Hammel, Frank. "Leadership 101: Teams Work." *Supermarket Business,* February 1996, pp. 127-130.

Hatcher, Timothy G. "The Ins and Outs of Self-Directed Learning." *Training & Development,* February 1997, pp. 34-39.

————."An Interview With Malcolm Knowles." *Training & Development,* February 1997, p. 37.

Hequet, Marc. "Fighting Fear." *Training,* July 1996, pp. 36-41.

"In Praise of Learning." *Wood & Wood Products,* May 1993, pp. 73-76.

Leander, Ellen. "Training Powerhouses: How A Handful of Companies are Developing Treasury Talent for the Rest of Corporate America." *Treasury & Risk Management,* October 21, 1996, p. 14.

Lynne, Don. "What's Your Solution?" *PC Week,* January 23, 1995, p. 70.

Miles, Chuck. "Training for Tomorrow's Technologies: Opportunities Abound in the Classroom and at the Computer." *Plan Engineering,* March 1997, p. 112.

"New Questionnaire Assesses Weaknesses of Training Participants." *HR Focus,* August 1994, p. 21.

Nweke, Kem M.C. "Training Needs and Methods of Training in Information Technology." *Information Services & Use,* July 1992, pp. 291-300.

Packard, Michael. "Alternative Training: The Home-Study Course." *RV Business,* November 1993, p. 38.

Philips, Glen. "Education and Training for the Adult." *Journal of Systems Management,* April 1989, pp. 8-9.

Piskurich, George M. "Developing Self-Directed Learning." *Training & Development,* March 1994, pp. 30-36.

Robotham, David Mark. "Self-Directed Learning: The Ultimate Learning Style?" *Journal of European Industrial Training,* July 1995, pp. 3-8.

Saunders, Marybeth K. "Training Tips." *Training & Development,* October 1990, pp. 18-21.

Sisco, Rebecca. "What to Teach Team Leaders?" *Training,* February 1993, pp. 62-68.

Steharsky, Charmaine Judy. "Understanding the Adult Learner: Implications for Effective Teaching of Proposal Preparation Skills." *Journal of the Society of Research Administrators,* Fall 1984, pp. 31-37.

Stern, Gary M. "Improving Verbal Communications." *Internal Auditor,* August 1993, pp. 49-55.

References & Resources

Books

Caffarella, Rosemary S. *Planning Programs for Adult Learners: A Practical Guide for Educators, Trainers, and Staff Developers.* San Francisco: Jossey-Bass, 1994.

Daniels, Aubrey C. *Bringing Out the Best in People: How To Apply the Astonishing Power of Positive Reinforcement.* New York: McGraw-Hill, 1994.

Draves, William A. *Energizing the Learning Environment.* Manhatten, KS: Learning Resources Network, 1995.

Gange, Robert M., and Karen L. Medsker. *The Conditions of Learning: Training Applications.* New York: Harcourt Brace, 1996.

Schwartz, Roger M. *The Skilled Facilitator: Practical Wisdom for Developing Effective Groups.* San Francisco: Jossey-Bass, 1994.

Smith, Phyl, and Lynn Kearny. *Creating Workplaces Where People Can Think.* San Francisco: Jossey-Bass, 1994.

Swanson, Richard A. *Analysis for Improving Performance: Tools for Diagnosing Organizations and Documenting Workplace Expertise.* San Francisco: Berrett-Koehler, 1995.

Info-lines

Bedrosian, Maggie. "How to Make a Large Group Presentation." No. 9102.

Bellman, Geoffrey, and Leslie A. Kelly. "Create Effective Workshops." No. 8604 (revised 1997).

Bensimon, Helen. "How to Accommodate Different Learning Styles." No. 9604.

Butruille, Susan G., ed. "Basic Training for Trainers." No. 8808 (revised 1998).

Darrough, Barbara, ed. "Coaching and Feedback." No. 9006 (revised 1997).

Eline, Leanne. "How to Prepare and Use Effective Visual Aids." No. 8410 (revised 1997).

Fairbanks, Deborah M. "Basics of Accelerated Learning." No. 9209 (revised 1998).

Garavaglia, Paul. "Transfer of Training." No. 9512 (revised 2000).

Kirrane, Diane, ed. "Training and Learning Styles." No. 8804 (revised 1998).

Liebman, Sophie. "The 3-5-3 Approach to Designing Creative Training." No. 9609.

Plattner, Francis. "Improve Your Communication and Speaking Skills." No. 9409 (revised 1997).

Priziosi, Robert. "Icebreakers." No. 8911 (revised 1999).

Smagala, Tina. "Theater-Based Training." No. 9411.

Thompson, Connie. "How to Motivate Employees." No. 9108 (revised 1998).

Wircenski, Jerry, and Richard Sullivan. "Make Every Presentation a Winner." No. 8606 (revised 1998).

"Survey Cites Need for Retraining, but Employers Offer Little Help." *HR Focus,* August 1994, p. 21.

van de Vliet, Anita. "Assess for Success." *Management Today,* July 1993, pp. 60-64.

Visser, Dana. "That's Using Your Brain!" *Training & Development,* September 1996, pp. 38-41.

Waddel. G. "Simulation: Balancing the Pros and Cons." *Training & Development Journal,* January 1982, pp. 80-83.

Weinrauch, J. Donald. "Educating the Entrepreneur: Understanding Adult Learning Behavior." *Journal of Small Business Management,* April 1984, pp. 32-37.

"Which Training Method Is Best? The Right Training Method Is as Important as Is the Skill With Which It Is Delivered." *Agency Sales Magazine,* August 1993, pp. 13-16.

Winslow, Charles D., and James C. Caldwell. "Integrated Performance Support: A New Educational Paradigm." *Information Systems Management,* Spring 1992, pp. 76-79.

Zemke, Ron, and Susan Zemke. "Adult Learning: What Do We Know For Sure?" *Training,* June 1995, pp. 31-38.

———. "30 Things We Know for Sure About Adult Learning." *Training,* July 1988, pp. 57-61.

Job Aid

Checklist for Presentation Skills

☐ Do you prepare an introduction that states the purpose of your presentation?

☐ Does the introduction orient learners to the subject matter of your talk?

☐ Have you chosen a presentation format or instructional strategy appropriate for your learners' education, experience, and level of comprehension?

☐ Is the type of presentation (lecture, demonstration, role play, and so on) right for the size of your group and the subject matter?

☐ Are you comfortable with this kind of presentation?

☐ Is the nature and amount of your material suited to learners' level of comprehension and experience?

☐ Is the material relevant to learners' jobs?

☐ During your presentation, do you ascertain whether learners are listening to and understanding your message by noting verbal and nonverbal (gestures, facial expressions, and so on) cues?

☐ Are these cues also useful in determining length, focus, pace, and activities?

☐ During the presentation, do you provide visual or verbal illustrations of your main points?

☐ Do you use analogies to illustrate or clarify particular points?

☐ Do your analogies fit logically into the context of your talk and are they well matched to learners' levels of comprehension and experience?

☐ Do you establish frames of reference during a talk and do they relate directly to points you are making?

☐ Are these frames of reference instrumental in relating the subject matter to the learners' jobs and are they well matched to learners' levels of comprehension and experience?

☐ At the end of the presentation, do you provide summaries of key ideas?

☐ Do you apply feedback from learners to evaluate the presentation?

☐ Are your presentation skills better than average? For example, do you speak clearly and loudly enough for a large group to hear everything you say? Is your tone of voice relaxed and natural? Are your mannerisms and expressions engaging rather than distracting? Do you maintain eye contact with your learners?

☐ Are you enthusiastic about the subject of your presentation and do you project this excitement?

☐ Do you communicate the credibility of your subject?

☐ Do you show learners that you respect their previous experience?

Facilities Planning

Issue 8504

Facilities Planning

REVISION CONSULTANTS

Coleman Finkel
President, The Coleman Center
810 Seventh Avenue, 23rd Floor
New York, NY 10019-5818
Tel: 212.541.4600
Fax: 212.541.4232

Coleman Finkel, an authority on designing and operating conference centers, has helped a variety of organizations plan and design their facilities.

Andrew D. Finkel
Diversified Technologies, Inc.
1092 Wilda Drive
Westminster, MD 22157
Tel: 410.526.5516, ext. 103
Fax: 410.549.3048

Andrew Finkel heads the commercial and residential sales, design, and CAD team at an electronics and communications integration company.

Editorial Staff for 8504

Editor
Madelyn R. Callahan

Revised 2000

Editor
Cat Sharpe Russo

Contributing Editor
Ann Bruen

Production Design
Leah Cohen

Facilities Planning

It is a common scenario: The meeting room is too hot, the lights are too dim, and the coffee is tepid. The speaker seems miles away, the slide projector does not focus, and employees attending the meeting grumble to one another in small groups about "a waste of time." Most workers in the United States can tell similar stories, but too often what they *cannot* seem to focus on is what they learned during the session.

The physical environment can have a major impact on the success of any training program. No matter how well designed, regardless of how talented and entertaining your presenters, a good session in a poor environment might add up to a waste of time and money for everyone involved. Take heart. Researchers have spent considerable time finding ways to create environments that actually help people learn, and experts have discovered how to remove some of the impediments that make learning difficult.

The learning environment most of us remember from our school experience required us to sit in fairly straight rows of hard desks and get talked at by a teacher who knew *everything*. Some of us, however, were lucky enough to take classes in which students met in small groups, and usually the effect was startling. It might not have been the subject matter or the teacher, but the simple fact that the environment, once changed, had a profound effect on our attitude toward the material being presented.

This issue of *Info-line* will look at ways you can make sure the physical environments of your training sessions are more like those fondly remembered group experiences and less like sterile and uncomfortable classrooms. Although the emphasis in this issue will be on facility planning and selection for training programs, the guidelines are applicable to all meetings and conferences.

A word of caution is in order for the current world of technological marvels: Today's meeting room should not so much emphasize technology but, more important, an approach to human well-being in an atmosphere of pressure and, often, boredom. Technology should be used only to augment, not take the place of the primary learning objective for a training program.

Planning Guidelines

When we were in school, a teacher stood before us and handed down knowledge. Our job was to sit still and absorb. Research tells us, however, that adults do not respond well to this approach. For many, it is boring; for others, frustrating. There are many methods you can use to meet your training goals, but matching the method to the participants calls for skill and sensitivity. Some learners prefer games and role playing (see *Info-line*s No. 8411, "10 Great Games and How to Use Them"; and No. 8412, "Simulation and Role Play"). Others prefer to learn using a hands-on approach. When determining participants' needs, consider these hints:

- Know your audience. Your needs analysis and task analysis will indicate specific learning needs and provide information about the required training and the participants. (For further information, see *Info-line* No. 8502, "Be a Better Needs Analyst.")

- Identify specific needs that the program should address.

- Find out the average education and experience levels of participants.

- Determine what type of stimulus is most likely to engage the learners (auditory, visual, physical, or a combination).

- Be familiar with the kinds of facilities most likely to be available, and the limitations of these facilities.

- Consider ways of effectively overcoming these limitations.

- Assess the impact of your actions on the participants and on your program design.

The Physical Environment

Planning the physical setting starts at the design phase. You will find that many of the questions you ask when designing a training program must also be asked when planning the physical environment—and the planned physical environment will affect your training design. Here are some items you should consider during the design phase:

- What presentation methods should be used to support the material and meet the needs of the participants?

- What are the anticipated audiovisual requirements?

- What are the computer connectivity needs regarding high-speed access?

- What level of physical activity is anticipated? Will the participants break into discussion groups; make presentations or demonstrations; be asked to write or take notes; or move from one location in the room to another?

- How much space will the leader require to conduct the training?

- How much privacy will be required? If participants will be asked to confer privately with instructors, can this be done in the same room, or must another location be arranged?

- Does the subject matter require any special security arrangements before or after the meeting?

- How will participants be dressed—casual or sports clothes, suits or dresses?

- If disabled persons will be attending the training session, make provisions for wheelchairs and guide dogs. For more information, consult the ADA (Americans with Disabilities Act) and ABA (American Building Association) guidelines or the Access Board in Washington, DC.

Select the Right Setting

Physical comfort is a prerequisite for mental alertness. People learn better in an environment where they are comfortable and the physical setting is appropriate to training. The proper physical environment can reinforce the material offered; a bad environment can make the best presentation almost worthless. Too much stimulation—bright lights, exposed audiovisual equipment, plush surroundings—can detract from the message being presented. It is disruptive to require participants to walk around equipment, extra chairs, and charts, or move a great distance from one location to the next.

If the training will take place in an auditorium or one principal meeting room, consider the following physical characteristics:

1. The room should help people concentrate. Avoid lots of decorations and pick something painted in subtle colors—but not flat white. All elements in the room should be designed to be comfortable while avoiding distraction.

2. Lighting should be bright, but not overpowering. Measure the light falling on a tabletop in several parts of the room. Too much light can produce shadows, squinting, and eye fatigue; too little may cause drowsiness.

3. If you are using audiovisual or television equipment, run through the program beforehand to identify any distracting echoes, shadows, or glare.

4. Check for proper electrical outlets.

5. Try to find rooms with separate heating and air conditioning controls.

6. Look for rooms that do not spread out the participants. Long, narrow rooms make participants in the back feel out of the action. Rooms that are too wide make it is difficult for a speaker to maintain eye contact with the entire audience.

7. Avoid rooms with clocks. Clocks can make a speaker's life miserable. Ten minutes before the end of the session, the speaker will notice the audience's attention drifting from his or her face to that of the clock.

8. If rooms have windows, make sure that they have lightproof curtains.

9. If you are designing a program in which participants will spend time learning individually in their own rooms, make sure the accommodations are suitable. Look for reading lamps with high-wattage bulbs, a lounge chair with a reading light, and a desk and chair that are comfortable and large enough to accommodate books, papers, and a lot of reading material. If participants will be using computers in their rooms, or need access to the Internet, make sure there are three-pronged outlets, modems, and sufficient space to set up a laptop computer.

10. If you are planning small-group learning in break-out rooms, make sure the rooms are the appropriate size to accommodate the break-out session participants.

11. Make sure the break-out room is not too far away from the central meeting site. The more walking and wandering people do, the less time they will spend learning.

12. If the group is small, try to arrange for special lounge chairs that can be placed in a circle. People with back problems find traditional hotel stack chairs uncomfortable for more than a few hours of use, leading to squirming and slouching and a lack of concentration.

13. If there are many participants who do not know one another, consider having a number of small rooms for breaks between sessions. Participants can discuss what they have just heard while having something to eat or drink.

14. Consider place cards and assigned seating at the first dinner or lunch. This avoids the "Where will I sit?" or "Will I have to eat alone?" anxiety.

15. Although the most common hotel dining table seats 10 people, if you want to enhance informal communication, try to arrange smaller tables of six to eight people. Ten people cannot keep one conversation going, especially if they are strangers. In a business setting, the shy participants tend to get lost as the more vocal and aggressive ones take over.

Avoiding Pitfalls

Every session planner has horror stories that they would rather forget. Everyone who plans meetings, conferences, or training programs is going to make a few mistakes, but the goal is to get tripped up as little as possible. Here are some suggestions:

- Do not hold meetings in rooms that are ornately decorated. Sometimes hotels offer rooms that have busy, flocked wallpaper, or mirrors and large pictures covering the walls. These can distract participants from the learning process.

- Beware of beautiful views. When difficult subject matter requires concentration, using a room with a panoramic view can be counterproductive. It is a lot more fun to stare out the window than focus on figures covering charts and graphs.

- Do not hold sessions in basement rooms where participants might feel trapped.

- Do not conduct training in long, narrow rooms if a lot of movement is part of the program.

- If you are catering to CEOs of profit-making corporations, choose upscale facilities. In general, hold sessions in rooms that have an environment similar to the workplace.

Arranging the Room

The single factor that determines the success of any training session is the seating. Placement of chairs and tables can contribute to accomplishing learning objectives.

Determining where people will sit can influence the level of participation. Some seating arrangements make it difficult—if not impossible—to interrupt a speaker. Other arrangements encourage participation of the entire group. So, depending on how much you want to control the group, or get their direct involvement, use one of these seating arrangements.

Let us first look at the seating arrangement that gives the audience the greatest involvement in the meeting, and then move on to the more traditional seating arrangements that give the speaker the most control.

■ The Circle

The plain circle of chairs often is used to foster an intimate relationship between participants in which they can interact in a friendlier kind of setting. This arrangement has no physical setting for a leader and creates an equality of participation.

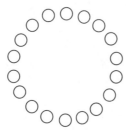

■ The Broken Circle

Many trainers use this configuration because it provides all the advantages of the full circle while affording a measure of control. This arrangement allows for a flipchart and a standing leader.

■ Circle and Table

This combination takes advantage of the informal aspects of the circle, but gives participants a place to put papers and books. The table also removes the sense of vulnerability some people feel in a plain circle of chairs. Studies show that when the same people sit at a round rather than square table, they participate more in the session, have more conversation, and shorter inputs.

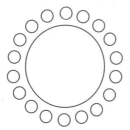

■ Square Tables

Square tables are a first full step toward a formal meeting arrangement. They are used when there are "sides" to be presented. Research indicates that a solid square table seems to encourage conversation across the table, while arranging tables so there will be a hole in the middle cuts down on cross-table conversations.

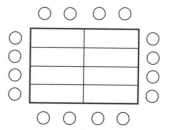

■ Rectangular Table

At a rectangular table, no one can see the faces of all the other people at the table, except perhaps for those seated at the ends of the table, whom participants expect to control the meeting. Rectangular tables can be very effective for some kinds of meetings, but they also can highlight the tensions felt by the two sides facing each other.

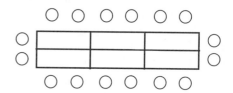

■ U-Shaped Tables

This configuration is extremely popular for seminars. A U-shaped table gives everyone taking part the sense that they are all equal. But such a layout also gives the center of the U a position of power and can provide space for someone at a flipchart to take notes. The person standing and taking notes can either lead the session or serve as a recorder.

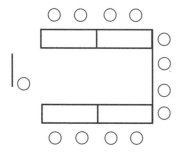

■ Classroom Style

For years, conferences have relied on the conventional classroom seating arrangement for training programs. This arrangement gives the leader—especially if standing on a raised platform—a lot of control, and it is hard for people to talk to anyone in the room except for those seated beside them. This arrangement accommodates a great many people in a relatively small room, however. It is also a familiar configuration, and effective for one-way communication.

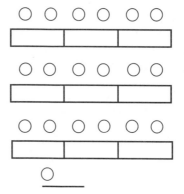

■ Circle the Wagons

The main advantage of this seating arrangement is that it can allow break-outs and small-group work without requiring participants to leave the room. If the entire group is seated through a lecture, and then each table is given an assignment and told to report back their findings to the entire group, this can all be done in the same room. A leader can assume a position of authority during the lecture time, but also move around the tables to help individual teams during these break-outs. As is the case with the round table, participants have direct sight lines to one another and can exchange ideas without a lot of movement.

■ Theater Style

Theater or auditorium seating is used when the planner wants to maximize the number of participants present in one room. It is not a good arrangement for stimulating group discussion.

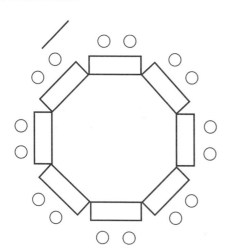

Selecting the Facility

Before you begin the facility selection process, identify the learning goals of the participants. Then plan the physical setting that matches those objectives. Remember that presentation techniques will need to be adapted to the ways that adults learn. For further information on learning styles and environments, see *Info-lines* No. 8506, "How to Create a Good Learning Environment"; No. 8804, "Training and Learning Styles"; and No. 8808, "Basic Training for Trainers."

Most rooms in which training takes place accommodate an amazing range of uses. They also serve as movie theaters, storage rooms, classrooms, even restaurants. Given the inevitable limitations, strive to make the facility the best you can. Be sure you can easily adjust room temperature. Chairs must make people comfortable (but not too comfortable), and tables must be capable of being moved, yet stable. Restroom facilities must be available for use by a large number of people in a short period of time. They also must be wheelchair accessible. Here are some other rules-of-thumb to guide you.

Space

Selecting the best space for your particular needs is no simple task. Remember to consider the following requirements, depending on what you are planning:

Type of Activity	Space Needed
Receptions	9-10 sq. ft. per person
Meals	12-13 sq. ft. per person
Theater seating	9-10 sq. ft. per person
Classroom seating	15-17 sq. ft. per person
Conference seating	23-25 sq. ft. per person
U-shaped seating	34-36 sq. ft. per person

Screens

Another way to check the adequacy of dimensions of a room is to judge all distances from the width of the screen to be used for visual presentations. Follow these guidelines:

● The distance from the screen to the last row of seats should not exceed six screen-widths.

● The distance to the front row of seats should be at least twice the width of the screen. Participants who are closer than that will experience discomfort and fatigue.

● The proper width of the viewing area is three screen-widths. No one should be more than one screen-width to the left or right of the screen.

● Ceiling height is important. The room's ceiling should be high enough—a minimum of nine feet—to permit people seated in the last row to see the bottom of the screen over, not around, the heads of those in front of them.

● Try to use screens that recede into the ceiling and that automatically raise and lower.

Peripheral Facilities

When making facility arrangements, you should understand the communication requirements of those involved in the meeting. Arrange to take messages and tell participants that outgoing calls can be made only during breaks. To facilitate this, take the following steps:

1. Make sure there is an operator available to take incoming messages.

2. Create a message board in a central location, and place messages on the board. Ask participants to check the board during each break.

3. Never install a telephone in a meeting room. If a telephone is already present in the room, have it disconnected.

Parking

One logistical problem often associated with meetings is how best to handle parking. Here are some guidelines to follow:

- If the training is held in an office building, make sure the additional cars will not place a burden on the normal parking facilities.

- If there is a parking problem, provide additional parking at a nearby location.

- If the training is held in the evening, parking may not be a problem, but security might be. Unguarded parking lots in most cities can be potential problem areas, so consider hiring security guards.

- If the organization has controlled parking lots, make sure you issue passes or gate permits for those attending.

- If the training session is held at a hotel or conference center, ask if there is a charge for parking. Determine who will pay for parking.

Restroom Facilities

If you are conducting your training in a location lacking sufficient nearby restrooms, you might want to direct people to facilities on other floors. Make sure you schedule enough time for this travel. If the meeting is in a hotel, ensure the restrooms are large enough to accommodate your group and are located nearby.

Evaluating the Quality of a Facility

Meticulous attention to detail, says Coleman Finkel, creates effective and adult-oriented facilities. Finkel was both founder and designer of The National Conference Center in New Jersey and is currently president of the New York-based conference center, The Coleman Center. He has developed a unique guide to help planners evaluate the quality of a facility using a numerical rating scale. This instrument focuses on key areas that may contribute to or limit the success of a training program. The following excerpt from his guide has been adapted for the purposes of this issue of *Info-line:*

The Facility Rating Guide

As a framework for your thinking, consider that you are evaluating an outside facility for a meeting of fewer than 50 people, who will be staying overnight. This checklist, however, can be adapted for evaluating your own meeting rooms, as well as for a program lasting eight hours, after which the participants go home for the night. To achieve the maximum number on this rating scale, you would have to check the highest score for every item on the checklist.

To maximize the value of a meeting, the planner should examine the ways in which participants will use the 24 hours of the session. The varied activities during those 24 hours occur in different places, seven of which are identified here (see *Relating Activities to Environments*). These environments should be considered separately, and designed differently if possible. Each should and can contribute to increasing the learning levels of participants—both in the informal as well as the formal activities of the program.

The facility rating process also includes a checklist for evaluating the quality of a meeting facility and its staff as they relate to the seven environments (two of which are detailed here; see *Evaluating Quality*). The items under each environment are ones that influence how each person in a meeting interacts, concentrates, relaxes, and studies, ultimately affecting his or her learning.

A rating scale for every item is listed in the right-hand column. There are separate ratings for each of the seven environments Note the range of numbers from which you should select (including "0"). Choose the number that represents the degree to which you feel the facility rates on that item. This listing is not intended to be all-inclusive. It does, however, cover most items that you should consider in a facility.

Relating Activities to Environments

Relating the activities that are part of the program to the environments in which they occur is the first step in the facilities evaluation process. List each activity first, then the environments in which it will take place. In the third column, identify all of the possible activities that will take place in each environment.

Activities During the Day	Environments	Activities in These Environments
1. Presentation and discussion in principal meeting room.	Meeting room in which the principal instruction, talks, discussions take place.	1, 2, 8
2. Work in small groups.		
3. Coffee breaks.	Break-out room in which project work occurs in small teams.	2, 3, 5
4. Three meals.	Sleeping room where participant meets others, studies, works, and relaxes.	2, 6, 8, 9, 10, 11
5. Cocktail party.		
6. Socializing with participants.	Indoor and outdoor areas where participant takes part in individual or group sports or games.	7
7. Recreation.		
8. Individual work related to program.	Break areas where participant can relax and socialize.	3, 4, 5, 6, 7
9. Washing, dressing, writing personal letters, making personal calls, watching television, reading.	Meal area.	4
	Meeting facility and its setting.	2, 3, 5, 6, 7, 8
10. Sleeping.		
11. Making business calls or writing business letters.		

Created by Coleman Finkel.

Evaluating Quality

Use this instrument to evaluate the quality of a meeting facility and its staff. The highest evaluation rating possible is achieved by checking the highest score for every item on the list.

I. Main Room Environment

Items	Rating (Circle one number for each item)
A. Square or slightly rectangular—not long and narrow so that participants in the rear are removed from the action in front.	0 1 2 3
B. Lighting is bright and evenly spread through the room. No spots of light. No high and low shadows on walls. No sconces or chandeliers.	0 1 2 3
C. No reflective surfaces from mirrors, glass, television monitors, crystal, or chrome—will cause eye fatigue and reduce perceptual levels.	0 1 2 3
D. Solid colors on floor covering. No plaids or stripes, which are fatiguing to the eye.	0 1 2 3
E. Ceiling at least 9 feet high, preferably close to 10 feet—to avoid feeling of compression and enable participants to view projection over the heads of others.	0 1 2 3
F. Comfortable chairs with arms, swivel, wheels, and recliner.	0 1 2 3
G. Tables that provide 2 1/2 feet between participants. Modesty panel on table. Rich-looking top requiring no covering and hard enough to write on.	0 1 2 3
H. No pictures or clocks on walls.	0 1 2 3
I. Light controls on front wall operated by communicator. Dimmers in room.	0 1 2 3
J. Audiovisual controls at front with communicator able to operate easily.	0 1 2 3
K. Air conditioning controls in room. Quiet system with good ventilation capabilities.	0 1 2 3
L. Comfortably sized for number of people in group.	0 1 2 3
YOUR TOTAL: _____	
MAXIMUM: _____	36

II. Break-Out Room Environment

Items	
A. Room appropriately sized for number of participants—not too large or small.	0 1 2 3
B. Room specially designed for small groups. Not a "make-do" room. Equipment on hand.	0 1 2 3
C. Comfortable seating.	0 1 2 3
D. Within easy walking distance of main meeting room.	0 1 2 3
E. Quiet area.	0 1 2 3
YOUR TOTAL: _____	
MAXIMUM: _____	15

Created by Coleman Finkel.

References & Resources

Articles

"Best Presentation Rooms." *Training,* May 1997, pp. A-Z.

Bishop, Kathleen A. "Tips for Making Your Seminar a Success." *Manage,* July 1988, pp. 22, 23, 37, 39.

Cothran, Tom. "Picking the Right Site." *Training,* November 1990, pp. 8-15.

Filipczak, Bob. "Make Room for Training." *Training,* October 1991, pp. 76-82.

Finkel, Coleman. "Meeting Facilities that Foster Learning." *Training & Development,* July 1997, pp. 36-41.

———. "A Room of One's Own: Climate Control." *Training & Development,* November 1989, pp. 31-33.

Green, Edward E., Paul F. Cook, and Lorraine Bolt. "Fitting New Technologies into Traditional Classrooms." *Educational Technology,* July-August 1996, pp. 27-38.

Holder, Robert J. "Creating a Training Space that Works: Space and Learning." *Journal for Quality & Participation,* June 1989, pp. 54-55.

Kasworm, Carol E. "The Learning Sanctuary as an Educational Environment." *New Directions for Adult & Continuing Education,* Summer 1990, pp. 27-39.

Linsley, Clyde. "Meeting Everyone's Needs." *Training,* July 1992, pp. 7-16.

Pappas, James P. "Environmental Psychology of the Learning Sanctuary." *New Directions for Adult & Continuing Education,* Summer 1990, pp. 41-52.

Price, Michael A. "Designing Video Classrooms." *Adult Learning,* January 1991, pp. 15-19.

Schurr, Tom. "Training Nightmares and How to Avoid Them." *Training & Development,* August 1992, pp. 18-19.

Sebrell, William. "Training Center Do's and Don'ts." *Computerworld,* January 22, 1990, p. 129.

Sheridan, David. "Making the Site Right." *Training,* November 1990, pp. 26-30.

———. "Yes but Where?" *Training,* July 1996, pp. 71-77.

Williams, Robert L. "Technology in the Learning Sanctuary." *New Directions for Adult & Continuing Education,* Summer 1990, pp. 63-73.

Books

Finkel, Coleman. "Meeting Facilities." In *The ASTD Training and Development Handbook: A Guide to Human Resource Development,* edited by Robert L. Craig. Alexandria, VA: ASTD, 1996.

———. *The Total Immersion Learning Environment: Its Critical Impact on Meeting Success.* New York: The Coleman Press, 1987.

Gayeski, Diane M., ed. *Designing Communication and Learning Environments.* Englewood Cliffs, NJ: Educational Technology Publications, 1995.

Terlaga, Kory L. *Training Room Solutions: A Guide to Planning the Learning Environment.* Trumbull, CT: Howe Furniture Corporation, 1990.

Info-lines

Buckner, Marilyn. "Simulation and Role Play." No. 8412 (revised 1999).

Butruille, Susan G., ed. "Basic Training for Trainers." No. 8808 (revised 1998).

Callahan, Madelyn R., ed. "10 Great Games and How to Use Them." No. 8411 (revised 1999).

———. "Be a Better Needs Analyst." No. 8502 (revised 1998).

Kirrane, Diane, ed. "Training and Learning Styles." No. 8804 (revised 1998).

Sharpe, Cat, ed. "How to Create a Good Learning Environment." No. 8506 (revised 1997).

Facilities Planning Checklist

To ensure a learning environment that will promote successful meetings, follow these guidelines. Keep in mind that for longer meetings, comfortable chairs are essential. Because there is increasing use of online education through the Internet and Web telecasting, planners should include such technology concerns in the evaluation process.

Location

☐ Is the meeting room located away from high-traffic areas that might lead to interruption?

☐ Are there signs directing people to meeting rooms, break-out rooms, dining facilities?

☐ Are there telephones available but away from the meeting room and in a place that will not disrupt other organizational functions?

☐ Is there a system set up to minimize outside interruptions?

☐ Is there a message board outside the meeting room?

☐ Have all telephones been disconnected from inside the meeting room?

☐ Can you easily control the temperature and ventilation in the room?

Room Size and Shape

☐ Is your room the correct size for the kinds of activities that will take place?

☐ Is there enough space for the instructor's work area and the books, handouts, and materials he or she might use?

☐ Is there enough room for the audiovisual equipment?

☐ Is there enough clearance space between tables and chairs?

☐ Are doorways wide enough for classroom furniture, audiovisual equipment, and disabled participants to pass easily?

Walls and Ceilings

☐ Can the walls accommodate charts and panels?

☐ Are the walls a neutral color that will not distract the learner?

☐ Are the ceilings high enough to accommodate projection screens?

☐ Do the walls contain enough electrical outlets? If computers are to be used, will antisurge electrical outlets be needed?

☐ Are light switches easily accessible?

☐ Can different parts of the room receive different kinds of lighting?

(Job Aid continued on page 90)

Job Aid

Noise Control

☐ Is the room too close to the street?

☐ Is the room near an alleyway or loading dock?

☐ Is the room located near building renovation, or where heavy machinery is being used?

☐ Are elevators too near the room?

☐ Is a noisy session scheduled for the adjoining room?

☐ Is there a dividing wall that does not shut out noise from an adjacent room?

Furniture

☐ Do chairs have wheels that permit them to be moved without noise?

☐ Are swivel chairs available?

☐ Do chairs have arms that allow people to rest their arms at a 90-degree angle?

☐ Are the seats made of fabric rather than vinyl, leather, or plastic?

☐ Are there sufficient whiteboards or flipcharts, as well as markers?

☐ Does the room have tables with modesty panels and separate tables to hold slide or overhead projectors?

☐ Have you checked the audiovisual equipment?

☐ Do you have extra light bulbs and extension cords?

☐ Do screens cover writing surfaces?

Use of Technology

☐ Are there flexible cable outlets for computer hookups?

☐ Are there in-floor jacks?

☐ Are there electrical in-floor outlets at least every eight feet?

Teaching SMEs to Train

Issue 9911

Teaching SMEs to Train

AUTHOR

Cat Sharpe Russo
Editor, Info-line
ASTD
1640 King Street
Box 1443
Alexandria, VA 22313-2043
Tel: 703.683.8136
Fax: 703.683.9203
Email: crusso@astd.org

Managing Editor
Sabrina E. Hicks

Production Design
Leah Cohen

Internal Consultant
Phil Anderson

Contributor
Sabrina Christian

What Is an SME?

The subject matter expert (SME), often pronounced *sh-mee*, is someone with more qualified expertise in performing a specific job, task, or skill than anyone else in your organization. Why are SMEs so important to training and performance? First, in today's environment of using less dollars to conduct top-notch training and get the biggest return-on-investment (ROI), using SMEs to train makes a lot of economic sense. Most organizations already employ SMEs to carry out their everyday business. Why not tap your internal smarts to benefit the organization as a whole?

Second, who better to conduct training than those individuals with the most expertise in a certain field? It can take training generalists weeks, if not months, to get up-to-speed sufficiently on a technical process or other job skill to prepare a curriculum. An SME, on the other hand, already knows this information, to use a old-fashioned phrase, "like the back of his hand." In addition, because the SME has performed the job often and well in a variety of situations, he or she can provide real-world examples of how to perform the trained skill or knowledge on the job. An SME's experience provides learners with concrete and visual images, and this increases the credibility and effectiveness of the training.

Last, many organizations can neither afford a large training staff nor have the luxury of time to take employees off the job to conduct training. On-the-job training (OJT) is now the norm. To keep your organization up and running, why not investigate the benefits of using SMEs—who are already performing vital business functions for your organization—to mentor OJT programs that train other employees?

You can use SMEs in the transfer of training or learning for the following:

- skills acquisition
- knowledge/information acquisition
- problem solving or attitude

Skills Acquisition

Skills acquisition refers to the transfer of skills and processes that you can easily observe, replicate, and document. In this role, an SME performs what is most commonly referred to as "technical and skills training." This training involves skills that are manipulative, calculable, or analytical (for example, learning computer spreadsheet software, running a piece of machinery in a plant, or completing a form). A trainer providing technical or skills training provides cognitive or conceptual information only to the extent required for participants to learn these skills.

Knowledge/Information Acquisition

Knowledge and information acquisition refers to the transfer of material that helps individuals perform their jobs, without necessarily being an observable skill. Here, the SME trainer is the possessor of knowledge and information about specific work. The SME shares this information with learners to enable them to perform better (for example, company history, mission and values, and HR policies).

Problem Solving or Attitude

The transfer of problem-solving or attitude skills refers to the transfer of new methods of dealing with work and management issues to help individuals or groups perform their jobs better. In this capacity, an SME acts as a facilitator, whose main focus is on the transfer of learning through group process (for example, improving group decision-making skills, solving a team conflict, or determining future work projects). Direct skill acquisition is not typically an objective of this type of learning.

So, it would appear that employing SMEs as trainers should be a major boon to management's on-going training issues. Unfortunately, SMEs are exactly what they purport to be: SMEs—not trainers. Too often, we ask SMEs to conduct training, but we never tell them what training really entails. For example, your SME, Pat Expert, might be well versed in programming and administering a computer network system, but Pat may not have the first clue how to help (that is, train) the 500 people who are linked to and must use the network.

This issue of *Info-line* will help managers, training and performance specialists, and consultants guide SMEs through the fundamentals of transferring learning and job skills. While doing this, it is important to keep in mind the mindset of today's business environment—an environment

Basic Design Terms

SMEs probably are not familiar with basic lesson design terminology. The following definitions, taken from the glossary of Donald V. McCain's book *Creating Training Courses (When You're Not a Trainer)*, should help SMEs get their design vocabulary up-to-speed in no time.

Case Study: a written account of a real or fictitious event or situation, including facts and opinions in enough detail for learners to analyze the problem or problems presented and make decisions to solve the problem. Generally, the closer the case depicts reality, the better the organization learning.

Design/Development: the process of structuring content, whether it be knowledge, information, theories, concepts, procedures, and so forth; instructional strategies; and media into meaningful learning experiences with the result of enhanced individual performance, business unit performance, or both.

Exercise: a structured learning experience supported by instructions and debrief explanation with application to the job; allows for discovery or application of concepts.

Evaluation: a process of training appraisal to determine and improve its value; the determination of the effectiveness of training programs; a measure of the extent to which objectives were met.

Instructional Strategies: activities that determine how learning will take place, including role plays, games, case studies, facilitative discussion, simulations, and so forth.

Modeling: the facilitator, or some other leader (as on videotapes), demonstrates a skill or behavior, which is then analyzed and practiced by the learners. The learners then receive feedback on their practice. The desired performance is scripted to provide a good example of the required behavior.

Simulation: a culminating activity that replicates reality and requires the learner to use what has been taught. Simulations are intended to provide opportunities to interact with realistic representations of reality.

Training: learning that is directly related to the person's current job. Training is required on the basis of a need for improved current job performance.

that requires employees to receive training when and how they need it, in an affordable, effective manner.

Selecting an SME Trainer

The first step in selecting an SME trainer is to identify what knowledge and skill the SME must have for you to consider him or her as trainer for your course. It stands to reason that you should base the required subject matter knowledge and skill on the content of the course. For example, selecting an SME based on his or her expertise in delivering excellent customer service does you little good if the subject of your course is the orders processing system.

To accurately identify the content of the course requires conducting a needs assessment. The end result of a needs assessment is to determine what specific job skills or knowledge you want transferred to participants. The needs assessment identifies the gap between your employees' current skill or knowledge level and the desired level. This information is the foundation for developing training objectives and the follow-up curriculum design.

You can select from a number of methods for conducting needs assessment. If conditions are right, a mini needs assessment can provide you with good information. For other situations, you will want to invest the time and resources for a full needs analysis. In the end, your needs analysis should answer the following questions:

- Is training the solution to your problem?
- What kind of training do you require?
- Which employees need training?
- What skills must trainees acquire?
- What are the specific job requirements?
- Do you need an SME to conduct the training?
- What materials/equipment do you need?

For more details on conducting needs analyses, refer to *Info-lines* No. 8502, "Be a Better Needs Analyst" and No. 9611, "Conducting a Mini Needs Assessment."

Once you decide to use an SME to conduct training, you will often base your SME selection on a single criterion: job performance. Excellent job performance, however, does not automatically equate to "good trainer." Following are selection criteria that you can use when selecting an SME to train. Recognize that it is rare for an SME to possess all of the criteria on this list. If you can select an SME who meets the first criterion fully and at least half the remaining requirements, consider yourself fortunate. An individual can acquire the knowledge and skills associated with the other criteria, perhaps not overnight, but certainly with time and appropriate resources.

■ Subject Matter Expertise

The SME trainer must have a thorough and comprehensive knowledge of the subject he or she is teaching. This means possessing the skills, knowledge, and ability to meet your minimum standard for conducting the designed training program. Ideally, the SME trainer exceeds these standards. While it is preferable to have an instructional designer design and develop the curriculum, the reality is that SMEs are often asked to design and deliver training. If you plan to ask the SME to both design and deliver the training, ensuring that the SME exceeds your standards is essential.

■ Communication Skills

A good SME trainer must be able to communicate with learners using these two skills:

1. Presence.

2. Relationships.

First, the SME must have a confident and inviting presence; he or she must be comfortable whether in front of a group of participants or in a one-on-one situation. Relationships, on the other hand, define how an individual establishes a rapport with another individual and how he or she interacts with that other person. To be an effective trainer, the SME must be empathic, sympathetic, yet confident, knowledgeable, and forceful enough to teach skills, behaviors, and impart information.

■ Adult Learning Principles

Your SME should have some foundational knowledge about adult learning principles and the characteristics of adult learning. Applying these principles to the training environment is a different skill set and comes with experience. Newly appointed SME trainers need to be aware of how adult learning principles, styles, and characteristics affect the transfer of learning. For more information, refer to the *Adult Learners* sidebar (on the following page) and *Info-line* No. 8804, "Training and Learning Styles."

■ Desire

Do not select an SME who does not want to be involved in the transfer of training. Reluctant trainers make bad trainers, and no one will gain from the experience. If your goal is to effect the transfer of learning, find an SME who is enthusiastic about his or her job and wants to impart his or her knowledge to others.

Preparing the SME to Train

Once you have selected the SME trainer, your first step is to make an inventory of his or her skills and qualifications and cross-reference these items against your training objectives. For example, do you want the SME to conduct training from an already designed curriculum, or do you need the SME to design a course and then teach it? Refer to the job aid at the back of this issue for an SME training inventory checklist you can use to help guide you through this assessment.

What Is the Training Outcome?

This question gets to the most basic element you are asking an SME to act on: Clearly define what the outcome of training is to be. Do not use convoluted words and concepts, or ask an SME to "just do it." Give clear parameters and definitions, such as the following:

● At the end of the training, participants will be able to demonstrate all the steps required to make Widget Y on the assembly line.

● When training is completed, learners will be able to discuss three different models of preparing strategic plans and assess environmental conditions to determine which model best suits the conditions.

Adult Learners

When subject matter experts (SMEs) are called upon to become trainers, they must have a fundamental understanding of how and why adults learn. What motivates one person may not necessarily motivate the next. In addition, the method by which one person learns best will probably not apply to the next person.

Adults are motivated to learn primarily when they have a need to do so. In terms of training, they want to know how it will help them—why must they learn the material or skill. Adult-learning theorists, like Malcolm S. Knowles, have conducted valuable research on this subject. This research has determined the following about adult learners:

- need to see the relevance of the training to their own life experience

- learn best when they have a measure of control over their own learning experience

- like to apply their own experience and knowledge to the learning

- are actively involved in the learning process

- benefit from task- or experience-oriented learning situations

- learn best in cooperative climates that encourage risk taking and experimentation

How adults learn is equally important, especially to the SME who has been tasked with training the adult learner. Typically, adults are influenced by their backgrounds— their cultural legacies, their adult experiences, their perceptions and skills, as well as their individual differences. When acquiring new knowledge and skills, adults gain information in two ways: **actively** (through direct involvement) or **passively** (through the absorption of information). Active involvement could be on-the-job training (OJT); passive involvement might be listening to a lecture. Individuals then process this new information either **deductively** (from the general to the specific) or **inductively** (from the specific to the general).

So what can the SME do to accommodate different learning styles? Given that the SME is one person, usually tasked with conducting one or two training sessions, the answer is that you probably cannot accommodate everyone. What you can do, however, is be constantly vigilant to the fact that each adult is an individual, with an individual learning style and a personal motivation for learning. By remembering this, the SME can show empathy, make a connection between himself or herself and the learner, and consequently enhance the learning experience for both the trainer and participant.

Use the following chart as a guideline to liken delivery methods with learning preferences.

	Gathering Information		Processing Information	
	Active	**Passive**	**Deductive**	**Inductive**
Lecture/presentation		X	X	
Group discussion	X		X	
Readings	X	X		
Simulation and role play	X			X
Programmed instruction	X			X
Games	X			X
Panels		X	X	
Demonstration		X		X
Case study	X		X	

Adapted from Info-line *No. 8808, "Basic Training for Trainers."*

- By the end of three sessions, participants will be able to describe alternative methods for resolving conflict between team members.

- When the week-long accounting and software training is finished, participants will be able to perform the following tasks:

  — prepare invoices using spreadsheet software
  — type in general ledger entries
  — chart accounts receivable payments
  — reconcile lockbox deposits

Who Is the Learning Audience?

Any trainer, SME or not, needs to know the defining qualities of the audience. This is more than "Is the audience composed of men or women?" At a minimum, the SME trainer should consider the following items:

- Is the audience one person, several people, or a large group?

- Are the participants more comfortable learning from a computer screen or from printed materials?

- What prerequisite knowledge do the learners have?

- Does the subject material allow for flexible learning styles?

Refer to the sidebar at left for more information on adult learners.

Methods of Delivery

Your SME trainer can select from a number of ways to deliver training to learners. These include, but are not limited to, the following suggestions:

■ *Lecture*
Lecturing is the most frequently used method for delivering training; therefore, SMEs must possess good presentation skills. Lectures (that is, speeches or presentations) usually lack interactivity between the lecturer and audience.

Selecting an SME

If you find yourself in the position of having many SMEs to choose from to conduct your training, you may need a little help getting started. Use the following checklist to help during the SME selection process:

☐ Have you completed the needs assessment for your training program?

☐ Does the SME exhibit excellent job performance?

☐ Does the SME have a thorough and comprehensive knowledge of the subject?

☐ Does the SME possess a confident and inviting presence? Is he or she comfortable in front of groups and working one-on-one with other employees?

☐ Is the SME able to establish good rapport with other individuals? Does he or she interact well with others?

☐ Is the SME knowledgeable about adult learning principles? Is he or she aware of adult learning characteristics?

☐ Is the SME enthusiastic about his or her job? Does he or she honestly desire to help others acquire knowledge?

Lectures, however, have their advantages:

- If the lecture is designed properly and if learners are motivated, you can use lectures to impart information to groups composed of mixed learners, fast and slow.

- You can disclose vast amounts of material quickly in a lecture.

- As long as the audience can see and hear the speaker, any size audience is acceptable.

- Lecturing positions the speaker "in control" because, as the speaker, he or she sets the tone and restricts interruptions.

There are also disadvantages to lecturing:

- Effective lecturing is very demanding; it requires practice and skill—a trainer must often sustain audience interest and concentration for several hours at a time.

- Audience participation is minimal; learning is passive.

- Lectures alone cannot facilitate skills training or any training topic that involves practical applications.

■ *Demonstration*

An SME trainer may select to use this method if he or she wants to clearly illustrate how to accomplish a task or process step-by-step. Typically, you use demonstrations to present skills and techniques in action. For example, demonstrations can show how machines and equipment operate.

Following are advantages of using demonstrations:

- The transfer of skills is high because you apply on-the-job skills during the demonstration.

- The method is flexible, and you can adjust it to accommodate learners' needs.

- If learners have practice time, the SME can correct errors before they become habitual.

Disadvantages include the following:

- Learners may lose interest during demonstrations because they are not directly participating.

- The demonstration itself may fail if the SME does not undertake careful preparation.

- You must keep audience size under 25 so everyone can see, unless you employ video equipment.

For more information on demonstration techniques, refer to *Info-line* No. 9804, "The Transfer of Skills Training."

■ *Discussion Groups*

This method is participatory and relies on the interaction and involvement of learners for success. Here, groups explore specific topics or issues by analyzing, evaluating, or reviewing subject matter. This method is valuable for problem-solving, decision-making, and brainstorming issues.

Advantages include the following:

- Discussion groups can be motivating and stimulating for all participants; everyone can contribute and feel involved.

- You can address real-life problems; participants can practice skills and responses to scenarios; and the learning environment often simulates participants' actual work place.

- Group input and choices in problem-solving and decision-making activities are more effective than individual contributions.

Disadvantages include the following:

- Discussions must be well-organized; otherwise, they lack direction and accomplish nothing.

- To be effective, groups can be no larger than 10 to 15 individuals.

- Group leaders often dominate; facilitators must intervene so all learners can participate.

- Discussions are time consuming and often run over if not controlled.

For more information on this topic, refer in *Info-line* No. 9906, "Group Decision Making."

■ *OJT*

Most SMEs are familiar with this delivery method because, as an organization's SME, they have probably been asked to help their fellow workers acquire or fine-tune a skill or task. Using OJT to deliver training simply means that training is provided by having an "expert" teach another employee how to perform a task. You can call this the "let me show you how to do it" delivery method. Usually, trainers provide OJT in a one-on-one situation.

Advantages of OJT include the following:

- Trainer uses checklists to ensure that he or she reviews all required skills.

- Checklists ensure that all employees receive the same training.

- Trainers present skills in manageable segments or "chunks."

Disadvantages of OJT include the following:

- Selected SME trainers performing OJT must have good interpersonal skills or OJT fails.

- OJT is not an appropriate delivery method if you need to train large numbers of employees or if your trainees are geographically disperse.

For more information, refer to *Info-line* No. 9708, "On-the-Job Training."

■ *Web-Based Training*
Whether you call it online instruction, Web-based training (WBT), or Internet/intranet learning, this delivery method benefits from use of intranets or the Internet to transfer knowledge. Due to the cost of most WBT programs, the decision to conduct training via this delivery method would probably be handed down to the SME trainer. Obviously, if this is the method of choice, the SME must be technologically savvy.

Below are some advantages:

- Both intranets and the Web provide learners with consistent information at a time that is convenient for them.

- Participants control their own learning.

- Distribution of training material is simplified.

- Trainers and learners can be geographically dispersed.

There are some disadvantages to this delivery method that are unique to the new workplace.

- The use of such technology could deter learners not familiar with technology.

- Learners must have a high sense of self-motivation to complete training.

- Those in charge of selecting the WBT program often do not evaluate the WBT programs well and end up with a visually stimulating yet unproductive training program.

- Organizations must have the hardware and software readily available.

For more information on this delivery method, refer to *Info-line* No. 9701, "Delivering Quick-Response IBT/CBT Training."

For additional methods, refer to the *Alternative Instructional Methods* sidebar on the following page, as well as *Info-line*, No. 8506, "How to Create a Good Learning Environment."

Course Design/Development for SMEs

Instructional Systems Development (ISD) is a process for creating, developing, and evaluating a training program. You selected an SME for his or her subject matter expertise, not for his or her instructional design ability. Too often, managers and organizations without training departments, forget this important fact. How do you get beyond this?

First, you need to ensure that your SME understands the basics of ISD. At its most fundamental level and to create an effective instructional program, follow these steps:

1. Conduct a needs analysis to determine your training requirements.

2. Design the training program.

3. Develop the instructional materials and test the program.

4. Deliver or implement the program.

5. Evaluate effectiveness of the training program.

Alternative Instructional Methods

Anyone who conducts training can use a variety of approaches to transfer knowledge or skills to learners. Each method has advantages and disadvantages. Select the method that best meets learners' needs as well as the knowledge or skills you must transfer.

Method	Purpose	Pro	Con
Lecture/Panel	Conveys facts or information to large groups.	Quick, easy, accommodates any size group.	Learning is passive. Learners may miss information. There are few opportunities for feedback.
Programmed Instruction	Printed, video, audio, CBT, Internet or intranet-based programs that allow learners to follow a sequence of planned instruction.	Effective for any size group—especially distance learning situations. Adds illustrations and examples; convenient and easy to use; learners can go back to get missed information.	Learner is passive and there is little interaction (unless the SME trainer facilitates the session). Several monitors are necessary in a large group situation.
Simulation/Role Play	SME trainer assigns learners with roles to act out in scenarios.	Shows how to solve problems and encourages understanding. Allows dramatization of feelings. Encourages personal growth and use of imagination. Safe environment for practicing skills.	Adults tend to resist play-acting. Inconsistent learning. Best if lead by skilled trainer—avoids confusion.
Games	Competitive activities that use preset rules to govern players' activities and determine outcomes.	Provides dynamic interaction, but is low-risk for participants. Used to demonstrate many concepts and applications.	Costly to develop and administer. Limits number of participants. Requires multiple copies.
Group Exercises	Use to communicate concepts and teamwork.	Learners accomplish the task by interacting, which becomes the basis for learning.	Requires monitoring and providing feedback to keep groups on track.
On-the-Job Training (OJT)	Use for teaching skill mastery, orientation to variety of tasks, and developing correct attitudes toward jobs.	Experts provide training in a real-world setting, providing practical application of skills.	Requires a knowledgeable trainer. If not planned carefully, can interfere with other work responsibilities.
Case Study	Facilitator explains a problem/case, which the group discusses to find a solution.	Flexible format. Stimulates and involves participants.	Outcome is hard to control without a skilled leader. Assumption that learning takes place.
Exercises/Tests	Use to evaluate new skills and knowledge.	Provides a clear picture of what participants have learned and what they still need to work on. Important for trying out new knowledge. Can affect motivation to learn. Can point out need for instructional improvement.	Need time to create test and to allow for test-taking.

You have already completed Step 1: You selected an SME because you conducted an analysis to determine your training requirements. Steps 2 and 3 can come in several flavors for the SME.

You could ask your SME trainer to perform the following tasks:

- design and develop the program based on his or her expertise

- assist an instructional designer to create the curriculum

- teach a program that is already designed

- attempt a combination of any or all of the above

SMEs are often asked to provide a combination of services. Asking an SME to teach an already designed program requires the least work for the SME. Requiring the SME to assist an instructional designer in curriculum creation allows the SME to work with an instructional design expert (another SME if you will). Here, the SME and the instructional designer create the program with the designer taking the SME's knowledge and developing a curriculum.

Often the SME is asked to take the lead to design and develop a program. Here is where things can fall apart—the SME is not an instructional designer. To carry out the ISD process with the least amount of headache, the SME can use the following model to get through the basic course design and development. At a minimum, all course design and development should consist of the following:

- budget
- design document
- objectives
- a project plan
- course instruction and lesson design

Budget

If funding has not been set, the SME trainer needs to request a budget. Your organization's training manager or department should be responsible for setting and allocating appropriate resources for course design and development.

Design Document

This document records broad design considerations and decisions as well as supports a budget request. Design documents vary in length, depending on what your organization requires. The SME should write a design document that answers the following questions:

1. Why does your organization need the course? Include here the course objectives and expected benefits for learners, managers, and clients.

2. Who will receive the training? What are the prerequisites (if necessary)? Who will conduct the training (that is, identify the SME—listing his or her experience)?

3. What aspects of learners' work must be coordinated and who will manage this task? This includes the following:

    - general course content

    - knowledge, skills, and attitudes (KSAs) to be learned or improved

    - proportion of cognitive learning (knowledge), psychomotor learning (skill), and affective learning (attitude) the course involves

    - how learners will demonstrate successful learning or completion of training

4. How should you sequence course content and what learning strategies should you use to engage participants? This includes learning events and activities and whether you conduct learning with individuals or in groups.

5. When will the course take place and how long will it run? This includes the following: how many times you will offer the course; the expected end date of each course; if course will run in segments or as a whole; if you will offer alternative design formats.

6. Where will the SME conduct the course—at a central site (such as corporate training centers, individual plants, or field sites) or on the Web? Does the SME require special facilities for demonstrations?

Objectives

Throughout the course, learners will work to meet certain objectives. The SME trainer can incorporate several kinds of objectives into his or her design:

● Terminal objectives or performance objectives that indicate what learners will be able to do after training, the conditions, and the standards or criteria they must meet.

● Subordinate or enabling objectives describing learning steps that lead to terminal objectives.

For more information on objectives, refer to *Info-line*s No. 9706, "Basics of ISD"; No. 9712, "Instructional Objectives"; No 8905, "Course Design and Development"; and No. 8906, "Lesson Design and Development."

A Project Plan

The SME's project plan needs to specify individual responsibilities and deadlines for course development. It should include the planning, directing, and controlling of resources for the period covering course development, implementation, and evaluation. For complete details on how to develop and manage a project plan, refer to *Info-line* No. 9004 "Project Management: A Guide."

Media and Materials Requirements

The SME trainer should develop a list of media, equipment, materials, and supplies needed to conduct the training program and then finalize this list as he or she completes the lesson plans. Often, decisions about media and materials require some trade-offs depending on budget limitations. Some of the considerations a trainer must think about include the following:

● audience size (small groups, large groups, or individuals)

● structure of instruction (OJT, apprenticeship, formalized mentoring, or coaching)

● place of instruction (field site, classroom, laboratory, or work station)

Course Instruction and Lesson Design

Typically, trainers structure and sequence instruction according to task, topics, or problems. A task structure, such as creating a budget spreadsheet, might follow a sequence of steps beginning with the following tasks:

1. Turn on the computer.

2. Open the spreadsheet software.

3. Open a new or existing file.

4. Enter numbers.

5. Create formulas.

6. Print the spreadsheet.

7. Save the file.

When grouping tasks into topics, instructions for a similar situation could involve the following:

● learning the basics of using a computer
● understanding spreadsheet mechanics
● creating and saving new files
● working with existing files
● manipulating spreadsheets

At the problem-solving level, the SME trainer can gear instruction toward the higher end-user—someone who has mastered the basics of spreadsheet software and now must create or use more sophisticated spreadsheet features, such as doing statistical analyses or multiple, linking spreadsheets.

When developing a lesson design, the SME should think of creating a blueprint to follow as he or she presents the program. Call it a detail agenda, a checklist of steps to cover, a sequential diagram of events, whatever you wish—lesson plans are the basic pieces that direct the curriculum. The SME should include the following elements in the lesson plan:

● Specify the lesson title and provide a one-line description of the lesson.

● State the lesson objectives (including the conditions under which learners will meet the objectives), the expected performance, and the criteria that you will use to establish satisfactory performance.

- Design, for each objective, a testing vehicle that can evaluate whether or not the objective has been met. This posttest should exactly match the conditions of each objective and contain instructions and specific items to be tested.

- Outline how the performance objectives will be achieved in the following: content, instructional methods, media, techniques, and learner activities.

- Build in some type of ongoing evaluation to assess learner progress.

- Create a lesson plan that lists learning activities, time allotted, and materials you will use. The plan will vary depending on the type of learning transfer required (KSAs).

For more detailed information on developing lesson plans, refer to *Info-line* No. 8906, "Lesson Design and Development."

Developing Course Materials

Part of the development phase includes selecting or creating media and materials. The SME trainer can use or adapt off-the-shelf materials as appropriate. If necessary, he or she may need to create materials. Unless specifically required, the SME should rely on the organization's training department to take the lead for creating course materials. Some typical materials include the following:

- written or electronic instructional guides providing introductory or background information

- bridges that lead from one instructional activity to another

- administrative aids (such as participant rosters, maps, material, equipment, supplies checklists, and name tags)

- evaluation materials

- participant guides (such as texts, workbooks, job aids, pretests, and posttest examples)

- activity aids (such as checklists, role-play scripts, case studies, and exercises)

- actual equipment and visual aids (such as paper, video equipment, VCRs, film, computers, Internet access, charts, pointers, flipcharts, markers, overheads, and spare parts)

A good point to remember is that learner comprehension and retention increase dramatically when you use visual aids and other materials in training programs. In addition to adding variety and emphasis to presentations, well-executed visual aids and materials can enhance an SME's professional image with learners.

For detailed information on preparing course materials, refer to *Info-line*s No. 9707, "High Performance Training Manuals"; No. 8410, "How to Prepare and Use Effective Visual Aids"; and No. 9711, "Create Effective Job Aids."

Stand Up and Deliver

The cardinal rule of any good training effort is the following: You need to prepare everything for the program in advance. The above guidelines for design and development help the SME trainer prepare a course program, but the SME is usually also asked to conduct the training. To prepare for this, the SME trainer must address two additional items:

1. Delivery preparation.

2. Facilities preparation.

A simple checklist (refer to the sidebar on facilities preparation) will help ease the SME's concerns about making sure everything is set up for a program. On the other hand, most people find it difficult to prepare for delivery. Preparation is especially hard on SMEs who have never had to present or teach in front of a group.

Facilities Preparation

The SME trainer must ensure in advance that the facility chosen for training has all the amenities he or she needs for a successful training environment. Have your SME use the following checklist to help develop his or her own facilities "precheck."

☐ Is the room an appropriate size for the setup you have chosen to meet your training goals? For the number of people you expect?

☐ Is the room large enough to handle small group discussions or one-on-one training or do you need additional rooms for those activities?

☐ Is the room large enough for audiovisual and computer equipment?

☐ Is Internet access available?

☐ If the room has airwalls, are they soundproof?

☐ Is the room free from obstructions (pillars and low hanging lights) to attendees' view of the speaker and audiovisual presentations?

☐ Is there a lectern and riser available if necessary?

☐ Are there individual room-heating, ventilation, air conditioning, and lighting controls?

☐ Are lights dimmable? Can the light over the screen be disconnected if necessary to avoid washing it out?

☐ Does the room have a built-in sound system for microphones and sound equipment amplification?

☐ If necessary, can you leave the room setup overnight? If not, is there secure storage available for training materials?

☐ Is there space for registration and security checks? For refreshment service?

☐ Are restrooms and telephones nearby?

☐ Are the training room and ancillary facilities accessible for persons with disabilities?

Oral presentation, whether speaking to one individual or a group, is one of the most important skills a trainer can possess. For an SME trainer, this is the most effective means of getting information across to learners. How an SME interacts, both verbally and nonverbally, will have a direct impact on how well participants learn and retain the information delivered.

Following are some basic qualities an SME trainer can strive for as a public speaker:

● Be honest.
● Have a sense of humor.
● Be prepared.
● Balance confidence with modesty.
● Read nonverbal cues from your audience.
● Dress appropriately.

The following guidelines will help your SME trainer deliver a top-notch training program.

■ *Good Voice*

A good voice is the primary means for communicating information. The SME needs to remember three important characteristics about the voice:

1. Quality.

2. Intelligibility.

3. Variability.

Keep a quality voice; do not become too infused with emotion or attitude. Articulate and pronounce words correctly and use proper grammar—this reconfirms credibility with an audience. Keep the rate of speaking to between 120 and 180 words a minute; the volume should not be overbearing and the force with which you speak should vary depending on what you need to emphasize.

■ *Nonverbal Clues*

The SME trainer's ability to convey information to his or her audience is often affected by what he or she communicates nonverbally. For example, your appearance (how you dress) can influence how the audience perceives you and your presentation style. As a general rule, trainers should dress in the most formal clothes they expect to see in their audience. If everyone is wearing jeans, do not come in a tuxedo or evening dress.

■ *Body Movements*

Body movement creates a language of its own. A static speaker is very boring; speakers who never stand still distract learners from the information they impart. Somewhere in-between, you will find movement as a means of holding an audience's attention. The SME should use it at points where he or she needs to make specific, important points. Gesturing with hands, arms, shoulders and head reinforces what is said. When used well, gestures add to the presentation; when used poorly, they distract.

■ *Eye Contact*

Eye contact with the audience, whether one person or a hundred, is vital for success. Listeners want a speaker to look at them when they are talking; this lets them know you are interested in their response. It enhances an SME trainer's credibility and lets the audience know who is in control. Eye contact also allows the SME to read nonverbal cues from his or her audience to see if the audience understands or if they are losing interest.

Helpful Hints

Recognize that public speaking causes most people to become nervous and anxious. Those individuals who have experience in public speaking offer the following hints for you to share with your SME to help alleviate uneasiness and prepare for the experience:

- Do not let your audience intimidate you. Most of the people in your audience are people with whom you could interact with everyday. Your audience is there to learn from you, not judge you.

- Do not rush to begin speaking.

- Use nervous energy to your advantage.

- Rehearse your presentation to a small group and accept constructive criticism.

- Be enthusiastic about the material you present. Nothing infuses more energy or passion into material than if a presenter is passionate about his or her topic.

- Use humor when appropriate and certainly as an icebreaker.

Follow Up Training Into Workplace

One of the overriding reasons why training fails to produce long-term improvement is inattention to the transfer of training to the workplace. Applying newly acquired skills to the job is not just the employee's responsibility; it is also the responsibility of the trainer and supervisor to guarantee that the learner has the opportunity, resources, and motivation to apply new skill. An SME trainer can use the following specific training activities to increase training transfer to the job:

- job aids that learners use on the job to refresh their memories

- checklists that the SME provides and uses during the training

- action plans that map out how and when employees will apply the new skills

- follow-up sessions at stipulated intervals (one month, three months, and six months after the training)

- mentoring programs

For more information on follow-up, refer to *Infolines* No. 9804, "The Transfer of Skills Training"; No. 9006, "Coaching and Feedback"; and No. 9809, "Scenario Planning."

Evaluating the Training Effort

The SME will often become involved with evaluating the training program he or she has conducted. This is true for many reasons:

- You must assess the training outcome (that is, did the training accomplish its goal?).

- You must assess the quality of training, as perceived by the learners, so the SME can receive feedback on his or her ability to be a "transferer" of learning. This assessment also gives the SME information for self-improvement.

Trainer Competencies

Based on work done by the International Board of Standards for Training, Performance and Instruction (IBSTPI), whose goal is to "promote high standards of professional practice in the areas of training, performance, and instruction," following is a summary list of 14 essential competencies or standards that every trainer should master.

1. Ability to analyze course materials and learner information.

2. Assure the preparation of the instructional site.

3. Establish and maintain credibility.

4. Manage the learning environment.

5. Demonstrate effective communication skills.

6. Demonstrate effective presentation skills.

7. Demonstrate effective questioning skills.

8. Respond appropriately to learners' needs for clarification or feedback.

9. Provide positive reinforcement and motivational incentives.

10. Use instructional methods appropriately.

11. Use media effectively.

12. Evaluate learner performance.

13. Evaluate delivery of instruction.

14. Report evaluation information.

● The evaluation provides participants an opportunity to report on the effectiveness of course materials and assignments, as well as the overall course design. It is also a mechanism for assessing learners' progress and attitudes toward the training.

The actual evaluation of training is not within the scope of this issue, but SMEs will want to acquaint themselves with the fundamentals so that they can grow and improve as trainers. For further information on evaluation, you may refer to *Info-line*s No. 9705, "Essentials for Evaluation"; No.8907; "Testing for Learning Outcomes"; No. 9813, "Level 1 Evaluation: Reaction and Planned Action"; No. 9814, "Level 2 Evaluation: Learning"; No. 9815, "Level 3 Evaluation: Application"; No. 9816, "Level 4 Evaluation: Business Results"; and No. 9805, "Level 5 Evaluation: Mastering ROI."

Get Your SME Off and Training

Transferring knowledge is not an easy task—even for those of us educated in the training field. So it should come as no surprise that if selected to design and deliver training, an SME may need additional guidance before he or she is ready to face learners. Use this *Info-line* to initiate SMEs to all that is foreign to them in the training profession: adult learner characteristics, delivery methods, course design and development, and so forth. Armed with this knowledge, your SME can figure out which topics he or she needs to investigate further in order to conduct successful training for your organization.

References & Resources

Articles

Filipczak, Bob. "Just Passing Through." *Training,* April 1996, pp. 60-64.

Hudspeth, Lauren, and Rick Sullivan. "Teaming to Design Interactive Multimedia." *Technical Training,* August/September 1997, pp. 22-28.

Ingram, Albert L., et al. "Working With Subject Matter Experts." *Performance & Instruction,* September 1994, pp. 17-22.

Katz, Cynthia, and Peter L. Katz. "A Training Solution for Lean and Mean Times." *Personnel Journal,* July 1996, pp. 8, 10+.

Kiser, Kim. "When Those Who 'Do,' Teach." *Training,* April 1999, pp. 42-48.

Marsh, P.J. "Training Trainers." *Technical & Skills Training,* October 1995, pp. 10-13.

Strandberg, John. "Training for a Technology Upgrade." *Training,* November 1997, pp. 36-38.

Books

Alden, Jay. *A Trainer's Guide to Web-Based Instruction.* Alexandria, VA: ASTD, 1998.

Goad, Tom W. *The First-Timer: a Step-by-Step Quick Guide for Managers, Supervisors, and New Training Professionals.* New York: AMACOM, 1997.

McCain, Don. *Creating Training Courses (When You're Not a Trainer).* Alexandria, VA: ASTD, 1999.

Sharpe, Cat, ed. *Info-line Guide to Training Evaluation.* Alexandria, VA: ASTD, 1999.

Weiss, Elaine. *The Accidental Trainer: You Know Computers, So They Want You to Teach Everyone Else.* San Francisco: Jossey-Bass, 1997.

Info-lines

Austin, Mary. "Needs Assessment by Focus Group." No. 9401 (revised 1998).

Bensimon, Helen. "How to Accommodate Different Learning Styles." No. 9604.

Butruille, Susan, ed. "Basic Training for Trainers." No. 8808 (revised 1998).

———. "Be A Better Job Analyst." No. 8903.

———. "Course Design and Development." No. 8905 (revised 1997).

———. "Lesson Design and Development." No. 8906 (revised 1999).

Callahan, Madeyln, ed. "Be a Better Needs Analyst." No. 8502 (revised 1998).

———. "Write Better Behavioral Objectives." No. 8505 (revised 1998).

Cassidy, Michael. "Group Decision Making." No. 9906.

Darraugh, Barbara, ed. "Coaching and Feedback." No. 9006 (revised 1997).

———. "How to Facilitate." No. 9406 (revised 1999).

Dent, Janice. "Technical Training." No. 9909.

Eline, Leanne. "How to Prepare and Use Effective Visual Aids." No. 8410 (revised 1997).

Gupta, Kavita. "Conducting a Mini Needs Assessment." No. 9611 (revised 1999).

Hacker, Deborah Grafinger. "Testing for Learning Outcomes." No. 8907 (revised 1998).

Hodell, Chuck. "Basics of Instructional Development Systems." No. 9706.

O'Neill, Mary. "Do's and Don'ts for the New Trainer." No. 9608 (revised 1998).

Plattner, Francis. "Improve Your Communication and Speaking Skills." No. 9409 (revised 1997).

———. "Instructional Objectives." No. 9712.

Preziosi, Robert. "Icebreakers." No. 8911 (revised 1999).

Russell, Susan. "Create Effective Job Aids." No. 9711.

———. "Training and Learning Styles." No. 8804 (revised 1998).

Sharpe, Cat, ed. "How to Create a Good Learning Environment." No. 8506 (revised 1997).

Sullivan, Rick. "The Transfer of Skills Training." No. 9804.

Thompson, Connie. "Project Management: A Guide." No. 9004 (revised 1998).

Waagen, Alice. "Essentials for Evaluation." No. 9705.

———. "Task Analysis." No. 9808.

Job Aid

SME Training Inventory Checklist

After deciding to use a subject matter expert (SME) to conduct training, use this checklist to help identify the strengths and weaknesses of your SME trainer candidates.

Skills	Yes	No	Notes
Possesses and demonstrates a thorough and comprehensive knowledge of the subject.	YES ☐	NO ☐	
Is confident in knowledge and can explain principles and skills easily.	YES ☐	NO ☐	
Is knowledgeable about adult learning principles.	YES ☐	NO ☐	
Is aware of adult learning characteristics.	YES ☐	NO ☐	
Has a confident and inviting presence.	YES ☐	NO ☐	
Is comfortable in front of groups and can facilitate a group.	YES ☐	NO ☐	
Is comfortable working one-on-one.	YES ☐	NO ☐	
Establishes good rapport with others.	YES ☐	NO ☐	
Interacts well with others.	YES ☐	NO ☐	
Speaks and enunciates clearly. Uses effective voice projection. Maintains a comfortable speaking pace.	YES ☐	NO ☐	
Maintains eye contact with others. Uses hand and arm gestures to reinforce points.	YES ☐	NO ☐	
Is familiar with using audiovisual equipment (overheads, easels, PC projector, etc.).	YES ☐	NO ☐	
Is enthusiastic about helping others acquire knowledge.	YES ☐	NO ☐	

Make Every Presentation a Winner

Issue 8606

Make Every Presentation a Winner

AUTHORS

Jerry L. Wircenski
College of Education
Department of Technology &
   Cognition
University of North Texas
P.O. Box 311337
Denton, TX 76203-1337
Tel. 940.565.2714
Fax: 940.565.2185
Email: wircensk@tac.coe.unt.edu

Richard L. Sullivan
Director of Training
JHPIEGO Corporation
Brown's Wharf
1615 Thames Street,
   Suite 200
Baltimore, MD 21231-3447
Tel. 410.614.3551
Fax: 410.614.0586
Email: rsullivan@jhpiego.org

Editorial Staff for 8606

Editor
Madelyn Callahan

ASTD Staff Consultant
Eileen West

Revised 1998

Editor
Cat Sharpe

Contributing Editor
Ann Bruen

Winning Presentations

In business, presentations are a fact of life, particularly in the field of training and development. They can range from brief presentations before management to a series of talks that constitute a training program. The three critical areas for successful presentations, say experts, are planning, delivery, and follow-up.

Planning includes understanding the audience; assessing training needs and establishing objectives or goals for the presentation; researching the topic; designing the instruction; and matching facilities to program requirements. Delivery includes the presenter's style and ability to involve participants in meaningful learning activities and should follow fundamental guidelines for verbal and nonverbal communication, questioning and reinforcement, group interaction, and the appropriate use of humor. Follow-up includes the presenter's availability to provide feedback during the training, assistance to participants on the job, and evaluating transfer of learning.

This issue of *Info-line* will introduce you to techniques for planning, presenting, and following up your training to better ensure learning transfer.

Planning

Effective presenters plan every detail to ensure the success of their presentations. Areas to consider during planning are audience profile, training needs and objectives, the most effective training approaches, and required training facilities.

Audience Profile

Developing an audience profile means becoming familiar with your intended audience. During this critical phase of the planning, consider the following suggestions:

- Get a sense of who your audience is by asking about their education, background, and experience. Other useful information includes median age, job titles, and cultural orientation.

- Find out about your participants' interests and abilities. This can help you develop relevant instruction to meet your participants' needs.

- Determine the gender and cultural mix of the audience.

- Identify any issues or topics that should be avoided when addressing your audience.

- Find out if any members of your audience can serve as special resources—perhaps as a discussion leader or facilitator for break-out sessions.

- If possible, survey your audience to find out about their preferred learning styles. This information can help you select instructional strategies and materials.

Topic Research

Topic research involves educating yourself thoroughly in the content and subject matter of your presentation. This includes gathering library research, consulting subject matter experts (SMEs), surveying learners, analyzing corporate files, and so forth. During this phase of the planning process, consider the following suggestions:

1. Review training goals and objectives to better focus your research directly on training content.

2. Think of ways to conduct your research effectively. Some examples include interviews with subject matter experts, direct observation, surveys, questionnaires, corporate files, and production/waste records.

3. Using research and an audience profile, select an effective and appropriate instructional approach. Many approaches are available to presenters. These include case studies, discussions, demonstrations and practice, games and simulations, role playing, and small-group activities. Your selection of one or more of these approaches will depend on other audience- and program-related variables such as your objectives for the presentation, audience needs, and time limits.

4. Draft a presentation plan that includes goals or objectives, suggestions for introducing the topic, an outline of the presentation content, and outlines for participant activities.

Preplanning Countdown

To make sure your investment of time and energy is worth your efforts, do some preliminary thinking and organizing. The following questions will help you make the best choices for preparing a successful presentation:

1. Who are your participants? Do they share the same background and level of experience?

2. Have participants attended presentations similar to yours? Do they have any knowledge or skills that pertain to the topic of your presentation?

3. How many participants will attend the presentation? How will you use this information for selection of instructional strategies, meeting room, facilities, and materials?

4. How were the participants selected to attend the presentation? Have they volunteered, or were they required to attend?

5. What are the participants' preferred learning styles? Do most prefer lectures, demonstrations, simulations, group activities, or a combination of these approaches?

6. Do some participants have special learning needs? Do any have visual, hearing, or mobility difficulties? How will you accommodate these learners?

7. What are the goals of the presentation? Have you developed objectives to inform them of what they are expected to know and do after the presentation?

8. How much time will you have for the presentation? Will you include a question-and-answer period?

9. How well do you know your subject area? How will you research and prepare for your presentation?

10. How much will the presentation cost? Will you need to add to the budget to buy or rent audiovisual equipment? Is your presentation cost effective?

11. Do you have the support of management? Will managers and supervisors reinforce the training back on the job? How will you assist them in following up?

5. Develop a "catchy" title for your presentation that reflects its purpose. For example, instead of calling your presentation "Computer-Aided Design," how about a title like "Egad! It's CAD!—Exploring Computer-Aided Design."

6. Always rehearse your presentation. Even a short run-through is preferable to walking in cold.

Facilities Planning

The most dynamic presenter can fail in poorly prepared facilities. Even when the presenter is aware of the participants' backgrounds and has comprehensive instructional plans, the presentation may still fail if, for example, it is delivered in an overcrowded, hot room. Consideration of the physical environment is a crucial part of the planning process. Here are some suggestions for establishing a comfortable physical and social environment:

- Determine your size requirements. How big should the facility be to accommodate your audience?

- If you require break-out rooms, arrange for the appropriate number.

- Make sure all rooms are accessible to all participants. Are the rest rooms located nearby, and are they accessible to all participants, including those with disabilities?

- Try to make the room comfortable. Is it relatively free of distractions and noise from adjoining rooms and hallways? Can the climate controls in the room be adjusted?

- Determine your lighting requirements? Where are the controls? Can the room be dimmed as opposed to darkened?

- Determine what type of support media you are going to need? Don't forget to place a request for a microphone, if needed.

- Ensure that the furniture—tables, chairs, and desks—are comfortable and appropriate for the learning. Do you need a podium and table up front for your handouts and materials?

- Arrange the room in a way that suits your objectives and presentation format. Some examples include U-shaped or horseshoe, classroom style, circle, multiple tables, and theater style. (For more information see *Info-line* No. 8504, "Facilities Planning.")

- Schedule enough time for meals, breaks, and phone calls, and have refreshments such as coffee, tea, water, and soft drinks available throughout the session.

Delivery

Even with solid research, good planning, and excellent facilities, some presentations still fail. Why? The presenter may not have a good, relaxed delivery style. Without that skill, participants quickly lose interest and become bored. Delivery style is important because presentations are primarily trainer centered. Three areas that presenters can work on to improve their delivery are verbal and nonverbal communication, questioning and reinforcement, and humor. But, first, they need to put the participants in a receptive mood.

Introduction Techniques

The introduction should both explain the topic of your presentation and capture the audience's attention. Do not attempt the second without covering the first. Remember, if your attention grabber does not tie into your topic, you will only confuse and distract the audience. Here are some suggestions for working up an interesting and effective introduction:

- State the purpose or goal of your presentation. All audiences want to know your objective(s).

- Make your introductions relevant to real-life experiences. This helps participants grasp the content of your presentation by relating it to something they understand.

- Ask questions to stimulate thinking on the topic of your presentation. Besides stimulating the thought process, this technique helps participants develop a focus on the topic. These might be rhetorical questions or a show of hands.

An On-Site Checklist

Before participants arrive, be sure to allow enough time to check the following:

☐ Locate the temperature and ventilation controls and regulate them so the environment is appropriate for your audience and equipment.

☐ Make sure the lighting is adequate. Know where the controls are so you can adjust the lighting easily for visual displays.

☐ Check the size of the tables to make sure there is sufficient space for participants to work with training materials.

☐ Test all audio, video, and demonstration equipment to be sure it is in working order.

☐ Check microphones to make sure they operate correctly and be sure you know how to adjust the volume.

☐ If you are using a writing board, be sure it is clean and that chalk or pens are available.

☐ Hang any posters, charts, or visuals applicable to your session. Make sure that these can be seen clearly from any location in the room.

☐ Set up a display of instructional material, projects, work samples, or other items relating to your presentation.

☐ Check information boards to make sure they are up to date with schedules, announcements, and other training-related notices.

☐ When appropriate, place name cards and training materials on tables before participants arrive.

☐ Have back-up supplies handy such as extra pens, paper, tape, and flipchart pads.

Caution: Introduction Ahead

A good introduction will get you started in the right direction. Here are some suggestions for preparing a strong beginning and getting your participants involved:

Give participants a clear picture of your presentation by discussing your objectives in the introduction. Use an overhead projector or blackboard and list each objective neatly and in simple terms.

Describe the activities and assignments you will expect participants to perform. Make sure they understand what will be expected of them—group tasks, projects, and other outcomes.

Describe in specific terms what participants will be expected to do during the presentation, in between sessions, and after the training. Should they take notes as you speak, bring assignments to each session, do outside reading and research, and so forth?

Explain the nature of the evaluation system you have planned. Tell them if they will have an opportunity to critique the presentation and your performance and how you will be evaluating their performance.

Give trainees a specific schedule outlining due dates for their assessments. Participants need to plan their time so they can complete and submit their work on time and to the right source.

Explain how you plan to deliver your presentation. Describe your approach. Will you be giving an illustrated talk, demonstration, group presentation, or another approach? When participants know how you intend to provide the information, there are fewer delays caused by misunderstandings and surprises.

Keep your personal introduction short and to the point. Avoid reading your entire résumé, focusing on your numerous accomplishments, ad-libbing, or starting with "I started work back in 1967. . . ."

● Share a personal experience or anecdote that is universal. You will spark participant interest if they have experienced something similar. But limit your "war" stories; too many can turn off interest.

● Create interest with an imaginative visual. Weekend comic strips or editorial pages are full of motivational tools. Remember to check the copyright laws, and if necessary, ask artists for permission to use their work.

● Make a provocative statement. When applicable, this technique generates comments and discussion to help introduce your topic. Be careful with this one! It can also turn off your audience if not handled well.

● Give a unique demonstration. This works well with technical topics. You can then proceed from the introduction to explanations of the "why" and "how" of your demonstration.

● Use an interesting or famous quotation, or perhaps turn this quotation around just a bit to fit your topic. For example: "Ask not what work teams can do for you, but what you can do for your work team."

● Relate the topic to previously covered content. Perhaps the speaker who preceded you has established the groundwork for your presentation topic. (For additional information, see *Info-line* No. 8911, "Icebreakers.")

Verbal and Nonverbal Communication

In any presentation, how you say something is just as important as what you say. Experts have observed that the techniques used to communicate information often determine whether or not the information is received. To improve your presentations consider these suggestions for re-sharpening verbal and nonverbal communication skills.

Verbal

Pay attention to the sound of your voice. Your projection—the pitch, tone, and volume of your voice—is crucial for effective delivery. Vary the pitch, tone, and volume to draw emphasis to key points. For example, voice inflection can capture and hold participant interest. Beware of sounding monotone; that is the easiest way to lose your audience. Avoid the use of repetitive words or phrases such as "OK," "ah," "now," "like," and "Do you know what I mean?" Try to break bad habits such as unconscious long pauses between sentences and using "um" or "uh" while pausing. Talk to, not at, your participants. Deliver key words and concepts slowly. Less important material can be covered more quickly. The recommended rate of speech is about 110 to 113 words per minute.

Begin by capturing the attention and interest of your audience. The first moments of your introduction should set the tone of your presentation. They should make your audience want to know more about the topic. Examples of effective introductions include the following:

- a provocative statement

- a unique demonstration

- an illustration of how the topic relates directly to work experiences

- a topic-related visual

Communicate on a personal level with your participants. Be sure to pronounce and spell words that are difficult or technical. Reinforce this by writing out new words on a board or flipchart. Accept and praise ideas offered by participants. These individuals should feel very positive about being involved in your presentation. Your acceptance of ideas and observations will encourage others to get involved and contribute to the presentations.

Emphasize key points through relevant examples, questioning techniques, appropriate application activities, and the use of visuals. Use sufficient and relevant examples to assist participants in understanding the subject of the presentation. Examples should relate to work activities, personal experiences, or current events. Make logical transitions between topics. If transitions are too abrupt, participants may get confused and lose interest. Topics should be in logical sequence with smooth transitions between each one.

Nonverbal

Dress appropriately for the presentation. First impressions are important. Experts say participants often form an opinion about a presenter based solely on appearance.

Use eye contact to "read" participants' faces to detect comprehension, boredom, or lack of understanding. From the participants' standpoint, eye contact with the presenter is essential in order to make them feel they are part of the presentation. Arrange the training area for maintaining optimal visual contact.

The effective use of body language and gestures contributes to communication—to emphasize, show agreement, and maintain audience interest. Important points about body language to remember include the following:

Use quick, positive, and energetic movements of the hands, arms, and head. Keep the attention of your audience by making your movements unpredictable. Walk rapidly, but alter the pace of your stride as you make points and reinforce them. Coordinate movement and gestures with your delivery.

Pay attention to unconscious body language. Some gestures and movements that can distract your audience include fidgeting, pacing, and jiggling keys or coins in pockets.

Observe your audience's body language. Facial expressions, down-turned eyes, fidgeting, or slouching are signals of boredom, disinterest, or lack of understanding.

Use positive facial expressions. These include smiles, expressive eyes, looks of concern, empathy, and encouragement. Look at your face in the mirror. How do you communicate feelings and emotions? How do you use your eyes, eyebrows, and mouth to express yourself?

Never sit behind a desk or stand behind a podium or lectern during your presentation. This establishes a barrier between you and your participants. Put more life into your presentation by moving freely about the room and down the aisles. Presenters who sequester themselves behind the podium and venture out occasionally to the writing board or flipchart appear less than enthusiastic.

Walk toward participants as they respond to your questions. This encourages them to continue. As a participant responds, nod your head slowly to show you understand what they are saying, approve of their comments, and invite them to continue.

To be effective, demonstrate enthusiasm about your subject and presentation. Remember, sincere enthusiasm is contagious; it generates interest and positive feelings. Illustrate your points with visuals such as real models, mock-ups, transparencies, videotapes, slides, computers, posters, charts, flipcharts, work samples, or writing boards. Besides being worth a thousand words, pictures lend variety and creativity to a presentation, making it more interesting and stimulating.

Give clear directions for all activities so that participants have the opportunity to apply the new information and practice new skills. Participants should not at any point be wondering what is next, what they are supposed to be doing, or how they should be conducting activities. Because training sessions are designed to provide participants with an opportunity to acquire new knowledge, skills, and attitudes, presenters must plan for appropriate application or follow-up activities that may take place during the session or back on the job.

Provide closure to main segments of your presentation by drawing together the main points in a good summary. Summaries should be complete and brief, and they should provide an opportunity for participant feedback. They can be used for clarification at points during the presentation as well as at the conclusion of the presentation. (For more information, see *Info-line* No. 9409, "Improve Your Communication and Speaking Skills.")

Questioning and Reinforcement

Questioning provides participants with an opportunity to display their understanding of key points. Participants' responses not only tell you how effective your presentation is but also indicate how to adjust your delivery. When posing questions, you can address participants by name and involve them in the presentation. Questioning also gives you the opportunity to provide the positive feedback and reinforcement that are essential for effective learning.

Advantages

The use of questioning and reinforcement is helpful for the following reasons:

- It involves all participants in the presentation.

- It stimulates and motivates participants.

- It provides participants an opportunity to display their understanding of the topic.

- It promotes active, not passive participation.

- Participants have an opportunity to apply the knowledge and skills you have presented.

- Responses to questions provide feedback to the presenter as to the effectiveness of the delivery.

- The questioning process helps you evaluate individual performance.

- Questions create variety in presentations.

Levels of Questions

Low

Memory: The participant is required only to recall or recognize information.

Comprehension: The participant demonstrates an understanding of the material or the idea being presented; discovers relationships between facts; makes generalizations; or explains meanings.

Application: The participant solves practical problems through the use of ideas, principles, or theories.

to

Analysis: The participant solves a problem by breaking it down into its component parts and determining the relationships between them.

Synthesis: The participant solves a problem by using original, creative thinking; and composes or combines parts or elements to form a whole.

High

Evaluation: The participant makes judgments on specific criteria rather than opinions.

Disadvantages

There are, however, some aspects of questioning and reinforcement that can detract from your presentation:

- The overuse of low-level or short-answer questions may not challenge the participants.

- Questioning can be time consuming.

- Some participants may not wish to get involved in the interaction process.

- Some participants may attempt to dominate the interaction process.

Questioning and Reinforcement Tips

Carefully formulate questions during the planning process and use the following guidelines:

1. Write questions at a variety of levels, from the simple *yes/no* kind to those that require more thought. Questions such as "Why?" and "What is your opinion?" stimulate a lot of discussion.

2. Phrase questions carefully. Avoid ambiguous or vague questions since they may confuse participants and cause them difficulty in responding.

3. Make questions short enough to remember. When questions are too long, presenters have to repeat them.

4. Design questions to focus on key points or concepts of the presentation. Do not waste time asking about secondary or less important information. You want to be sure participants comprehend the most significant material.

5. Design questions so they do not suggest the answer and state them in a way that eliminates guessing.

6. State questions clearly for the entire group. Pause for a volunteer response or direct your questions to specific participants. Address participants by name, and then ask your questions.

7. Repeat participant questions and responses, especially if you are addressing a large group. This ensures that everyone can hear. It also gives the presenter an opportunity to clarify questions and responses and provides positive reinforcement to the participant.

8. On occasion, handle participant questions by pausing and then redirecting the question to another participant. This involves more participants in the discussions and creates more interaction.

Humor

Humor and laughter help improve, maintain, and enhance participant interest. Camaraderie begins to develop when presenter and participants share a pun, story, or other common experience. Humor fosters a "team" atmosphere and promotes a positive learning experience. You can integrate humor into your presentations in the following ways:

- Use topic-related cartoons, stories, puns, and anecdotes to emphasize and reinforce points throughout your presentations.

- Maintain a file of humorous stories, pictures, drawing, and related materials.

- Avoid humor that might offend or alienate your participants.

- Practice telling stories *before* your presentation.

- Laugh *with* not *at* others.

- Laugh at yourself, particularly when a story or pun flops. This puts your audience at ease and indicates you are comfortable with the group and self-confident about your presentation.

Follow-Up

Follow-up requires the presenter to be available for instructional feedback and performance evaluation both during training and in the workplace.

During Training

Effective presenters often find that participants want to discuss various features of the presentation before, during, and after sessions. When presenters make themselves accessible to participants, they can resolve individual questions and concerns. By being available for feedback, presenters help to tie the session together, summarize important points, and provide closure. Here are some hints for making yourself accessible to participants:

- Take the time to greet and talk with participants as they gather before the presentation actually begins.

- Remain in the room during breaks to answer questions and interact with participants.

- Stay after the presentation ends to address individual questions and concerns.

Instructional Feedback

Presentations or training sessions that require assignments, projects, or evaluations give the presenter an opportunity for keeping participants apprised of their progress. Here are some suggestions for giving feedback on learning:

- Give participants clear written and oral instructions for all assignments and activities.

- Return participant assignments and materials with positive written and oral comments and suggestions. It is important to include encouraging remarks and reinforce participants' successes, particularly for participants who are experiencing difficulty.

- Return all assignments and materials promptly. Participants are anxious to know about their progress and begin working on weak performance areas. If you wait too long, they may lose enthusiasm.

- If appropriate, use a progress chart to map participants' activities and accomplishments.

- When session activities yield products such as projects, written material, or action plans, invite the authors to display or discuss their work. This motivates participants, and the materials serve as samples of satisfactory work products.

In the Workplace

Some presenters reinforce training with follow-up activities in the workplace. For example, on-the-job training or coaching would be effective follow-up activities for a variety of jobs, from management to manufacturing. Besides on-the-job training and coaching, presenters can assist managers and supervisors with actual workplace implementation and application of skills and knowledge gained from the presentation.

Posttraining evaluation is the presenter's most crucial follow-up task. To measure training success, presenters determine the degrees to which learners have accomplished training objectives. This determination is based on a comparison of work levels before and after the training. Pretraining assessment consists of determining the difference between expected and actual performance. If, for example, that difference is 10 percent, the presenter will want the posttraining to be significantly lower, say 0 to 4 percent, indicating little or no difference between the expected and actual performance. The best result, of course, would be a negative value indication that learners have exceeded the expected performance.

Knowing how to deliver your presentation in a more productive manner is a skill that anyone can learn. In today's corporate environment, flatter structures and more emphasis on teamwork mean communications skills are essential for all employees. Making use of the above suggestions for planning, delivery, and follow-up should result in winning presentations. All you need are forethought, practice, and follow-through in order to be successful.

References & Resources

Articles

Brody, Marjorie. "Visual, Vocal and Verbal Cues Can Make You More Effective." *Presentations,* October 1997, p. 34.

Brown, David A. "Delivering Power Presentations." *Security Management,* March 1997, pp. 29-30.

Bryant, Sue. "Speak for Yourself." *Marketing,* October 31, 1996, pp. 29-30.

Carey, James F. "Speak Out, Stand Out." *Journal of Management Consulting,* May 1997, pp. 39-44.

Daley, Kevin, and Irene Kim. "Don't Shy Away from Presentations." *Chemical Engineering,* November 1997, pp. 155-158.

Dervarics, Charles. "On Target: On Your Mark. Get Set. Present!" *Technical & Skills Training,* July 1995, pp. 6-8.

Harris, Richard M. "Practically Perfect Presentations." *Training & Development,* July 1994, pp. 55-57.

Luke, Robert A. Jr. "Managing Bunny Trails." *Training & Development,* January 1994, pp. 19-21.

Malouf, Doug. "The Seven Deadly Sins of Speakers." *Training & Development,* November 1995, pp. 13-15.

Smith, Terry C. "Listen Up." *Technical & Skills Training,* August/September 1994, pp. 21-23.

Warman, Wendy. "Six-Step Guarantee for Powerful Presentations." *Technical & Skills Training,* July 1977, p. 5.

Books

Bartel, C. *Instructional Analysis and Material Development.* Chicago: American Technical Society, 1976.

Bender, Peter U. *Secrets of Power Presentations.* Buffalo, New York: Firefly Books, 1995.

Broadwell, M.M. *The Supervisor and On-the-Job Training.* 4th edition. Reading, MA: Addison-Wesley, 1994.

Denham, Wendy, and Elizabeth Sansom. *Presentation Skills Training.* New York: McGraw Hill, 1997.

Draves, William A. *Energizing the Learning Environment.* Manhattan, KS: Learning Resources Network, 1995.

———. *The Successful Presenter.* Manhattan, KS: Learning Resources Network, 1994.

Finch, C.R., and J.R. Crunkilton. *Curriculum Development in Vocational and Technical Education.* 4th edition. Boston: Allyn and Bacon, 1992.

Gilbert, Frederick. *PowerSpeaking.* Redwood City, CA: Frederick Gilbert Associates, 1996.

Jeary, Tony. *Inspire Any Audience.* Dallas: Trophy Publishing, 1996.

Jeffries, J.R., and J.D. Bates. *The Executive's Guide to Meetings, Conferences, & Audiovisual Presentations.* New York: McGraw-Hill, 1983 (out of print).

Laird, D. *Approaches to Training and Development.* 2d edition. Reading, MA: Addison-Wesley, 1985.

Lauffer, A. *Doing Continuing Education and Staff Development.* New York: McGraw-Hill, 1978 (out of print).

Krathwohl, David, and B.S. Bloom. *A Taxonomy of Educational Objectives. Handbook I: Cognitive Domain.* London: Longman, 1984.

Miller, H., and J.R. Verduin. *The Adult Educator.* Houston: Gulf Publishing, 1979 (out of print).

Mills, H.R. *Teaching and Training.* New York: John Wiley & Sons, 1977 (out of print).

Nadler, L., ed. *The Handbook of Human Resource Development.* New York: John Wiley & Sons, 1984.

Pike, Robert W. *High Impact Presentations.* West Des Moines, IA: American Media Publishing, 1995.

Sullivan, R.L., and J.L. Wircenski. *Technical Presentation Workbook.* New York: ASME Press, 1996.

Van Ments, M. *The Effective Use of Role-Play.* London: Kogan Page, 1983.

Verduin, J.R. Jr., et al. *Adults Teaching Adults.* Austin, TX: Learning Concepts, 1977 (out of print).

Wilder, Claudyne. *The Presentation Kit: 10 Steps for Selling Your Ideas.* New York: John Wiley & Sons, 1994.

Info-lines

Finkel, Coleman, and Andrew D. Finkel. "Facilities Planning." No. 8504 (revised 2000).

Plattner, Francis. "Improve Your Communications and Speaking Skills." No. 9409 (revised 1997).

Preziosi, Robert. "Icebreakers." No. 8911 (revised 1999).

Job Aid

Presentation Planner

Here is a checklist to help you work on presentation planning, delivery, and follow up. **Directions:** Complete the checklist by checking yes or no next to each item. Note that "no" answers may indicate weaknesses in your process. Record possible solutions and ways to improve your presentation in the section for comments.

Planning

	Yes	No	Comments

Audience Profile

1. Determined number of participants and planned to accommodate that number.

2. Took into account participants' reasons for attending the presentation.

3. Reviewed audience background and experience and considered this information in planning of presentation.

4. Planned to include preferred learning styles of participants.

5. Identified participants' unique learning needs.

Topic Research

1. Established goals and objectives.

2. Reviewed presentation content for accuracy, relevance, and comprehensiveness.

3. Selected appropriate instructional strategies.

4. Allotted sufficient time for the presentation.

5. Developed instructional plans to accomplish stated goals and objectives.

Facilities Planning

1. Meeting room was comfortable. Temperature, lighting, were adequate.

2. Tables and chairs were arranged to suit participants' needs.

3. Training materials and name cards were clearly printed and ready in time for the presentation.

4. Participants used name tags.

5. All audiovisual equipment was checked and working in good order.

6. Writing boards and flipcharts were available.

7. Break-out rooms were available.

8. Meals and breaks were scheduled and refreshments were arranged for.

	Yes	No	Comments

Facilities Planning *(continued)*

9. Information and bulletin boards were up to date.

10. As participants arrived for the training, presenter greeted them at the door.

Delivery

Verbal and Nonverbal Communications

1. Dressed appropriately.

2. Had satisfactory voice projection, pitch, tone, and volume.

3. Introduced presentation effectively; captured audience attention and interest in the rest of the presentation.

4. Maintained eye contact.

5. Used body language to express confidence and enhance presentation.

6. Used facial expressions effectively; engaged participants in discussions and invited them to contribute ideas and comments.

7. Moved around the room and gestured to emphasize and reinforce key points of the presentation.

8. Showed sincere enthusiasm.

9. Used gestures that were not distracting.

10. Communicated on a personal level.

11. Emphasized key points and used relevant examples.

12. Used effective visual materials.

13. Made logical, smooth transitions between topics.

14. Provided a comprehensive, easy-to-follow summary.

15. Gave clear directions for all activities.

Questioning and Reinforcement

1. Asked key questions.

2. Directed questions to the entire group.

3. Presenter targeted questions to individuals.

4. Addressed individuals by name.

5. Walked toward individuals when addressing them.

6. Offered participants praise and reinforcement.

(Job Aid continued on page 122)

Job Aid

Questioning and Reinforcement *(continued)*	Yes	No	Comments
7. Asked questions on a variety of levels.			
8. Increased participation and interaction by directing participants' questions to others in the group.			
9. Repeated or restated participants' responses for the benefit of the group.			

Humor

	Yes	No	Comments
1. Used humor effectively. Jokes and stories illustrated key points.			
2. Used humor that was acceptable to the group and never offensive.			
3. Laughed with individuals, never at them.			
4. Used topic-related cartoons, drawings, and illustrations to reinforce training points.			

Follow-Up

During Training

	Yes	No	Comments
1. Greeted participants as they gathered to attend the presentation.			
2. Stood at the door and welcomed each participant individually.			
3. Was available during breaks to answer participants' questions.			
4. Was available after the presentation to answer additional questions and discuss concerns.			

Instructional Feedback

	Yes	No	Comments
1. Provided clear oral and written instructions for all assignments and activities.			
2. Returned participant work promptly.			
3. Returned participant assignments and other materials with positive written and oral comments.			
4. Used a progress chart to map participant progress and illustrate their rate of achievement.			
5. Displayed exemplary participant works as reference materials for the rest of the group.			

In the Workplace

	Yes	No	Comments
1. Arranged or conducted on-the-job training or coaching.			
2. Assisted supervisors and managers with implementing the training.			

Icebreakers

Icebreakers

AUTHOR

Robert C. Preziosi
Professor of Management
  Education
School of Business &
  Entrepreneurship
Nova Southeastern University
Ft. Lauderdale, FL 33315
Tel.: 954.262.5111
Fax: 954.262.3965

Editorial Staff for 8911
Barbara Darraugh

Revised 1999

Editor
Cat Sharpe Russo

Contributing Editor
Ann Bruen

Production Design
Anne Morgan

Using Icebreakers

How often have you attended training sessions where all the housekeeping details and introductions took up the first half-hour? Too often. Many sessions begin with a standard "Why don't you give us your name and tell us a little bit about yourself?" After such introductions, however, participants may still feel isolated and may not remember the other participants' names. These sessions start off slowly and then challenge the trainer to pick up the tempo.

One way to get people involved immediately is with an icebreaker. Julius Eitington in *The Winning Trainer* defines icebreakers as "start-up activities that help participants ease into the program." Sue Forbess-Greene, author of *The Encyclopedia of Icebreakers*, defines icebreakers as "tools that enable the group leader to foster interaction, stimulate creative thinking, challenge basic assumptions, illustrate new concepts, and introduce specific materials."

Whatever the definition, icebreakers make participants participatory and give them a strong message that they must be involved in their own learning. While it is certainly possible that some trainees have not been involved and do not want to be, the trainer must establish the norm of active engagement up front.

There are several different kinds of icebreakers. This *Info-line* will focus on openers, acquainters, games, and brainstorming. It will provide examples of the favorite activities of several practitioners as well as tips for conducting successful icebreakers and information on designing your own activities.

In *The Encyclopedia of Icebreakers*, Forbess-Greene divides icebreakers into several different categories. Each type of icebreaker serves a different purpose.

■ *Openers and Warm-Ups*
These icebreakers warm up the group by stimulating, challenging, and motivating the participants. They can be used to begin a session, start a discussion, prime the group after a break, ready the trainees for new material, or shift the topic focus.

■ *Getting Acquainted*
These icebreakers serve two functions: They establish nonthreatening introductory contacts, and they increase participants' familiarity with one another. Although they usually are not tied to the course content directly, these activities can be adapted to meet the specific needs of the participants and the training program.

■ *Energizers and Tension Reducers*
These icebreakers are used when the participants appear overly stressed or when the group is "flat." When participants feel more relaxed, they will be receptive to a more open dialogue about the information, issues, and skills that are to be introduced.

■ *Games and Brainteasers*
Games and brainteasers are effective warm-ups. Games can function as introductions to problem solving, competition, team building, and consensus-seeking activities, while brainteasers "reduce learning overload when the material being presented becomes cumbersome or draining."

■ *Feedback and Disclosure*
These icebreakers differ from others in that they are used to demonstrate "communication variables rather than as a means for developing ongoing interpersonal relationships between participants." Forbess-Greene defines feedback as "the reception of corrective or evaluative information by the original source," and disclosure as the "sharing of personal thoughts and/or feelings."

In addition to the above, icebreakers can do the following things:

● Define the group personality.

● Identify interaction patterns among group members that may enhance or inhibit learning.

● Build group identity.

● Build or maintain participant self-esteem.

● Develop trust among the participants.

● Establish a baseline on the group—how comfortable they feel with the level of participation.

Selecting Icebreakers

To help you choose an icebreaker appropriate to your audience and course content, ask yourself the following questions:

1. Do I have enough time?

2. How well does it fit my content flow?

3. Does it allow for a high rate of learner success?

4. Will it help build openness and trust?

5. Will it be fun and energizing?

6. Will any learner feel uncomfortable?

7. Are the logistics easy to manage?

8. How will learners feel when it ends?

9. How will the trainer feel when it ends?

- Increase awareness of trainees' level of knowledge or skill.

- Let participants know their trainer and help develop the trainer's credibility.

- Set program tone.

- Open communications.

- Move into a new content area.

- Evaluate training style.

The icebreaker also can serve as a source of additional data about the learners. For example, you can find out:

- how well the group is getting along
- supplementary personal information
- learner reaction to material
- the extent to which the group is bonding
- if any cliques are forming
- the energy level of the group
- if people like to have fun in training

Variables

Several considerations come into play once the trainer decides to use an icebreaker. Plan carefully, based on the following variables:

Group composition. This information includes age range, cultural background, gender, and education level.

Target audience. Salespeople, who are normally extroverted, probably don't require an exercise designed to foster introductions, while other groups may need a nudge to get things started.

Program length. Short courses (half-day) may spare only five or 10 minutes for icebreaking; day-long course icebreakers may last 15 to 20 minutes; in courses of four or five days, icebreaking may involve up to two hours.

Program content. Topics should echo the content of the course, but they may not be tied to it directly. Openers may summarize what has preceded or act as a transition to the next course segment. Openers also may contribute to participants becoming better acquainted.

Trainer's style. This determines what type of ice-breaker to use. More experienced trainers—those who don't fear losing control of the participants or sight of the subject—may opt for novel or experimental exercises that allow for more free flow. Less experienced trainers might use more structured exercises.

Although icebreakers are marvelous training tools, they can be misused. To minimize risks and maximize benefits, Forbess-Greene recommends the following:

- Trainers should encourage the active participation of all group members.

- Data or information generated during an exercise may be deeply personal and intended only for the group. Trainers should warn participants to keep such information "in the room."

- The trainer's active participation may help reduce the participant's initial inhibitions and promote risk taking.

Barriers to Successful Use of Icebreakers

Here are a few obstacles to the effectiveness of icebreakers and some suggestions for overcoming them:

Barriers	Solutions
Lack of clarity in the trainer's explanation of the process or exercise content, or both.	Be very clear and specific about instructions and expectations.
Previously existing relationships among participants.	Take an active role in encouraging everyone to talk with as many other participants as possible.
Differences in job type or status among group members.	Establish behavioral guidelines that require some heterogeneous interaction.
Devaluing of a person's contribution by someone (trainer or another participant) during the process.	Emphasize the importance of positive behavior and a nonjudgmental attitude during the icebreaker.
Charisma of one or more participants that causes trainees to focus their attention solely on them.	Stress that the icebreaker is nothing more than an introductory or fun exercise.
Participant's individual attitudes, including "I don't want to participate or don't feel like participating, and the trainer won't notice"; and "I'm not a good communicator; I always become too self-conscious and worry about people liking me."	Approach any nonparticipants and "pull" them into the activity.

● The trainer must carefully evaluate an icebreaker's appropriateness to the audience, subject matter, and climate.

● The trainer should remain attuned to the development of participants and of the group. Issues such as disclosure, cohesiveness, trust, team building, risk taking, control, and dependence should be closely monitored.

Openers

Openers differ from acquainters in that they introduce or tie in to the subject matter being taught. Eitington notes that openers are intended to "set the stage, to avoid abrupt starts, and generally to make participants comfortable with the formal program they are about to experience." Openers also may energize the group after coffee breaks and luncheons and may be used to open sessions that occur on the second or third day of the program. Here are some examples of openers.

■ Introductions/Expectations
The following exercise, although not an icebreaking game, provides an excellent way to warm up a new class. This exercise allows instructors to match participant expectations with the program's objectives, providing an excellent lead-in to the program topic.

How to Use:

● Ask participants to introduce themselves. As part of the introduction, have them state their expectations for the course.

● Write individual expectations on a flipchart. When all participants have spoken, compare their expectations to the course objectives that have been written on another flipchart. This provides the trainer with an excellent way to tailor the material covered in the course and to personalize content by matching topics to individual expectations.

How to Modify:

- Have participants pair off. Allow a few minutes for the pairs to interview each other about where they are from and why they are there.

- Have one participant introduce the other, using the information garnered in the interview. The trainer should record these on a flipchart or whiteboard.

- Have the just-introduced participants repeat introductions and statement of objectives for the other partner.

■ *The Successful Role Model*

Bob Preziosi uses "The Successful Role Model" to help set content expectations at the beginning of the program.

How to Use:

- After initial introductions, break the class into small groups of four to six people. Provide each group with a marker and two sheets of newsprint.

- Ask the group two questions: "Who was the most successful [blank] you have ever known, and what did he or she do to make you think of him or her as the best?" and "How did he or she make you feel?"

  Note: The trainer fills in the blank based on course content. If the program is sales training, for example, use the word "salesperson." The exercise's purpose is to have the groups build a model for the role or behavior that is covered by the training program. The term that fills in the blank serves as an introduction to the content that follows.

- Tell the groups to write the key points of their discussion of the first question on one sheet of newsprint. The other sheet is for the second question.

- Give the groups 12 to 15 minutes to discuss and write their answers. As each group finishes, the reporter should post their sheets along the walls. Or, each group can report on its findings when everyone is finished.

- Summarize the exercise by connecting each point to the program content.

■ *Collecting Autographs*

Michele Wyman of Effectiveness By Design (Phoenix, AZ) uses "Collecting Autographs" to bridge from cursory introductions into subject matter.

How to Use:

- After the preliminary introductions, tell participants they will now get to know one another better.

- Distribute the worksheet at right and read aloud the instructions that appear at the top of the page. Explain that you are available to sign participants' worksheets.

- After about 10 minutes, have participants return to their seats. Take a few minutes to find out who was able to collect the most autographs. Trainers may draw up a list of "correct" answers, based on registration information, or may see how many different people can claim the different characteristics.

- Use one of the subject-related items on the worksheet to lead into the overview of what will be covered during the course. A sales course, for example, could include characteristics such as "holds the record for the most cold calls made," "exceeded quota three years' running," or "walking encyclopedia of product information." These characteristics could be used to introduce techniques for making cold calls, closing skills, and product information sessions.

Autographs Worksheet

[This version is used in a writing skills workshop.]

Instructions: During the autograph-seeking session, you will be interviewing people to find out who fits each of the categories listed below. You will then obtain that person's autograph in the appropriate space. You must have a different autograph for each item. You may not sign your own worksheet. Try to obtain as many autographs as possible during the next 10 minutes.

1. Enjoys writing letters. _____

2. Does volunteer work. _____

3. Writes creatively in his or her spare time. _____

4. Knows somebody famous. _____

5. Wrote a memo or letter within the last week. _____

6. Is new to his or her job. _____

7. Once got an "A" in an English course. _____

8. Is born under my astrological sign. _____

9. Uses his or her ear to punctuate correctly. _____

10. Recently quit smoking. _____

11. Finds it difficult to put thoughts on paper. _____

12. Has performed on stage. _____

13. Knows what word contains three double letters in a row. _____

14. Thinks the president is doing a good job. _____

15. Can correctly pronounce "facetious." _____

16. Has been to Mexico. _____

17. Could explain what a dangling modifier is. _____

18. Is a grandparent. _____

19. Is at a training program for the first time. _____

20. Spends at least 25 percent of on-the-job time writing. _____

Trainer Behavior During Icebreakers

To maximize your use of icebreakers, follow these guidelines:

● Listen. Maintain good eye contact with speakers.

● Refer to trainee comments, addressing them by name.

● Focus on what the trainee needs.

● Turn questions back to the group.

● Be enthusiastic.

● Remember that trainees need to know the reasons why they are doing an activity.

● Make positive statements about individual and group processes.

● Avoid public arguments.

● Ask questions that are capable of being answered.

● Nod when someone gives an appropriate response.

● Give precise directions.

● Start on time.

● Enhance every trainee's self-esteem.

● Avoid personality conflicts.

● Avoid being impatient or indifferent.

● Be polite and courteous.

How to Modify:

About every other item on the worksheet is related to the subject matter that will be covered during training. To make the autograph-collecting exercise work best, change the items to fit the training topic.

■ What's Your Problem?

This icebreaker was designed for a course on problem solving. The exercise was created to help raise awareness of existing problems.

How to Use:

● Provide each participant with an 8.5-by-11-inch piece of card stock paper. Participants divide the paper into three sections:

My problem is...
Barriers to doing it are...
I am good at solving problems that...

● Participants fill these out and hold them in front of them while they circulate to music.

● The trainer debriefs by leading a discussion on three questions: "How big really are these problems? How can barriers be overcome? Who would be a good resource person for your problem?"

■ Converting the Tough Audience

Don Wetmore, professional speaker at time management seminars, offers this opener for those occasions when you are dealing with a "tough audience"—one that is required to attend and may not appreciate what the seminar can do for them.

How to Use:

- Ask participants to rate their personal productivity on a scale of 1–10, with 10 being perfect. (The answers will typically be in the 6–8 range.)

- Then ask them: "What is keeping you from being at a higher number?" Allow them several minutes to think this through. Most will identify several things that are keeping them from being at a higher level of productivity.

- Finally, ask them: "What is it costing you to stay at that lower number?" This will take a few minutes of reflection.

As they answer the question, Wetmore says, "arms tend to unfold and the ears perk up as I explain how I will address those specific issues during the seminar." The process takes 15–20 minutes, but turns a tough audience into a receptive one.

■ *I Am*

Peter Renner suggests using icebreakers to help participants find out who session members are, thus increasing their degree of belonging and level of trust. He recommends the following warm-up:

How to Use:

- Give each participant an 8.5-by-11-inch piece of paper with "I am…" printed at the top. Ask everyone to finish the statement in at least six different ways. For example, one might read:

I am. . .
an engineer
a father
a stamp collector
feeling a bit silly
fun
a nonsmoker

- When everyone is finished writing, distribute a piece of masking tape to all participants. Have them tape their list to the front of their clothing.

- Instruct participants to get up and see who is there. They should spend at least 30 seconds with each person, reading their lists. No talking is allowed. (You may have to remind the class of the "no talking" rule.) Play along and model the instructions.

- After everyone has had a chance to circulate, ask the participants to post their lists on the wall. Invite them to "browse" during breaks and before going home.

How to Modify:

- Ask participants to write six areas or subjects in which they have some expertise. These areas or subjects should be confined to course content.

- Mention that this is your way of finding out what backgrounds the participants have and that you are always surprised by the talents of adult students.

- Keep the sheets after the posting period is over. The information can then be used to relate course material to specific participants.

Reprinted with permission from
The Instructor's Survival Kit *by Peter Renner,*
copyright Training Associates, 1983.

Acquainters

Acquainters may have no relation to the subject matter being taught. They are designed to put participants at ease and relieve the initial anxiety that comes with any new beginning. Here are some favorite acquainter exercises used by trainers.

■ *Fancy Sayings*

This exercise, suggested by Forbess-Greene, challenges participants to "translate" written communications.

How to Use:

- Give each participant a copy of a "Fancy Sayings" worksheet containing questions such as the following:

  — A feathered vertebrate enclosed in the grasping organ has an estimated worth that is higher than a duo encapsulated in the branched shrub. (A bird in the hand is worth two in the bush.)

  — It is sufficiently more tolerable to bestow upon than to come into possession. (It is better to give than to receive.)

  — The medium of exchange is the origin or source of the amount of sorrow, distress, and calamity. (Money is the root of all evil.)

  — A monetary unit equal to 1/100 of a pound that is stored aside is a monetary unit equal to 1/100 of a pound that is brought in by way of returns. (A penny saved is a penny earned.)

- Have trainees work alone to "decode" the famous sayings that have been obscured by the "fancy" language. Allow 10 minutes.

How to Modify:

Rather than translating the obscure sayings, pick some well-known sayings or slogans and ask participants to rewrite them in obscure language.

■ *Life Map*

In this icebreaker, participants prepare a map showing the significant events in their lives.

How to Use:

- Ask participants to think about the things they consider the significant events in their lives. While they are thinking, pass out colored markers and sheets of newsprint to each.

- Ask participants to list those events in the order they occurred on one sheet of newsprint. On the other sheet, ask them to prepare maps that reflect the events that have led them to where they are in life. (See opposite for an example of a life map.) Allow 10 minutes.

- Have the participants pair off and discuss their maps with their partners.

How to Modify:

Participants may map their careers or significant events in the past year.

Games

In addition to their usefulness as warm-ups and energizers, games are enjoyable ways to focus participants on the subject matter of the course.

■ *Let's Make a Deal*

Susan Boyd, president of a training consultant firm, suggests this game for fostering group interaction.

How to Use:

- Divide the class into four- to eight-person teams.

- Make up a worksheet listing six to eight items that each team's members would likely have with them, making one or two of the items more uncommon things. Suggestions include: a photo, a calculator, a pencil, more than three credit cards, an unusual key chain, something red, and so forth.

Life Map

Use this acquainter to help participants get to know one another by tracking the significant events in their lives.

| BEGIN | | Born July 26, 1955 | | Learned to sail |

Moved from Missouri to Connecticut

Placed in high school honors classes and developed a love of language

Studied in Austria and hitchhiked through Europe

Taught English

Switched to a career in publishing

Took up tennis

Married

OVERWORKED

Moved to Kansas

Had two children

Back to work

PRESENT

From The Encyclopedia of Icebreakers *by Sue Forbess-Greene, copyright Applied Skills Press, 1983.*

- Assign a recorder based on some criterion (for example, the person with the oldest car, whose birthday is next, who has the longest last name).

- Teams get points for having each of the listed items—count only one of each item per person. The team with the most points wins and receives an award.

■ *Jeopardy*

Jim Leogue and John Macchi of JKL Associates (Coral Springs, FL) like to use a trainer-designed game similar to the popular *Jeopardy* television show as a way to begin the second session of a course (whether it is the beginning of the second day or the beginning of the afternoon). The questions for each session can be limited to the material covered in the previous session or can be a combination of material covered to date in the course, supplemented by material that generally should be known by the participants. For example, if the seminar is for company sales training, topics might include company products, the competition, and sales policies.

How to Use:

- Before the session starts, glue 25 envelopes to poster board in a 5-by-5-inch matrix. Label each column with a subject heading and each row with a monetary value. Subject categories should stress the learning activity. Develop questions based on course material and enter the questions (and their answers) on 3-by-5-inch cards. (Remember that in Jeopardy, players are given the answers and have to provide the questions.) Assign dollar amounts to the questions based on their difficulty and insert the cards into the appropriate envelopes.

- Divide the class into teams of equal numbers of participants, and have the team appoint a spokesperson—the only person who can give an answer. If another team member gives an answer, it is invalid.

- Give each team play money to begin the game. The moderator should decide on the amount of money given to each team; that amount should be sufficient to ensure that bankruptcy is almost impossible, since bankruptcy removes a team from play. Allow an hour to complete the exercise to take advantage of the full value of the game and the team building that takes place.

- Have a team begin by picking a question by category and dollar amount. They then have a minute to give their "question" to the "answer." If the team answers correctly, they receive the dollar amount in play money. If they answer incorrectly or fail to answer, the next team is given a chance to answer the question. The question passes from team to team until a correct answer is given or until all teams pass. If a team answers the question incorrectly, they are penalized by giving the moderator the dollar amount of the question.

"Double Jeopardy" exists when the team selects a question that includes a wild card—a 3-by-5-inch card that doubles the dollar value of the question. One or two of these cards should be placed randomly on the playing board.

- The game ends when all the questions have been answered. The team with the most money at the end of the game wins. A small reward as recognition is appropriate for winning team members, but the euphoria of winning and the camaraderie that builds during the game is the most rewarding aspect of this game. Moreover, the participants have had a fun—and challenging—review of course material.

Humor in Icebreakers

Since humor is a basic communications tool, it can be of immeasurable value in an icebreaker. Humor is a right-brain, creative activity that can help trainers emphasize or reinforce main topics or points of discussion. Humor provides an entirely different perspective for an icebreaker. It can help relax people in tension-producing situations; it can be a "breath of fresh air" in activities that are encrusted with learned ritual and predictable patterns. It can even make a marginally interesting activity or subject more interesting, even exciting.

Before forcing humor into a training activity, a word of caution is in order. As with any activity, any references to ethnicity, religion, politics, or gender should be avoided. Slapstick is also inappropriate. In any use of humor, participants must maintain their sense of personal dignity. People are more likely to risk humor if they can maintain their self-esteem.

The appropriate use of humor in icebreakers, then, is important for the positive development of a group of trainees. It establishes an important norm for the duration of the training experience: Humor is fine. Learning is fun. The effectiveness of humor—throughout the course or within the icebreaker—is a function of many variables:

- Trainees should trust one another.

- Group members should be supportive, and competitiveness should be avoided.

- Humor should be objective, not subjective.

- Humor should flow naturally from the course or discussion topic.

- Humor should be kept focused on the ultimate learning objective.

- Alternatives to the humorous activity should be available, if the humor is not working.

Attitudinal barriers may exist among the participants that hinder your efforts at injecting humor into icebreakers. Some of these are:

- Training is work, and work is serious.

- Humor is a waste of serious work time.

- People who have fun at work are immature.

- People who enjoy humor are not tough enough to be executives.

- Only bosses should be humorous.

- "I didn't come here for a comedy show."

- A focus on humor indicates that we don't have our priorities straight.

- "No one likes my sense of humor."

These attitudes can certainly hamper efforts to inject humor into an icebreaker, but they should not prevent the use of humor. Build the acceptance of humor as a norm through the use of the opening icebreaker, and these barriers are less likely to be problematic. Should a barrier rear its ugly head, the trainer can reiterate the value of humor or provide some positive feedback to the overly "serious" participant.

Brainstorming

You can use brainstorming to break the ice and to identify problems the group may have with a topic.

■ *Team Brainstorming*

To help everyone feel equal and set the stage for later group activities on the course topics, Susan Boyd suggests this activity.

How to Use:

- Ask teams of four to six people to list things that are round, things associated with a holiday, things that are red, things you can make out of tires or coat hangers, excuses for speeding, and so forth. Allow no discussion; just list items!

- Assign a recorder based on some criterion that was set before the exercise began (for example, last person in the group who stands, person with the smallest or largest hands) to record the team lists. The team with the most items wins a prize.

■ *Beach Ball Brainstorming*

Susan Boyd likes to use this activity to get people up and moving, especially in the afternoon to break up a long session.

How to Use:

- Announce a topic to the whole group (for example, things associated with a season, a holiday, the course content, the company).

- Have everyone stand and pass around an inflatable beach ball. When someone catches the ball, he or she shouts out something related to the topic and then tosses the ball to someone else. If the group is small, the participants can pass the ball in a circle.

■ *Introducing Something New*

Peter Renner provides this example in *The Instructor's Survival Kit*. "The trainer's task was to introduce a new registration form to a group of government employees. For many this could seem like a dull topic, and a threatening one if you were being asked to give up a beloved old form for a new one.

The trainer 'warmed' the group to the topic and each other by asking them to brainstorm on the range of problems the new form was likely to present. After 10 minutes of this, everyone in the class had had a chance to speak, even those who would otherwise have been silent. Then he distributed the new form and explained its features. Next, the group again looked at the flipchart listing potential problem areas and, with the help of the trainer, was able to see how these were dealt with on the new form. Their acceptance of the new form was thus greatly enhanced."

Designing Your Own Icebreakers

Sometimes "canned" icebreakers or warm-ups just don't fit the need, and a trainer must either design his or her own—or not use the tool. Training consultant Marie Morgan provides the following guide on designing icebreakers for specific courses:

The central principle in designing content-related icebreakers is to make certain the icebreaker is integral to both the subject and the purpose of the day.

Once the importance of the icebreaker is established, trainers can ask "subquestions" such as "How high or low is the trust level of the group?" and "When in the sequence shall I plan to use this activity?" Answers to these questions also can indicate the size of the group each person will speak to—for example, a partner, a group of four, or the whole group.

When designing the icebreaker, the question that must remain constantly in the forefront is "What am I trying to create here?" Until the answer to this question can be stated in one sentence or less, the design will be muddled. In a course on stress, for example, the response to this question would be "To decrease participants' stress, to increase their power to handle their lives more healthfully, and to turn negative energy into empowering energy." Every exercise (as well as the choice and setup of the room, the type of nametags, and so forth) needs to serve the stated purpose.

In a stress-reduction course, trainers need to begin by putting people at ease as quickly and gently as possible, so that the class experience itself is not unduly stressful. In order to develop trust gradually, trainers may choose to have people introduce themselves to just one neighbor, rather than to the entire group, particularly if they are not part of the same work group or if there is a wide mix of hourly, middle management, and professional workers.

In time management and personal organization courses, trainers may invite people to tell their name and position and whether they are primarily interruption driven, project driven, or meeting driven, and whether they are away from their desks or workstations a lot. The next questions for this group are: "Why am I here? What do I really want to learn today? What do I need to accomplish?" With affirming body language and feedback, encourage those who, early on, dare to really confess to the mess on their desk.

The rationale for this personal sharing is that people learn better when their minds and spirits are relaxed. If each person imagines they are in the presence of perfectionist high-achievers, they will have more trouble admitting to themselves how much help they need and will be defensive about some of the suggested changes.

The more trainers can develop the camaraderie of "We're all in this together," the more receptive the group will be to learning. Two additional reasons for asking these introductory questions are: Each learner establishes his or her own learning goal for the day; and the trainer can tailor examples and discussion as much as possible to individual challenges and questions.

If the stated purpose of the day is to establish annual goals for the group, trainees should reflect on their own personal goals as a way of introducing themselves. In this case, the trainer's initial question may be "Tell us your name, one reasonable goal you have for the coming year (either business or personal), and about your dream." Encourage participation by asking trainees what they would do if they had no time or money restrictions and no responsibility.

The "dream" discussions add interest. One chief financial officer confessed to wanting to spend a year in Tibet studying meditation, and one vice president of operations wanted to publish his poetry. Often, the dreams provide information about participants that their co-workers had no previous inkling about. Inviting dream discussions stimulates creative, out-of-the-box thinking that contributes to the expansive discussion of group goals later on in the session.

Encouraging Equal Participation

If the question asked is not immediately answerable by the participants, use a simple writing technique before soliciting responses. Ask a question related to course content or for general information. Invite each person to write his or her responses for a couple of minutes before anyone speaks. This helps those who find it difficult to speak extemporaneously.

Extroverts figure out what they mean by listening to what they say; introverts reflect internally for a while before they are ready to speak. If immediate responses are requested, the introverts may not be ready to respond when the extroverts are ready to move on. This simple technique encourages equal participation, regardless of personal cognitive style.

On the Subject of Trust

Icebreakers are an effective way of building trust—both during the training session and afterward in the workplace. As the training session continues, icebreakers evolve into trust builders. Whenever a transition from one subject to another occurs, trainers can invite more self-disclosure by using openers.

Variables in the Design Process

When you are designing your own icebreakers, take into consideration these principles:

Who Speaks to Whom

There are three ways trainees can participate in the training: They can talk to the entire group, a group of three or four, or a partner. Speaking to one partner would seem to be the least threatening, but sometimes groups of three or four are less threatening, especially if the partner is a "frosty" supervisor or a person with limited English skills. Having more people in the group may lessen the tension, giving the participant someone more accepting with whom to make eye contact, or providing colleagues to help draw out a hesitant participant.

Who Is Spotlighted

Participants can introduce themselves, introduce their partners, or introduce others to the group. They can disclose information about themselves, or ask the group to "Find the person who. . . ." They can play roles, or they can be themselves. Trainers can highlight everyone equally, or some persons more (group reporters, for example).

Subject Matter

The possibilities of subject matter for icebreakers are virtually endless. A few examples are:

● Metaphor or simile: "What kind of plant would you be? What kind of animal? Why?"

● Historical information: "Where did you live when you were seven years old? Where were you when the first man walked on the moon?"

● Personal inventories: "What unusual hobby do you have?"

Methods of Accessing Information

You can access important data by using any of the following means: external models and instruments, such as personality inventories, physical activities, or nonverbal activities.

In a typical team building workshop among peers, a personality styles inventory can be used to help people see themselves, their strengths, what they bring to a team effort, and what others bring. During feedback, the trainer invites each person to reveal one characteristic of his or her type that he or she is most proud of. Shy people can point to the traits published in the inventory, where they might be reluctant to point out their most pleasing trait in ordinary conversation.

Later in the workshop, trainers can invite each person to reveal a trait they are less than proud of. If a compassionate and understanding atmosphere has developed, the participants will listen well and encourage this new behavior. By having everyone speak, all participants feel the vulnerability of admitting to a "short suit" and have the chance to be an encourager.

A variation on the central principle is to integrate the activity into the subject at hand, even if the connection is not readily apparent. In a course on professional presence, for example, the trainer can move beyond the obvious "dress for success" level to examine deeper issues of "personhood" that people project. The trainer asks each person in the group to give his or her name and tell what plant or animal they would like to be. At this point, the participants are not allowed to explain why they chose their plant, although most are anxious to do so. There is a remarkable congruence between the plant or animal chosen and the way other participants perceive that person. This acquainter helps the trainee focus on his or her own self-perception and opens the door for positive feedback from the group.

On the surface, this is a fun, no-wrong-answers introduction, and the person has total control of how they wish to present themselves. The question invites a surprising level of honesty and self-disclosure, however, bringing the group to a deeper level of learning. Later, the trainer can revisit this exercise and invite people to tell their small group why they chose their particular plants or animals. This enhances the trust level in small groups.

For more information on designing your own icebreakers, see *Variables in the Design Process* at left.

References & Resources

Articles

Berry, Bart A. "Getting Training Started on the Right Foot." *Training & Development*, February 1994, pp. 19-22.

Boyd, Susan. "Ten Ways to Break the Ice Before and During Class." *Technical Training*, May/June 1998, pp. 6-7.

Dahmer, Bart. "Kinder, Gentler Icebreakers." *Training & Development*, August 1992, pp. 47-49.

Mattimore, Bryan W. "Imagine That!" *Training & Development,* July 1994, pp. 28-32.

Sisco, Burton R. "Setting the Climate for Effective Teaching and Learning." *New Directions in Adult & Continuing Education*, Summer 1991, pp. 41-50.

Sonnesyn, Susan. "Games to Train By." *Training & Development Journal*, January 1990, pp. 22-30.

Books

Eitington, Julius E. *The Winning Trainer: Winning Ways to Involve People in Learning.* 3d edition. Houston: Gulf Publishing, 1996.

Forbess-Greene, Sue. *The Encyclopedia of Icebreakers*. San Diego: Applied Skills Press, 1983.

Jones, Ken. *Icebreakers: A Sourcebook of Games, Exercises and Simulations*. London: Kogan Page, 1991.

Newstrom, John W., and Edward E. Scannell. *Games Trainers Play*. New York: McGraw-Hill, 1980.

———. *Still More Games Trainers Play*. New York: McGraw-Hill, 1991.

Renner, Peter F. *The Instructor's Survival Kit*. Vancouver, BC: Training Associates, 1983.

Scannell, Edward E., and John W. Newstrom. *Even More Games Trainers Play*. New York: McGraw-Hill, 1994.

Info-lines

Callahan, Madelyn R., ed. "10 Great Games and How to Use Them." No. 8411 (revised 1999).

Sugar, Steve. "More Great Games." No. 9106 (revised 2000).

Job Aid

Analyzing the Success of Icebreakers

Trainers should thoroughly consider each of these questions as soon after the conclusion of the icebreaker as possible. Reasons for each answer should be analyzed so that improvements, if necessary, can be made before an icebreaker is used again.

1. Did it start and end in accordance with the lesson plan?

2. Did it achieve the stated objective(s) from the lesson plan?

3. Were participants able to keep on track?

4. Were the directions clear and focused?

5. Did every trainee have the opportunity to participate?

6. Were any problems that surfaced given appropriate time and solved?

7. Did the trainer take full notice of the interaction patterns that developed?

8. Was the trainer flexible enough to change the process, if needed, as it unfolded?

9. Was the trainer able to maintain the proper amount of control or free flow, or both?

10. Did every question that arose before, during, or after the exercise get an appropriate answer?

11. Was the level of self-esteem of every trainee maintained or enhanced?

12. Were materials used appropriate for the activity?

13. If any participants played a special role, how well was it handled?

14. What parts were most and least effective?

15. Was the mix of process and content appropriate?

16. Did every aspect of the activity get processed appropriately so that closure was achieved?

17. Was trainer behavior appropriate in all respects?

18. Would anything be done differently the next time that this icebreaker is used?

19. Was this icebreaker appropriate to the level of knowledge and interpersonal experience of the participants?

20. Was the trainer comfortable with the process and the results?

10 Great Games and How to Use Them

10 Great Games and How to Use Them

Editorial Staff for 8411

Editor
Madelyn R. Callahan

Revised 1999

Editor
Cat Sharpe

Contributing Editor
Ann Bruen

Production Design
Anne Morgan

Selecting and Designing Games

Trainers have long believed in the adage "live and learn." Not surprisingly, they have always known that experience is often the best teacher. Experiential learning in the form of trainer-conducted games is frequently more effective than traditional classroom methods in increasing learning and retention. Research shows that adults learn more effectively by doing—by using their new knowledge and skills—than by passively listening or reading.

One study concluded that within one year, adults are likely to forget 50 percent of what they have learned through exclusively passive methods. Another study indicated that approximately half of one day's learning may be lost during the ensuing 24 hours. In two weeks, an additional 25 percent may be lost.

Games frequently provide the basis for successful training programs. They aid in program preparation, instruction, and evaluation. Their strongest feature is the element of fun that relaxes, motivates, and involves every participant from the outset, making learning enjoyable and productive. Games also use the five basic senses, particularly sight, sound, and touch, making for a more comprehensive and effective learning experience.

Strictly speaking, games are competitive activities governed by rules that define players' actions and determine outcomes. For the purposes of this discussion, we will employ a broad definition of *games* that includes the formalized, competitive activities and various exercises, activities, or demonstrations (also known as structured experiences or participative group exercises).

Other experiential exercises, such as simulation, role play, and simulation games, are addressed in other *Info-line*s. These exercises represent a number of either very simple or extremely sophisticated and complex activities. Role play and simulation exercises use real-life situations and applications. Simulation games are both reality based and competitive.

Simple games appeal to a large number of trainers for the following reasons:

■ *Versatility*
Game components can be interchanged easily to create a new focus or an entirely new game, and many different versions of a game can be built on one model.

■ *Cost Effectiveness*
Resource materials for these games are easy to produce and obtain. Some games require no materials at all, and most games involve little more than paper and pencils, which every training budget can afford.

■ *Transfer of Learning*
Learning proceeds from group interaction, with the instructor serving as a guide or resource rather than a detached lecturer or presenter. The instructor facilitates the learning and is an active integral part of the training process.

This issue of *Info-line* will acquaint you with various types of games, their special uses and features, as well as when to use and how to implement them. It will discuss the effective designs and uses of the four most widely used games:

- icebreakers
- competitive games
- exercises
- puzzles

Effective games can have significant impact on your audience. They can sharpen your training session so that your group will comprehend the materials on several levels—cognitive, affective, and empathetic. Such meaningful experiences will increase participation and learning. To accomplish this, be sure to carry out each phase of the game properly and completely.

Start by choosing a room that will accommodate your group comfortably. Check the noise level inside and outside the building. Prepare the seating arrangements in advance, and test acoustics and audiovisual equipment.

Designing Games

Find out as much as you can about your audience, facility, and available resources. Become familiar with a variety of games—their content, time limits, themes, style, format, and required supporting materials. Then decide how you would like to use the game: to identify, examine, critique, or discuss a problem; to develop skills such as empathetic listening, communication, problem solving, decision making, or management; or to start up, conclude, or refresh a program.

Organize your activity by establishing clear and specific objectives. You can proceed on a logical course once you know where you are going. Design resource materials to fit the content, and compile a list of materials for every phase of the game: instruments, forms, information sheets, background reading, diagrams, charts, and props, such as matchsticks, toothpicks, cards, blocks.

Consider the participants' level of interactive training experience to determine how they may respond to particular games. Plan in sequence; each phase of an activity should enhance the next one. Ask another trainer's opinion of your design, and pilot your design by using a test group.

Build into the design ways to gather data: listeners, observers, or questionnaires, for example. Always be certain that games are adaptable to the needs of participants with physical limitations. Determine physical constraints of the game, particularly those that involve movement.

Design Hints

To design games that will enhance your training sessions, follow these tips for success:

- Use a flowchart to plan your steps, and time each step.

- Choose a basic structure—introduction, stages, conclusions—and then add detailed content.

- Prepare all handouts in advance and have them ready.

- Plan for the worst; have back-up activities in case your group is too slow, too quick, or too familiar with your first-choice game.

- Make sure that participants are always actively engaged and challenged.

- Schedule sufficient time for breaks and discussions to alleviate tension.

- Play the game before you use it to make sure you are prepared to administer it properly.

- Be flexible; your game is a learning experience that should evolve naturally.

Conducting Games

Clarify expectations at the beginning of your session and make sure that trainees understand the objectives and game rules. Misunderstanding can lead to resistance and disruptions. Make a contract with the group, agreeing on expectations, roles, responsibilities, and norms. Then make a checklist of participants' expectations; post them and refer to them during the game.

Intervene only when necessary; encourage participants to be assertive and not to rely on you to defend or protect them. Give support and be willing to accept it from the group. Ask for feedback and respond to it (see *Giving and Receiving Feedback* opposite). Be sensitive to whether trainees are comfortable with open or experimental activities. Pick up cues from their behavior and comments. Be prepared to handle participant needs as they arise (see the *The Inevitable Gremlins* on the following page).

Experiment with and learn from your experiences as a facilitator. Maintain good listening skills and a respectful attitude toward trainees by keeping eye contact, repeating for clarity, and answering questions objectively. Be spontaneous and flexible. Whatever the outcome of the game, turn it into a learning experience. Reassure participants that mistakes are part of learning and that they will not be penalized for failures. Finally, close your activities properly by helping participants resolve problems and apply their learning.

The Don'ts of Game Presentation

Guard against these common mistakes made by trainers:

- using excessively difficult or threatening games

- distancing yourself from trainees (share breaks and meals with them)

- using the same techniques repeatedly

- giving long explanations

- changing the game to appease a few people in the group

- becoming more concerned with the game than the learning goals

Facilitating Games

Experts agree that this is the most important step of the learning process. This is the point at which participants examine their experience systematically. Facilitation methods may include a combination of discussion, observer's reports, instrumentation (questionnaires and surveys), and feedback and analysis. Without your planning and guidance, trainees cannot learn adequately. To ensure success, you should do the following things:

- Choose your role in the presentation. Will you act as leader, participant, or observer?

- Decide how trainees will participate: individually, in small groups, or as an entire group?

- Give participants a focus. Should you focus on specific behaviors, attitudes, or problems?

- Decide when to intervene *during* the activity in addition to providing wrap-up procedures.

- Provide supplies such as paper, pencils, markers, flipcharts, forms, and graphs.

Giving and Receiving Feedback

Games, like any learning situation, benefit greatly from constructive feedback. The following considerations will help you improve your group's productivity and participation:

- Establish a climate for testing new behaviors, taking risks, sharing information, and exploring alternatives.

- Establish feedback norms for listening, asking questions, and describing behaviors.

- Listen to and try to understand others' points of view without personal bias.

- Ask questions to get a thorough understanding of the problem. Show your interest with open-ended questions that invite comprehensive rather than yes-or-no answers.

- Be specific. Focus feedback on participants' behavior rather than on their qualities.

- Focus feedback on observations rather than inferences, on what you can see or hear rather than interpretations and conclusions. If you share interpretations and conclusions (it is sometimes valuable to do this), identify them as such.

- Describe the particular behaviors exhibited *during the game*. Do not be concerned with general or known behaviors associated with group members.

- Specify strengths first, then offer concrete suggestions for improving other areas. For example, say, "You are very articulate and observant, but you are most effective when you focus directly on particular discussion themes."

- Ask for a reaction to your suggestion. The trainee may not accept or may want to modify your suggestion.

- Try to close your discussions with agreements, particularly during the processing of competitive games. If you have listened to one another and clarified your ideas, you should be able to agree on specific changes and plans for improvement.

The Inevitable Gremlins

Every trainer must confront the dreaded gremlins of training sessions: the clowns, the hecklers, the disagreeable know-it-alls who manage to disrupt at least 10 minutes of your presentation. If it has not happened already, it is bound to sooner than you think. Take a look at the following pointers; they may make your life easier some day.

● Listen to the disruptive participants and let them know you are interested in their opinions.

● Give them responsibilities by asking them to be observers and to record others' viewpoints. Disruptive behavior is often an attempt to be heard; tell your dissidents that you welcome their *positive* contributions.

● Ask questions to find out what the problem participant really feels and needs.

● If personal problems cause the behavior, speak to the participant privately. Disrupters may become more cooperative once they have talked through problems.

● Reward cooperation and serious contributions.

● Never argue. Restate hostile questions in mild language and direct your answers to the group rather than the heckler. Remain calm and patient. If you lose your temper, your audience may decide to support the heckler.

● Rephrase superficial or hostile questions as statements so that the questioner must take a position.

● Form groups of two to five participants so the disrupter will no longer influence the entire group.

● Use processing time to discuss the activity or program in progress and to emphasize expectations and norms. The discussion will undoubtedly include the problem of disruptive behavior.

● Turn the disrupter over to the group. If a participant wants to argue with you, ask for responses from the group.

● Tell persistent arguers that you would like to hear more of their opinions during a break or after the exercise.

● Ask the disrupter to compare theirs and other members' ideas and to restate others' ideas. This will force the disrupter to listen to and understand other perspectives.

● Compliment the opinions of your talkative participants, but make it a point to solicit the input of less vocal members.

● Deal with class clowns by asking them to explain their remarks in objective terms so that everyone can comprehend their statements.

● Control sidetracking by asking the disrupter and the group to relate off-subject comments to discussion themes.

Facilitating Hints

There are a number of guidelines that are specific to facilitating games. Assess actual learning and determine the degree of goal accomplishment; then examine the reasons for similarities and differences in these two areas. Share discoveries about the learning process as well as personal discoveries, and analyze impressions of how the group worked together. Identify strengths and areas for improvement.

Decide how to apply the training to jobs. Examine personal and job-related changes and make specific plans to implement the changes. Finally, suggest ways to improve the game.

Icebreakers

Whatever the facilitator does at the beginning of a presentation sets the tone for the rest of the training. Thus there is a need for some sort of activity that will get your participants warmed up—an icebreaker.

Icebreakers present program materials in a more interesting way than introductory lectures by instantly involving the entire group; participants become acquainted by sharing personal attitudes, values, and concerns. Nonthreatening activities relax participants and reduce anxiety, encouraging spontaneity even among timid and shy trainees.

Icebreakers establish the pace and tone of the program and help build enthusiasm. They motivate the group quickly with activities that involve physical and emotional energy. In addition, they orient participants to the group's resources and give the group a sense of identity, helping to build trust. Finally, they establish the identity of the trainer as a facilitator rather than a lecturer. For examples of icebreakers, see *What's My Line* at right and *Roles of a Good Trainee* on the next page.

Icebreakers acquaint participants with one another and put them at ease (trainees are more receptive when they are ready to learn). These nonthreatening warm-up activities make a smooth start by introducing and focusing the program. They let participants know that *they* are responsible for their learning and that the trainer's job is to facilitate the learning. They also show participants what kind of trainer you are—demonstrative or reserved, conventional or innovative, program or participant oriented.

15 Icebreaker Tips

To properly set the stage for your training program, follow these icebreaker guidelines:

1. Develop an environment conducive to group interaction by providing a common experience or helping the group share experiences.

2. Never *insist* that participants share personal data.

3. If a trainee is using too much time during a personal statement, intervene tactfully and put the group back on course.

4. Determine the length of your opening activities by estimating the duration of the program (a four-hour session would require only six or seven minutes of icebreakers).

5. Consider your group's expectations when determining the level of activity and involvement of your icebreakers.

What's My Line?

Objective

To illustrate the importance of first impressions and stereotyping.

Procedure

This is a variation of the self-introduction game, using name, job, and favorite hobby. Instead of introducing themselves, however, participants are asked to introduce the person on their right, using strictly guesswork—that is, no clues are exchanged.

After a brief observation of the person on their right, ask participants to introduce him or her with a first name, job, and favorite hobby that they "think" he or she has, giving brief reasons for their guesses.

The person being guessed will then respond with the correct information before proceeding with his or her own introduction. Continue around the circle until everyone has been introduced. (If participants have done the first part of this exercise in a small group, have them return to a large group setting, positioning themselves so that the same person is still on their right. Participants will then introduce the person on their right to the larger group.)

Discussion Questions

1. How accurate are first impressions? What do we base them on?

2. Have you ever opted not to meet someone, based on your first impressions?

3. What are stereotypes? Why do we make them?

4. Do you now feel more comfortable with this group than when you arrived?

5. Do you know more about the people here than when you first arrived?

Materials Required

None.

Approximate Time Required

20–30 minutes.

Jacqueline V. Markus, Department of Communication, Arizona State University, Tempe, AZ

Roles of a Good Trainee

Objective

To create a constructive climate for discussion in a training session.

Procedure

In many groups of entry-level trainees, the participants have previously attended few, if any, formal training programs. Therefore, it is often helpful to establish clear norms for what constitutes acceptable (productive) trainee behavior.

One way to accomplish this quickly, with a certainty of hitting the "right" rules, is to present (orally, by handout, or by overhead transparency) a set of predeveloped guidelines for behaviors that trainees would ideally engage in or avoid. This approach has the advantage of clarity, but has the potential danger of creating a limiting, rule-filled environment. Presented in a positive manner, however, with the use of a handout such as the following example (especially when it is "spiced up" with some humorous illustrations), this exercise can have considerable success.

Example:

Roles of a Trainer (Facilitator)

1. Challenges thinking.

2. Creates lists.

3. Summarizes.

4. Shares ideas.

5. Provides handouts.

6. Serves as a model.

7. Raises questions.

8. Guides discussion.

9. Restates ideas.

10. Provides constructive criticism.

Alternative Procedures

1. Engage the group (early in the session) in a discussion of the productive and nonproductive behaviors they have seen (or can think of) on the part of seminar participants. This has the value of involving them in the creation of their own norms for their behavior.

2. Prepare printed tent cards with participants' names on the front and five rules of appropriate seminar behavior on the back. While the name faces outward to the trainer and other trainees, the rules are visually present to the trainee at all times as a constant reminder.

Materials Required

Possible handout, transparency, or tent cards.

Approximate Time Required

5–10 minutes.

From Games Trainers Play, *by E.E. Scannell and J.W. Newstrom. Copyright 1980 by McGraw-Hill Book Company, New York. Used with permission. All rights reserved.*

6. Select activities that will be appealing to specific kinds of groups. For instance, machine operators might not be as receptive to activities involving fantasies or imagination as would therapists.

7. Consider the background of your group and temper innovative activities with the knowledge of their cultural preferences.

8. Choose opening activities that are appropriate for the particular program. Employee motivation programs, for example, may use more flexible activities than management development programs.

9. Use icebreakers that involve physical energy to stimulate your group.

10. Use icebreakers as an opportunity for *you* to become acquainted with your group.

11. Use them to indicate what will be expected of the group and what the group can expect of the program.

12. Use them to show how you intend to participate in the program.

13. Choose icebreakers that will establish an environment for discussion.

14. Use icebreakers you are comfortable with. Some experiential activities may take time and participants' attention away from the specific subject matter. If you prefer more conventional methods that give you more control, use them.

15. Avoid using icebreakers for very large groups in which they will lose their intensity.

Competitive Games

Turning games into competitions helps to break up the routine of your training session. Participants can have fun and learn at the same time.

Competitive games are active, experiential forms of learning; that is, participants learn from their own actions rather than from what others tell them. This active involvement is motivational—most trainees respond to competition and the incentive to win. In addition, games appeal to learners of differing abilities, because everyone has the opportunity for involvement, and the valuable experience gained from games makes everyone a winner. Moreover, games provide a safe atmosphere for taking risks, away from real-world penalties for mistakes.

Games help trainees retain information and encourage unself-conscious behavior that can be analyzed in discussions. Games are social as well as educational tools, providing participants information about their own behavior in relation to others. For examples of competitive games, see *The Number Game* and *Archeological Game* on the following pages.

Games energize participants and promote interaction. They engage participants' interest and attention and provide them with a common experience. Games reinforce learning and training by demonstration. Among the skills they develop are strategic and critical thinking, communication, negotiation, problem solving, and decision making. Competitive games can inject energy into a low point of the program after lunch or at the end of the day, or they can be used to recap important points and close a presentation.

15 Competitive Game Tips

To use competitive games to best advantage, follow these guidelines:

1. Keep games in line with learning objectives.

2. Be familiar with your game. Trainees cannot be enthusiastic if they are interrupted constantly with corrections of game instructions.

3. Prepare by playing the game several times with friends.

The Number Game

Objective

To allow participants to discover (or reinforce) some principles of adult learning through hands-on activity.

Procedure

Distribute eight copies of "The Number Game" to each participant. Ask them to place a blank sheet of paper over the numbers so they cannot see the placement of the numbers. Tell them this is a simple hand-eye coordination exercise in which they are to work as fast as they can within a given time period. Then tell the participants: "Remove the blank sheet of paper. With pen or pencil, draw a line from No. 1 to No. 2, to No. 3, and so forth, until I say 'Stop.' OK? Go!"

Allow 60 seconds, and then say: "Stop. Please circle the highest number you reached and jot down the number '1' in the upper right-hand corner."

Repeat this procedure seven more times, each time allowing 60 seconds. Make sure each sheet is numbered in sequence.

Discussion Questions

1. In all candor, how did you feel when you were going through the exercise? (*Note:* Responses will be "nervous," "frustrated," "upset," "mad," and so forth.)

2. "Practice makes perfect." If this is really true, we all should have shown a consistent increase in the number attained with each attempt. Is that true for each of you? If not, why?

3. Did anyone have an increase every time?

4. Many of us experienced a slight decline, or "learning plateau." What might cause this?

5. If our trainees are likely to experience these plateaus, how can we be more understanding of these situations and adapt to them?

Materials Required

A quantity of "The Number Game" sheets (4 per person, printed on both sides).

Approximate Time Required

15 minutes.

From Games Trainers Play, *by E.E. Scannell and J.W. Newstrom. Copyright 1980 by McGraw-Hill Book Company, New York. Used with permission. All rights reserved.*

Archeological Game

Objective

To point up how our screening mechanism filters out unwanted data, details, minutiae. This is important so we can get through the day and get our tasks accomplished without being sidetracked by trivia bombardment.

Note: This objective is *not* given to participants, since this perceptual phenomenon is what they will learn from the game.

Procedure

Give the participants the following instructions:

1. "You are to function as archeologists. This means you are interested in reconstructing a given culture based on artifacts you discover.

2. The culture you are concerned with is the United States in the year 7000.

3. You are in a 'dig' and come up with a small, flat, round object. It has a man's face on it; the man has a beard. The object is a U.S. penny and has this year's date on it.

4. *Without* reaching for a penny from your pocket or purse, come up with as many characteristics of the U.S. coin and culture at that date as you can. This is what archeologists do all the time. You will have to rely on your memory to recall the data on the penny. You are in competition with the other teams. You have five minutes for the task."

At the five-minute mark, call time and ask participants to total their cultural characteristics. (The totals typically run in the "teens.") Get a verbal report from the team with the highest number of characteristics, and list its data on a flipchart. Anticipate items such as these:

- bilingual (English and Latin)
- architecture (if Lincoln Memorial is on rear)
- system of writing
- appearance conscious (Lincoln's beard)
- liberty loving (liberty)
- metallurgy
- calendar
- coinage system

- hero worship (Lincoln)
- a federal government ("E Pluribus Unum")
- religion ("In God We Trust")
- mining
- sewing skills or tailoring (Lincoln's shirt and coat)
- cloth production
- dress conscious (coat, tie)
- system of numbers
- agriculture (if a "wheat" penny)
- patriarchal society

Also anticipate friendly rivalry—the losing team will deny the validity of certain cultural traits listed by the winning team. Add (new) items from the other teams to your flipchart list.

Discussion

To process the game, ask participants what was learned. Some possible responses from the groups (list on a flipchart) are: importance of teamwork (several heads are better than one); a group leader is not necessary; importance of background or perception (different groups see different things).

At this point, add: "I'd like to pick up on the perception aspect. Was the task difficult to do, relying solely on memory?" [Participants respond "Yes."] "Why was it difficult to remember what is on an object that you handle *daily?*" [Pause at this point, for this is *the* profound question of the game.] Some possible participant answers are: "We don't pay attention to it. It's not important information. We take it for granted."

At this point, say: "Yes, we overlook the detail, the trivia, because we have a mechanism in our heads (phenomenon of perceptual choice or selective attention) that screens out the unimportant. This is a tremendously helpful device because it allows us to get through the day without getting bogged down by the innumerable stimuli that bombard us constantly—trees, signs, houses, stores, cars, clothing, colors. But at the same time, our screening mechanism may work the other way. It may screen out data we *should be cognizant of*—for example, to call old Harry to our meeting. We forget him, and he gets mad at us. So our screening device works for good and for less than good. We must be aware of this perceptual process and try to keep it from overlooking the important stimuli, which also are out there."

4. Organize all game materials and keep extra supplies of paper, pencils, and other items that are used up quickly or are easily misplaced.

5. If you are using handouts, know when to distribute them for greatest impact and least disruption.

6. Choose comfortable and workable seating and space arrangements.

7. Play the game at the time when participants will benefit most—during the introduction, instruction, or conclusion of your program.

8. Do not over-explain the game; introduce it briefly. If you use a written statement, make sure it is clear and precise.

9. Take questions only after you have completed your explanation. This will also give you time to ease into the game.

10. Choose a method of forming groups that best suits your particular game. If your objective is to build trust, random selection would produce groups of unacquainted individuals. Groups of two or three are ideal for sharing personal data. Groups of people who are wearing one or more of the same colors may also agree on other topics and work well as a team.

11. Refrain from intervening in the game frequently. Participants are playing the game to learn from their interaction with one another.

12. Avoid the role of trainer as authority figure or expert.

13. Assess learning and outcomes without appearing as a strict "evaluator."

14. Remind participants of the time five to 10 minutes before the game is scheduled to end.

15. Allow sufficient time for the entire activity when you plan your program schedule. Games that must be continued later lose momentum, and participants may lose interest before the outcomes.

Exercises

Exercises are structured learning experiences that help to enhance the training atmosphere. They are versatile instruments that can be used in a variety of ways.

Exercises accommodate a wide range of formats and purposes—short or long, simple or complex. They are conducted by the trainer, the group, or both. Exercises can be oriented either toward individuals or groups (of any size). Some exercises involve physical movement while others focus on discussion or writing, but they do not all require supporting materials. They can be made into games by adding competition.

Numerous sources for exercises exist—publishers, colleagues, or training programs—but they also can be created by trainers to suit specific needs, or they can use input from the group members themselves or from supervisors. For examples of exercises, see *Hand to Chin Exercise, One- and Two-Way Communication, What Do People Want from Their Jobs?* and *The Lemon Exchange.*

Exercises can be used to open or close a presentation, to illustrate specific learning goals, or to reinforce learning. They put participants at ease and maintain high participant involvement. In addition, exercises generate information for analyzing a particular problem or behavior and facilitate general and personal learning.

16 Exercise Tips

To make sure that you use exercises to their fullest advantage, follow these guidelines:

1. Select exercises that will fulfill your learning objectives best. Then consider the element of fun.

2. Organize all resource materials and equipment in advance.

3. Make sure the group understands instructions. Hand out written instructions if necessary.

4. Be straightforward.

5. Use relevant practical content that trainees can apply to their personal or job-related goals.

6. Use realistic time frames.

7. Choose the most effective time during the program to use your exercise. If you use it too early in the program, participants may miss the point; too late, and they may be less attentive.

8. Avoid covering too much material. If participants appear overwhelmed, edit extraneous material without causing breaks or long pauses in the activity.

9. Determine when to intervene *during* the exercise, particularly for the longer, more complex exercises.

10. Remind the group of the learning objectives throughout the activity.

11. Clarify your role in the learning process so trainees will know how you can assist them.

12. Show trainees that you identify with the group and are interested in learning with them. Sometimes this may include participating in the exercise.

13. If the exercise is long and multifaceted, use a summary sheet to help reinforce the training.

14. Use facilitation procedures that are appropriate for your group.

15. If you use observers, prepare them adequately with background information.

16. Avoid serious conflicts, too much emphasis on fun, or the generation of too much data. These problems will inhibit discussion and facilitation.

Hand to Chin Exercise

Objective

To illustrate that actions may speak louder than words.

Procedure

As you demonstrate, ask the group to extend their right arms parallel to the floor. Say, "Now, make a circle with your thumb and forefinger." [Demonstrate the action as you speak.] Then continue, "Now, very firmly bring your hand to your chin." [*Note:* As you say, "Bring your hand to your chin," bring your hand to your *cheek,* not your chin.] Pause. [Most of the group will have done what you have, that is, brought their hands to their cheeks.] Look around, but say nothing. After 5–10 seconds, a few in the group will realize their error and move their hands to their chins. After a few more seconds, more people will join in the laughter, and your point can then be verbally reinforced—a trainer's actions may speak louder than words.

Discussion Questions

1. Did you ever hear the saying, "Don't do as I do; do as I say"? Do we practice this as trainers?

2. We all know actions speak louder than words. How can we use this knowledge in our jobs to help ensure better understanding?

3. Communication is always a scapegoat for performance problems. What other barriers to effective communication does this exercise suggest?

Materials Required

None.

Approximate Time Required

5 minutes.

From Games Trainers Play, *by E.E. Scannell and J.W. Newstrom. Copyright 1980 by McGraw-Hill Book Company, New York. Used with permission. All rights reserved.*

One- and Two-Way Communication

Objective

To demonstrate the many problems of misunderstanding that can occur in a one-way communication.

Procedure

Prepare a diagram similar to the one shown here. Ask a volunteer to assist in this demonstration. Explain to the group that the volunteer is going to describe something to them, and their task is to simply follow instructions in sketching out the illustration.

Give the volunteer the figure. Have the volunteer turn his or her back to the audience so no eye contact is possible. The volunteer can use only verbal communication (no gestures, hand signals). Furthermore, no questions are allowed on the part of the group. In brief, only one-way communication is allowed. When the exercise is completed, project the correct figure on the overhead projector and ask participants to judge whether their drawings are at all similar to it.

Discussion Questions

1. How many of us got confused and just quit listening? Why?

2. Why was the one-way communication so difficult to follow?

3. Even two-way communication cannot ensure complete understanding. How can we make our communication efforts more effective?

One-Way Communication Diagram

(*Note:* If time permits, this activity can be immediately followed with another volunteer using a comparable illustration but allowing for full and free two-way communication.)

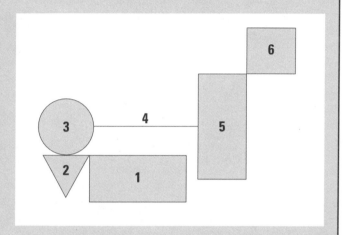

Materials Required

Diagram, as shown.

Approximate Time Required

10–20 minutes.

What Do People Want from Their Jobs?

Objective

To give participants an opportunity to discuss what factors motivate employees.

Procedure

Distribute copies of the form, "What Do People Want from Their Jobs?" Divide the group into subgroups of three to five people each. Ask each person to indicate which of the 10 items listed is thought to be of *most* importance in contributing to employee morale. Weight the items from 1 through 10, assigning 10 to the most important item, 9 for the next, and so forth, in a reverse order so that all 10 numbers are used.

Have each group total the individual weights within their group. Rank the 10 items under the column marked "Group."

Advise the group that this same scale has been given to thousands of workers around the country. In comparing rankings of both employees and supervisors, the typical supervisory group is ranked in the order shown under "Factors."

When employees are given the same exercise, however, and asked what affects their morale the most, their answers tend to follow this pattern [mark in the "Employees" column]:

1. Full appreciation of work done.

2. Feeling of being in on things.

3. Help on personal problems.

4. Job security.

5. High wages.

6. Interesting work.

7. Promotion in the company.

8. Personal loyalty of supervisor.

9. Good working conditions.

10. Tactful discipline.

Note that the top three items marked by the employees are the last three thought to be important for them by their supervisors.

Discussion Questions

1. In comparing your group's ratings with those of other groups ("Employees" column), what factors might account for differences of opinion?

2. Why might supervisory evaluations ("Supervisors" column) be so different from their employees ("Employees" column)?

3. If this form were to be used in your department or office, how similar would the results be?

Materials Required

Copies of the form "What Do People Want from Their Jobs?"

Approximate Time Required

20 minutes.

What Do People Want from Their Jobs?

Individual	Group	Factors	Supervisors	Employees
		High Wages		
		Job Security		
		Promotion in the Company		
		Good Working Conditions		
		Interesting Work		
		Personal Loyalty of Supervisor		
		Tactful Discipline		
		Full Appreciation of Work Done		
		Help on Personal Problems		
		Feeling of Being in on Things		

The Lemon Exchange

Objective

To vividly illustrate the importance of individual differences, the need for astute observational skills, and sensitivity to personal characteristics.

Procedure

Bring an adequate supply of lemons (or almost any fruit).

1. Distribute one to each member of the group. Direct each person to examine his or her lemon carefully by rolling it, squeezing it, and so forth. Ask them to *get to know their lemon* (always good for a few laughs). Tell them to pick a name for it. Encourage them to identify in their minds the strengths and weaknesses of their lemon.

2. Collect all the lemons and mix them up in front of the group.

3. Spread out all the lemons on a table and ask participants to come forward and select their original lemon. If conflicts develop over their choices, assist the parties in reconciling their differences, or simply note the failure to agree and use that as a basis for later discussion. (*Note:* In smaller groups of up to 25 people, the vast majority successfully identify their own lemons.)

Discussion Questions

1. How many are very sure they reclaimed their original lemon? How do you know?

2. What parallels are there between differentiating many lemons and differentiating many people? What differences are there?

3. Why can't we get to know people just as rapidly as we did our lemons? What role does the skin play (for lemons and for people)?

4. What human behavior does this bring to light?

Materials Required

A sufficient quantity of lemons (or other appropriate substitute).

Approximate Time Required

20–30 minutes.

From Games Trainers Play, *by E.E. Scannell and J.W. Newstrom.*
Copyright 1980 by McGraw-Hill, New York.
Used with permission. All rights reserved.

Puzzles

Puzzles are another valuable means of enhancing your learning environment. Like icebreakers, competitive games, and exercises, they encourage active participation.

Puzzles are versatile in form and use, and can be used as either solo or group games. They can be solved orally; visually—with handouts, charts, or blackboards; or physically—with blocks, straws, or sticks. Puzzles are more comfortable ways of exploring ability than stressful, inhibiting exams. They encourage imaginative solutions to problems without the pressure to "be creative." By illustrating alternatives, puzzles point out the value of investigating possibilities in areas such as career planning, taking risks, and assessing the potential of others.

Puzzles illustrate that effective approaches to problem solving use personal touch as well as logical thought. Participants can see themselves improve as they become better at solving the puzzles. This builds confidence and helps develop skills for planning strategies. Puzzles also let people know how they compare with others. For an example, see *Cake Cutting Puzzle,* opposite.

Puzzles involve everyone in an activity and engage the participants' curiosity and imagination. By providing variety and novelty, they show that learning can be exciting and interesting. Puzzles reinforce learning by explaining subject matter or by introducing and demonstrating the importance of both creative and logical approaches to problem solving. They also can be used to break the ice and put participants at ease.

12 Puzzle Tips

To use puzzles effectively, follow these guidelines:

1. De-emphasize the idea that "brain teasers," word games, crossword puzzles, and other puzzles require superior cognitive skills. Less confident participants may avoid puzzles that reveal shortcomings.

2. Use moderately difficult puzzles to stimulate your audience. Extremely difficult puzzles will frustrate and alienate trainees.

Cake Cutting Puzzle

Procedure

Draw an aerial view of a cake on the flipchart as shown in figure 1. Tell the group: "A woman had baked a cake for her party to be attended by eight guests. Her (and your) task is to produce eight pieces of cake with only three cuts of the knife."

Figure 1. Can you produce eight pieces of cake with only three cuts of the knife?

Bird's eye view

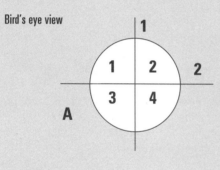

Lateral view

Figure 2. Lateral Cut Method: (A) Right angle intersecting cuts produce four pieces; (B) a lateral cut produces eight pieces.

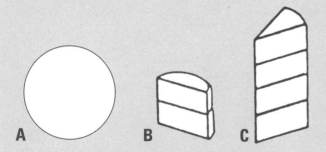

Figure 3. Stacking Method: (A) A vertical cut down the middle produces two pieces; (B) stacking the two pieces and cutting them vertically produces four pieces; (C) a final stacking and cutting of the pieces produces eight pieces.

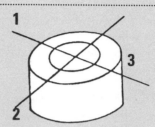

Figure 4. Center Cut Method: Two vertical cuts and then a center circular cut are made to produce eight pieces.

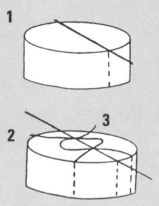

Figure 5. Disgustingly Sneaky Method: Two curved lines and a center straight cut produce eight unequal pieces.

Note: No one said the pieces had to be equal or the cuts made via a straight line. Remember, this is her party with her guests, and she can cut the cake any way she wishes.

Discussion

Ask: "What does the puzzle tell us?" Some answers are: "There may be more options than we think; let's stretch our imaginations and we can produce solutions that are varied and unique."

The puzzle may be used to stimulate thinking about problem solving, creating approaches, and alternative seeking.

From The Winning Trainer *by J.E. Eitington.*
Copyright 1984 by Gulf Publishing, Houston, TX.
Used with permission. All rights reserved.

3. Choose a straightforward puzzle. Some puzzles distance the activity from its purpose.

4. Explain objectives clearly and succinctly at the beginning so that these can be reinforced throughout the activity and the entire training program.

5. Always have a back-up puzzle in case too many trainees are familiar with your first choice.

6. Encourage trainees to approach the puzzles with the intention of taking risks and exceeding their self-imposed limitations.

7. Select a puzzle with a variety of solutions so that the activity is open to creative approaches.

8. Challenge your trainees to find new approaches and options.

9. Make them aware of the valuable uses of right-brain, creative thinking, but point out that there are times when logical left-brain thinking is more appropriate.

10. Keep a large stock of supplies. Participants often make several attempts and many mistakes before they solve puzzles.

11. Always budget enough time to integrate the experience into the training. Most puzzles are representative and must be interpreted at the conclusion.

12. Use puzzles simply for fun, as a change of pace, or to relax or stimulate participants. Puzzles offer a refreshing break from learning, enabling participants to resume their training with renewed energy.

Playing Those Mind Games

Researcher David Meier conducted a study that focused on the use of *mental imagery*—"the guided, self-controlled or spontaneous imagining of any thing or situation that can be seen, touched, smelled, heard, tasted, or experienced in any way." Through his research, he concluded that learning tools using fantasy and the imagination improve retention and recall.

Meier also described a mental imagery training technique, known as *guided imagery,* by which trainers use mental imagery to help trainees do the following:

● develop management skills

● set goals

● reduce stress

● increase confidence and assertiveness

● improve memory, communication, and problem-solving skills

● augment conventional training

These techniques provide experiential activities that are guided by a facilitator and carried out with a partner or by the entire group. For an example of how to use mental imagery, see Meier's professional development game opposite.

Development Through Mental Imagery

This game can be played with groups of any size. Its purpose is to help people identify their unique talents and strengths and discover how best to use them in their professional lives. The group leader can use the following script as a guide, varying it with experience to fit the needs of each specific group. The total time for this procedure is approximately 45 minutes.

■ *Introduction*
In just 45 minutes you will have a better understanding of what your unique talents and strengths are, and you will have a wealth of ideas of how best to use them to achieve higher levels of professional success and satisfaction. You will gain insight and a positive new sense of direction in your career. And you will come out of this experience with a set of guidelines for developing and enriching your professional life over the next year or so. This insight and direction will not come from me, but from you. I will provide the form, but you will provide 100 percent of the content. You will probably find the form to be fun. We will use mental imagery followed by reflection and analysis. In the first imagery session, we will ask you to vividly review in your mind three peak experiences of your life and to become aware of the unique strengths and talents you exhibited in those experiences. Then, after analysis, we will ask you to step into the future and see yourself exhibiting those strengths and talents flawlessly and effortlessly in your professional life. We will ask you to observe what you are doing, and from that, to design your own marching orders for peak performance over the next year.

(*Note:* In the script that follows, the virgule (/) indicates a pause. Most pauses can be for three to five seconds, but follow your intuition when you are in the situation.)

■ *Preparation*
To prepare for the first imagery experience, just get comfortable and relaxed. You can do this easily by breathing a bit more deeply than usual and becoming aware of your breath/ just concentrate on your breath/ just let your whole attention focus on the feeling of the air coming into your body/ notice how pleasurable it is to breathe/ concentrate on the pleasure of breathing/ as you breathe in, feel your whole body being refreshed/ a tingling sensation/ energy/ and each time you exhale, let go/ relax/ inhale and receive pleasure and new energy/ exhale and relax/ becoming more filled with quiet energy/ becoming more deeply relaxed with every breath/ continue doing this for a moment, closing your eyes and getting ready to enter the rich world of your deep inner mind.

■ *First Imagery Session (five minutes)*
Return in your imagination now to a peak experience of your life. Relive a time when your unique strengths and talents shone without obstruction—a time when you were filled with energy and an easy flowing personal power—a time when you were free, open, fulfilled, fully alive, fully

yourself in all your strength/ relive this situation now/ how old are you?/ where are you?/ what are you doing, saying, feeling?/ be totally back there now/ and observe what strengths you are manifesting and how this feels/ take a moment to relive this experience fully now, with total recall and total awareness/// (pause for about one minute).

Now move away from this scene and pick a second time and place in your past that was a peak experience—a time when you were filled with energy and an easy flowing personal power/ (continue as above).

Now move away from this scene and pick a third and final time and place in your life that was a peak experience for you—a time when you were filled with energy and an easy flowing personal power/ (continue as above).

■ *Analysis*
We will bring the imagery session to a close now and ask that when you are ready, you return to this time and place, open your eyes gradually, and get ready to reflect on the experiences you have just had.

Divide a piece of paper sideways into three columns. In each column, record your deepest impressions of each of your three imagery experiences. Use words, pictures, or a combination of both. Just capture in any way you can some of the most important elements of each experience. Reflect particularly on what each experience has to teach you about your unique talents and strengths. Work quickly and without criticism. We will allow three or four minutes for this.

Now debrief with a partner. Find a partner and share your experience and insight at any level you care to. Most important, help each other find the common thread that runs through your three peak experiences. Help each other determine what all three experiences are saying about your unique talents and strengths. We will take about five minutes for this.

Now by yourself, spend the next two minutes synthesizing everything you have experienced thus far down into its essence. Create an annotated list of what you now perceive to be your main unique strengths and talents.

■ *Second Imagery Session (five minutes)*
You have now identified your unique talents and strengths. We want you to enter the world of your imagination a second time now to experience what it is like to manifest these

talents and strengths fully in your professional life over the next year or so. You will enter the future and actually experience yourself exercising these talents and strengths in new and creative ways in your professional life. Out of this experience will come some rich and valuable insights regarding how you can direct your professional life for the maximum benefit both to you and to the organization and people you serve.

Your deeper mind already knows what you can do and must do to fully manifest your unique strengths and talents in your professional life. Through an imagery experience, you will now discover what that is.

Let's begin by becoming comfortable and deeply relaxed. (Repeat the instructions of the initial preparation session above.)

Now just let yourself become aware of the needs, problems, and opportunities that exist in your organization or your profession for which your unique talents and strengths are a good fit. Project yourself forward now to a situation where you have successfully met one of these needs, problems, or opportunities in a creative and exceptional way. You have shone. You have that feeling of success and fulfillment and deep satisfaction. You have been able to bring some of your unique talent and strength to bear, and it has worked beautifully. Be in that situation now/ feel how good it is to exercise your unique talents fully, to be fully alive, confident, successful, satisfied/ imagine yourself in that situation now/ what does it feel like?/ what do you see and hear around you?/ what is it that you have done?/ how have you done it?/ what were the steps that led up to your high performance, your success?/ see it all very vividly now/ and take a minute or so to observe everything you can about this situation in great detail/// (pause for about one minute).

Move away from this scene now and enter another one that speaks to another need, problem, or opportunity. Create a second situation, experiencing it even more deeply and vividly, where you have successfully exercised your unique strength and talent in your professional life. You have just turned in a truly exceptional performance/ feel the pride and the quiet satisfaction/ where are you now?/ what do you see and hear and feel?/ what, specifically, were you so successful at?/ what did you do?/ how did that come about?/ what were the specific steps that led up to your success and your sense of full satisfaction that you have now?/ experience this fully for a minute or so and observe everything with total awareness/// (pause for about one minute).

■ *Analysis*

We will bring the imagery session to a close now and ask that when you are ready, you return to this time and place, open your eyes gradually, and get ready to reflect on the experiences you have just had.

Now write nonstop for four minutes about your experience. What did you do? How did you do it? What were the steps that led up to your success? What allowed your talents and strengths to be fully exercised? What product, services, or benefits resulted from what you did? Write first on your first episode. Use words, pictures, anything to capture the essence of that experience. I will stop you in two minutes and ask you to go on to your second episode/// (pause for two minutes).

Now go on to your second episode, capturing in words and pictures as quickly as you can the essence of that experience. What strength and talent did you exercise? How did this manifest itself? What did you do and how did you do it? Write nonstop for two minutes/// (pause for two minutes).

Now debrief with your partner for five minutes, each of you sharing your experience at any level you care to.

(*Note:* At this point, distribute a handout to the participants that is a blank piece of paper with the following written on top: **Specific things I will do in the next year to exercise my talents to the fullest and be exceptionally successful and fulfilled in my work.**)

For the final exercise, complete this handout in any way that is most meaningful and useful to you. Be specific. What do you plan to do? How do you plan to do it? Mention specific people, places, dates, products, services, outcomes—whatever is most appropriate to your situation. You will be creating your job description, your marching orders, your professional development plan, for the next year or so. Be as detailed as you can, and use additional paper if you need it. We will take about 10 minutes to complete this final exercise.

■ *Close*

(*Note:* There are a number of options for closing this session, depending on the nature of the group and the amount of time remaining. Participants could have a final five-minute debriefing with a partner—preferably a different one than they had been working with. Or participants could share their main goals with the entire group for further feedback, suggestions, and refinement.)

Then, with a sense of how your unique strengths can be used to best advantage, go out and do it.

Contributed by David Meier

References & Resources

Articles

Abbott, Katherine. "Games That Work with Techies." *Inside Technology Training,* September 1998, p. 24.

Berry, Bart A. "Getting Training Started on the Right Foot." *Training & Development,* February 1994, pp. 19-22.

Boyd, Susan. "Ten Ways to Break the Ice Before and During Class." *Technical Training,* May/June 1998, pp. 6-7.

Duffy, Joseph R. "Creative Management: Does It Work?" *Quality Digest,* July 1991, pp. 58-67.

Ensher, Ellen A., and Jeanne Hartley. "The Employee Relations Game." *Training & Development,* December 1992, pp. 21-23.

Gunsch, Dawn. "Games Augment Diversity Training." *Personnel Journal,* June 1993, pp. 78-83.

Ireland, Karin. "The Ethics Game." *Personnel Journal,* March 1991, pp. 72-75.

Kirk, James J. "Playing Games Productively." *Training & Development,* August 1997, pp. 11-12.

Mattimore, Bryan W. "Imagine That!" *Training & Development,* July 1994, pp. 28-32.

McIlvaine, Andrew R. "Work Ethics." *Human Resource Executive,* August 1998, pp. 30-34.

Phoon, Annie. "Memory Massage: Review Games That Enhance Retention." *Technical & Skills Training,* January 1997, p. 4.

Thiagarajan, Sivasailam. "A Game for Cooperative Learning." *Training & Development,* May 1992, pp. 35-41.

West, Karen L. "Effective Training for a Revolving Door." *Training & Development,* September 1996, pp. 50-52.

Books

Baridon, Andrea, and David R. Eyler. *Sexual Harassment Awareness Training: 60 Practical Activities for Trainers.* New York: McGraw-Hill, 1996.

Boyan, Lee, and Rosalind Enright. *High-Performance Sales Training: 64 Interactive Projects.* New York: AMACOM, 1992.

Consalvo, Carmine M. *Outdoor Games for Trainers.* Brookfield, VT: Gower, 1995.

Eitington, Julius E. *The Winning Trainer.* Houston: Gulf Publishing, 1984.

Elgood, Chris. *Handbook of Management Games.* 5th edition. Aldershot, Hampshire, UK: Gower Press, 1993.

Engel, Herbert M. *Handbook of Creative Learning Exercises.* Amherst, MA: HRD Press, 1994.

Kirby, Andy. *Encyclopedia of Games for Trainers.* Amherst, MA: HRD Press, 1992.

Kirk, James J., and Lynne D. Kirk. *Training Games for Career Development.* New York: McGraw-Hill, 1995.

Newstrom, John W., and Edward E. Scannell. *Still More Games Trainers Play: Experiential Learning Exercises.* New York: McGraw-Hill, 1991.

Nilson, Carolyn D. *Games That Drive Change.* New York: McGraw-Hill, 1995.

———. *More Team Games for Trainers.* New York: McGraw-Hill, 1998.

———. *Team Games for Trainers.* New York: McGraw-Hill, 1993.

Scannell, Edward E., and John W. Newstrom. *Even More Games Trainers Play.* New York: McGraw-Hill, 1994.

———. *Games Trainers Play.* New York: McGraw-Hill, 1980.

Sikes, Sam. *Feeding the Zircon Gorilla.* Tulsa, OK: Learning Unlimited, 1995.

Thiagarajan, Sivasailam, and Raja Thiagarajan. *Each Teach: Harnessing the Power of Team Learning.* Amherst, MA: HRD Press, 1995.

———. *Interactive Lectures: Add Participation to Your Presentation.* Amherst, MA: HRD Press, 1995.

———. *Take Five: A Participatory Strategy for Better Brainstorming.* Amherst, MA: HRD Press, 1995.

Ukens, Lorraine L. *Getting Together: Icebreakers and Group Energizers.* San Francisco: Jossey-Bass, 1996.

———. *Working Together: 55 Team Games.* San Francisco: Jossey-Bass, 1996.

Info-lines

Preziosi, Robert. "Icebreakers." No. 8911 (revised 1999).

Sugar, Steve. "More Great Games." No. 9106 (revised 2000).

Game Selection Checklist

The appropriate game can make your presentation or training session one of the most memorable and productive experiences of your trainees' careers—but before you select a particular game, know the answers to the following questions:

☐ What is your purpose for using the game? What should it communicate to the group?

_____

_____

☐ What is the game's central focus? How does it serve your learning goals for the group?

_____

_____

☐ How large is your training group? What are their backgrounds? Are they familiar with the training material? With each other?

_____

_____

☐ Is the game adaptable to the needs of your training program? Can you use it to introduce, demonstrate, or reinforce the training?

_____

_____

☐ How "playable" is the game? Try it. How is it organized? Does it work according to its instructions? Is it fun?

_____

_____

☐ Do you have the resources and facilities for the game?

_____

_____

☐ Is this game the best way to achieve your objectives?

_____

_____

More Great Games

More Great Games

A U T H O R

Steve Sugar
The Game Group
10320 Kettledrum Court
Ellicott, MD 21042
Tel: 410.418.4930
Fax: 410.418.4162
Web: www.thegamegroup.com

Steve Sugar is president of The Game Group. He is the author of *Games That Teach* and co-author of *Games That Teach Teams*. He has developed instructional games and contributed to numerous publications.

Editorial Staff of 9106

Editor
Barbara Darraugh

Revised 2000

Editor
Cat Sharpe Russo

Contributing Editor
Ann Bruen

Production Design
Leah Cohen

Why Games?

I stand here singing my song. And, you leave here humming it…I hope.

—Anonymous

Today's learner does not want to hear you lecture, and they are too busy to read your instruction guide, so how can you tell them what they need to know? The answer is learning games—games that have a practical, instructional purpose. Participants like to have fun while they learn, and a well-designed learning game brings fun into the learning environment. In addition, games create interactive learning by transforming participants into active players and translating inactive information into enjoyable learning episodes. Learning occurs at three levels:

1. Players interact with the content, demonstrating their knowledge and ability to apply the information.

2. Players observe their own behavior and that of others during game play. Post-game debriefings give insights into those behaviors in thoughtful vignettes and examples observed during the game experience.

3. Discussion of newly acquired awareness guides the learner to the discovery of personal and work site applications.

Features of an Effective Learning Game

Balance. The game format should present an appropriate mix of chance and skill. Too much chance makes the game boring and mindless; too much emphasis on knowledge reduces the game to a test.

Easily adaptable. An effective game format should be "open" to your content and can be written to the level of any audience. Some games even allow you to adjust the level of competition you wish to bring to your audience.

User-friendly. The game format is easily understood, so participants are quickly converted into active players.

Fun to play. The game promotes player involvement and continued interest.

Flexible. The game can be modified to fit into almost any training facility and any time schedule.

Selecting and preparing a new learning game to use in your training can be a risky procedure. To help you experience the preparation and play of a learning game, this issue of *Info-line* offers you five fully adaptable learning games, selected to fill a specific, yet differing function in the training plan. Each game will be presented in terms of its learning objectives, features, and mode of play.

With the exception of "Lecture Bingo" by Sivasailam Thiagarajan, these games were created by this issue's author and are adapted from his books, *Games That Teach* and *Games That Teach Teams*. To expand your understanding and application of learning games further, consult the list of references and resources at the end of this issue. Finally, to help you prepare your own learning game, use the job aid *Adapt-and-Play Guidelines*—also developed by the author. It is a valuable worksheet that you can use over and over again, incorporating your own content.

Shape Up!

Situation: You want to bring focus to your group with an exercise that will introduce your topic in a climate of energy and playfulness. You would like to divide your group into teams that will generate ideas about your content. You hope this event will create an ongoing interest in the topic that will carry you through the entire program.

Purpose: This icebreaker activity will establish a problem-solving climate and bring participants into problem-solving groups.

Time: 15 to 30 minutes.

Number of Participants: 15 to 32.

Supplies Needed:

☐ One or more newsprint flipcharts and felt-tipped markers.

☐ A set of task assignments prepared in advance by the facilitator.

☐ Paper and pencils for the participants.

Sample Task Assignments

If you plan to use the game "Shape Up!" in your training, here are some examples of task assignments to write on the shapes. (These samples are appropriate for a time management training session.)

● Name seven reasons to keep a written journal of meetings.

● List seven ways to get more out of your desktop computer.

● List five ways to deal with an unwanted drop-in visitors.

● List nine important things you can accomplish in a seven-minute period of time.

● Name seven ways to make your next meeting more productive.

● Name five ways to get better use of the first hour of the workday.

● Name five ways to get better use of the last hour of the workday.

● List seven timesaving tips for using the telephone.

● List seven reasons why you should create a computer back-up system.

☐ Three sheets each of different color construction paper.

☐ Two or more fine-tipped permanent markers.

☐ Scissors or paper cutter.

☐ Four or more No. 10 envelopes.

☐ Masking tape.

Preparing for the Activity:

☐ Determine the number of task assignments you want resolved and choose a shape for each task.

☐ Write the tasks you wish each subgroup to accomplish on the appropriate shape.

☐ Determine the number of participants you want in each subgroup. Then cut the shape into the appropriate number of irregular pieces. For example, if you want four members in each subgroup, cut each shape into four pieces. (See the figure *Shape Up!* for an example.)

☐ In accordance with your group size, determine the number of tasks and the number of participants in each subgroup. For a group of 16, plan four tasks and four participants in each subgroup. This requires four different shapes (circle, square, star, and heart), each cut into four pieces. For larger groups, consider using more than one color for each shape.

Overview of Player Activity:

1. Distribute one piece of a shape to each player.

2. Have participants find other players whose pieces complete the shape.

3. Give each subgroup six minutes to complete the task written on the shape.

4. Call time at the end of six minutes.

5. Have each subgroup report on its task assignment.

6. Award one point for each item developed. The subgroup with the most points is declared the winner (optional).

7. Debrief and discuss the activity, as required.

Variations:

● Focus the debrief questions on identifying which participants took leadership, and post the results.

● Switch the task assignment after each subgroup has reported. Assign another subgroup to expand on the solutions devised by the original problem-solving group.

● Omit one piece from each shape to determine how participants handle ambiguity.

● Assign one point for each item presented. Determine if awarding points adds too much competition to the activity.

● Allow the group to vote for the most creative or most practical solutions, and award prizes.

Lecture Bingo

Situation: You have prepared a lecture containing vital information about your topic and want to ensure participant interest. Although you have taken great pains to support your material with appropriate overhead graphics, you are concerned that the lecture, in itself, will not be as interactive as it should be. You need demonstrated feedback to occur *during* key points of the lecture.

Purpose: Use this game to introduce the workshop topic, establish immediate work teams, and to motivate participants to interact with the lecture.

Time: 15 to 50 minutes.

Number of Participants: 15 or more.

Supplies Needed:

☐ One newsprint flipchart and felt-tipped markers.

☐ One bingo card per team of players (see the next page for an example).

☐ Paper and pencils for the participants.

☐ Prizes (optional).

Preparing for the Activity:

☐ Select 25 or more items from your lecture. Prepare these in "bite-size" statements or ideas.

☐ Prepare one bingo game sheet per two participants.

Overview of Player Activity:

1. Divide the group into teams of two to three players each.

2. Distribute one bingo card and pencil to each team.

3. Tell participants that they are to identify items from your lecture and mark these items on their bingo cards.

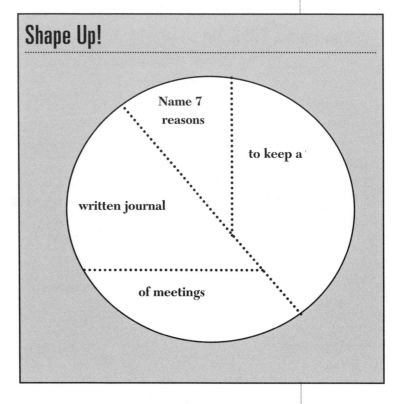

Shape Up!

Name 7 reasons

to keep a

written journal

of meetings

4. Present your lecture. The first team to identify and mark five items in a row from your lecture wins.

Variations:

● Replace key items with short-answer questions. Pause in your lecture and ask participants to see if they can answer a question on the bingo sheet. Give the correct response. Teams get to mark the box only if they give the correct response.

● Refrain from mentioning several key items to see if participants question you about those items in order to bring them into discussion.

● Require your participants to complete variations of items in a row, such as a total blackout card, an "X", a line of items forming a "T", or other configurations.

● Distribute bingo cards to groups, ranging from one to five, to demonstrate levels of effectiveness of different-size groups.

Source: *Zingo-2.* © 2000 Workshops by Thiagi, Bloomington, IN.

Lecture Bingo: Time Management

Rewards and punishment	Closed-door policy	Focus, focus, focus	Online meetings	TV, or not TV, that is the question
Telephone interruptions	My personal filing system	Virtual teams	The 80-20 rule	No. 1 time waster
Computer back-up system	5 is the "magic" number	My friend, the telephone	Chat room	Tele-conferencing
Just the fax, Ma'am	Coffee break	Internet connections	Email with attachment converter	Quiet time
Video/ teleconferencing	Journal keeping	Shared responsibility	Websites	Just say "no"

Brain Frame

Situation: You want to create a lively, energetic, creative atmosphere to unblock thinking or to generate new ideas about the topic. You also want to use this exercise after a luncheon to jump-start the module, by requiring participants to demonstrate their understanding by associating items that are part of the theme of the exercise. Finally, you want to demonstrate an easy-to-use brainstorming structure.

Purpose: Use this game to motivate participants to create as many options as possible for learning topics. It demonstrates an easy brainstorming structure and provides a method to get people to think outside the box.

Time: 30 to 45 minutes.

Number of Participants: Nine or more.

Supplies Needed:

☐ One or more newsprint flipcharts and felt-tipped markers.

☐ One flipchart-size game sheet for each team, prepared in advance by the facilitator.

☐ One set of felt-tipped markers for each team.

☐ Masking tape, to post the game sheets.

Preparing for the Activity:

☐ Prepare one newsprint flipchart game sheet per team, using the example found in the sidebar *Improving Plant Safety* as a sample format.

☐ Select a theme topic: Improving Plant Safety.

☐ Draw a 3-by-3 matrix.

☐ On the vertical axis, list three categories: Clothing, Materials, Activities.

☐ On the horizontal axis, select three letters: A, M, P.

Overview of Player Activity:

1. Divide the group into teams of three to five players each.

2. Have each team meet at one of the posted game sheets.

3. Give teams seven minutes to create as many items as they can, using the letters and categories on the matrix of the game sheet.

4. Call time at the end of seven minutes.

5. Award one point for each correctly identified item on the game sheet.

6. Award a three-point bonus for any item not found on an opponent's game sheet.

7. Debrief and discuss the activity, as required.

Variations:

● Create random rounds by placing letters in one hat and categories in another, and then have teams draw to create a random brainstorming round.

● Use game sheets as a take-home exercise to reinforce reading assignments. Have everyone fill them out after reading the material.

● Accommodate different categories or numbers of topics by using different matrix designs, such as 2-by-2, 2-by-3, 3-by-4, 4-by-4, and so forth.

● Rotate the game sheets among the teams for each round of play. Continue until all teams have played on all game sheets.

● Award 10 bonus points to each team that places at least one item in each square on the game sheet.

● Use numbers or dates on the horizontal axis instead of letters. Teams can use the Brain Frame grid to identify stages, dates, or milestones of a project or process.

● Use words on both axes to make the forced association challenge more difficult.

● Play as a cyber team using your chat room function. Create the matrix using a spreadsheet program, and assign one player as recorder to write down the words and ideas.

Improving Plant Safety

	A	M	P
Clothing			
Materials			
Activities			

Classify

Situation: You want a game that will get your participants out of their chairs and highly active, especially after breaks. You also want a game that quickly reviews the specifics of categorized material—that is, material that can be sorted into two or more categories, such as political parties, safety procedures, milestones, or stages of a production, inventory, or management process.

Purpose: This game demonstrates differences among similar items or processes and creates a dynamic exercise that requires players to sort items correctly.

Time: 15 to 30 minutes.

Number of Participants: 10 or more.

Supplies Needed:

☐ One or more newsprint flipcharts and felt-tipped markers.

☐ One newsprint flipchart game sheet for each team, with the names of the categories to be used in the activity, prepared in advance by the facilitator.

☐ One or more sets of item cards for each team, written on 3-by-5-inch cards, prepared in advance by the facilitator.

☐ Masking tape—tear strips of tape for each team. The teams will affix the tape to the backs of the index cards.

☐ Pins or thumbtacks (an appropriate amount to each team).

☐ A stopwatch or other timing device.

Preparing for the Activity:

☐ Select your topic, determine the number of categories (usually two or three), and then determine the number of items to be categorized.

☐ Determine the duration of the game by dividing the number of items to be categorized by 13. Allow one minute for every 12 to 15 item cards.

☐ Prepare one set of item cards for each team. This can be done by selected software programs or by generating a label for each item and pasting it onto the index card.

☐ Prepare one newsprint game sheet for each team. If creating two choices, draw a vertical line down the middle of the sheet; then write the two choices at the top of the sheet. If creating three choices, draw two vertical lines down the sheet.

☐ If possible, place each game sheet near a conference table to serve as a team's "base of operations" during game play.

☐ Distribute supplies for affixing the items onto the game sheet: masking tape and thumbtacks.

Overview of Player Activity:

1. Divide the group into two or more teams of five to 10 players each.

2. Place one prepared game sheet on the wall.

3. Place one complete set of item cards, face down, and strips of masking tape by each team's game sheet.

4. Have each team meet at one game sheet.

5. Tell players that this is a "relay" exercise, in which each team will be given one minute to attach all their item cards to the game sheet.

6. Allow each team to prepare their masking tape strips and line up for the round of play.

7. When told to start, the first player will turn over the first item card and place it into one of the categories. Warn players that there might be an item card that fits more than one category. In that case, they will want to place their card on the line dividing the two categories (see the sidebar *Cupper's Dilemma*).

8. Once a card is turned over, it must be played. Once a card has been placed, it cannot be moved. Only after the first card is placed may the second player turn over the second card.

9. Play will continue in this fashion until the team has placed all their cards on the game sheet or time has expired.

Cupper's Dilemma

Tea		Coffee

Tea

First served iced at 1904 expo

Britain's most popular drink

Pekoe, Darjeeling, Oolong, Earl Grey

Discovered when leaves fell into Shen Nung's hot water

Japanese Cha-no-yu ceremony

Sullivan's silk sample bags, 1908

Largest exporters India and China

Finest grown at higher altitudes

Coffee

Introduced to S. America in 1700s

Largest per capita user is U.S.

Mocha, java, French Roast

Discovered by Kaldi, the goatherd

Name from Arabic word "qahway"

Largest exporters Brazil and Columbia

---

10. Call time at the end of one minute.

11. Award one point for each correctly categorized item card. If you have used item cards that can be placed in more than one category, award a three-point bonus for any card correctly placed on the line between the two appropriate categories. The team with the most points is declared the winner.

12. Debrief and discuss the activity, as required.

Variations:

● Change the scoring so that one point is deducted for incorrect answers. This creates a more competitive dynamic during play.

● Although only one player may touch the item card, allow the rest of the team to coach their players as they are making their decision.

● Allow more or less time, depending on the difficulty of the material or the number of item cards.

Deadlines

Situation: You want a dynamic game that requires your participants to demonstrate their understanding of the topic under one of the following conditions:

1. After a lecture or readings about a specific module. This will give you data about how much participants understood and what material needs to be covered in more detail.

2. To preview the format of actual examination material in a less threatening environment. This can be very helpful in certification programs that require post-criterion testing.

3. At the beginning of your program. This can help you establish a baseline of how much your participants understand about the topic.

4. When you want this game to be easily played and generate a challenging, yet fun-filled environment, so that you can use the game over and over with the same or different audiences.

Purpose: Use this game to create a contract-and-challenge environment. Participants can predict how accurately their team can answer sets of questions pertaining to a certain topic and collect points based on the accuracy of both the predictions and the answers.

Time: 30 to 90 minutes.

Number of Participants: 10 or more.

Supplies Needed:

☐ One or more newsprint flipcharts and felt-tipped markers.

☐ One set of question sheets for each team, prepared in advance by the facilitator.

☐ Paper and pencils for each participant.

Preparing for the Activity:

☐ Prepare a test bank of questions on your topic. Then, select sets of seven questions and put these questions on a question sheet. For instance, if you select 21 questions, place the first set of seven on question sheet No. 1, the second set of seven on question sheet No. 2, and the third set of seven on question sheet No. 3. (Past experience has shown that this game works best with three sets of question sheets. Teams enjoy the challenge of adjusting their estimates on subsequent rounds.)

☐ Prepare a "key" for each question sheet with the appropriate answers and additional information to reinforce the answers, as needed.

☐ Prepare one set of question sheets for each playing team. All teams may receive the same set of questions. This will allow you to focus on the same information for all teams at the same time.

Overview of Player Activity:

1. Divide the group into teams of three to five players each.

2. Distribute paper and pencils to each team.

3. Round 1:

   • Tell teams that they will be given five minutes to answer seven questions on the topic.

   • Have each team estimate how many correct responses they will provide for the seven questions.

   • Post each team's prediction on the newsprint flipchart.

   • Distribute one set of question sheets to each team.

   • After five minutes, call time.

- Collect one completed question sheet from each team.

- Go over the correct responses with the participants.

- Have participants compute their scores according to the scoring matrix (at right).

- Record each team's points on the newsprint flipchart.

4. Play each second and succeeding rounds in the same fashion.

5. End of Game:

- Total all team points. The team with the most points is declared the winner.

- Debrief and discuss the activity, as required.

Variations:

- Adjust the time allowed for answers, depending on the complexity of the questions or size of the group.

- Vary the number of rounds to match the available time or the amount of material you wish to cover.

- Prepare question sets of four, five, or six using the same scoring system.

- After the participants have answered the questions and handed in their responses, give the teams the option of revising their original estimates of the number of correct answers. This allows the participants to reflect on how well they were able to answer the questions. But only the original estimate counts in determining the winner.

Scoring Matrix for Deadlines

Estimated Number of Correct Responses	Total Points
1	1
2	4
3	9
4	16
5	25
6	36
7	49

If a team does not accomplish its contract, it receives 2 points for each correct response. If a team exceeds its contract, it receives an additional 2 points for every correct response above the estimate.

- Team "A" estimates it will provide five correct responses. It actually provides six correct responses. Team "A" receives 25 points for meeting its estimate plus two points for the extra correct response, for a total of 27 points.

- Team "B" estimates it will provide five correct responses. It actually provides only four correct responses. Team "B" receives two points for each correct response, for a total of 4 x 2 = 8 points.

References & Resources

Articles

"Are Games a Waste of Time?" *Training & Development*, January 1996, p. 26.

Feldstein, Michael, and Kevin Kruse. "The Power of Multimedia Games." *Training & Development*, February 1998, pp. 62-63.

Filipczak, Bob. "Training Gets Doomed." *Training*, August 1997, pp. 24-31.

Fister, Sarah. "Fun and Games CBT." *Training*, May 1999, pp. 68-78.

Fowler, Alan. "How to: Use Games to Choose Winners." *People Management*, June 13, 1996, pp. 42-43.

"Games Trainers Play." *Sales & Marketing Training*, July-August 1990, pp. 12-13.

Geber, Beverly. "Let the Games Begin." *Training* (Supplement), April 1994, pp. 10-15.

Gunsch, Dawn. "Games Augment Diversity Training." *Personnel Journal*, June 1993, pp. 78-83.

Hequet, Marc. "Games That Teach." *Training*, July 1995, pp. 53-58.

Kirk, James J. "Playing Games Productively." *Training & Development*, August 1997, pp. 11-12.

Miller, Cyndee. "Training Pays Off—in Cash." *Marketing News*, July 22, 1991, p. 23.

Phoon, Annie. "Memory Massage: Review Games That Enhance Retention." *Technical & Skills Training*, January 1997, p. 4.

Prensky, Marc. "Bankers Trust: Training Is All Fun and Games." *HRFocus*, October 1998, pp. 11-12.

Richter, Alan. "Board Games for Managers." *Training & Development Journal*, July 1990, pp. 95-97.

Rubis, Leon. "Let the Games Begin." *HRMagazine*, December 1996, pp. 59-64.

Salopek, Jennifer J. "Stop Playing Games." *Training & Development*, February 1999, pp. 28-38.

Sonnesyn, Susan. "Games to Train By." *Training & Development Journal*, January 1990, pp. 22-30.

Sugar, Steve. "Training's the Name of the Game." *Training & Development Journal*, December 1987, pp. 67-73.

Takacs, George, and Steve Sugar. "Games That Teach Teams: Tale of the RAT." *Quality and Participation*, September-October 1999, pp. 54-55.

Thiagarajan, Sivasailam. "Board Games Excite Bored Learners." *Thiagi Game Letter*, November-December 1998, pp. 3-4.

———. "Games are on a Roll!" *Thiagi Game Letter*, July 1999, pp. 1-2.

———. "So Many Games." *Thiagi Game Letter*, September 1998, pp. 1-2.

———. "The Year in Games." *Thiagi Game Letter*, February 1999, pp. 1-2.

Walker, Kate. "Bring on the Entertainment." *Personnel Journal*, July 1995, pp. 84-90.

West, Karen L. "Effective Training for a Revolving Door." *Training & Development*, September 1996, pp. 50-52.

Books

Annual: Volume 1: Training. San Francisco: Jossey-Bass/Pfeiffer, 1972-present.

Annual: Volume 2: Consulting. San Francisco: Jossey-Bass/Pfeiffer, 1972-present.

Baridon, Andrea P., and David R. Eyler. *Sexual Harassment Awareness Training: 60 Practical Activities for Trainers*. New York: McGraw-Hill, 1996.

Consalvo, Carmine M. *Outdoor Games for Trainers*. Brookfield, VT: Gower, 1995.

Bond, Tim. *Games for Social and Life Skills*. New York: Nichols Publishing, 1986.

Christopher, Elizabeth M., and Larry E. Smith. *Leadership Training Through Gaming*. New York: Nichols Publishing, 1987.

Gredler, Margaret. *Designing and Evaluating Games and Simulations: A Process Approach*. Houston: Gulf Publishing, 1992.

Greenblat, Cathy Stein. *Designing Games and Simulations*. Beverly Hills, CA: Sage Publications, 1988.

Greenwich, Carolyn. *The Fun Factor*. Sydney, AS: McGraw-Hill, 1997.

Keiser, Thomas C., and John H. Seeler. "Games and Simulations." In *The ASTD Handbook for Training and Development*, edited by Robert L. Craig. New York: McGraw-Hill, 1987.

Kirby, Andy. *Encyclopedia of Games for Trainers*. Amherst, MA: HRD Press, 1992.

Kirk, James J., and Lynne D. Kirk. *Training Games for Career Development*. New York: McGraw-Hill, 1995.

Lawson, Karen. *The Trainer's Handbook.* San Francisco: Jossey-Bass/Pfeiffer, 1998.

Newstrom, John W., and Edward. E. Scannell. *Games Trainers Play.* New York: McGraw-Hill, 1980.

Nilson, Carolyn D. *Games That Drive Change.* New York: McGraw-Hill, 1995.

———. *More Team Games for Trainers.* New York: McGraw-Hill, 1998.

———. *Team Games for Trainers.* New York: McGraw-Hill, 1993.

Piskurich, George M. "Customizing a Board Game with Your Classroom Material." In *The ASTD Handbook of Instructional Technology.* Edited by George M. Piskurich. New York: McGraw-Hill, 1993.

———. "Using Games to Energize Dry Material," in *The ASTD Handbook of Training Design and Delivery*, edited by George M. Piskurich. New York: McGraw-Hill, 1999.

Scannell, Edward E., and John W. Newstrom. *Even More Games Trainers Play.* New York: McGraw-Hill, 1994.

———. *More Games Trainers Play.* New York: McGraw-Hill, 1983.

———. *Still More Games Trainers Play.* New York: McGraw-Hill, 1991.

Sikes, Sam. *Feeding the Zircon Gorilla...& Other Teambuilding Activities.* Amherst, MA: HRD Press, 1995.

Silberman, Mel, and Karen Lawson. *101 Ways to Make Training Active.* San Francisco: Jossey-Bass/Pfeiffer, 1995.

Sugar, Steve. *Games That Teach.* San Francisco: Jossey-Bass/Pfeiffer, 1998.

Sugar, Steve, and George Takacs. *Games That Teach Teams.* San Francisco: Jossey-Bass/Pfeiffer, 1999.

Thiagarajan, Sivasailam. *Games by Thiagi* (booklet series). Amherst, MA: HRD Press, 1994.

———. *Interactive Experiential Training.* Bloomington, IN: Workshops by Thiagi, 1998.

———. *Interactive Strategies for Improving Performance.* Bloomington, IN: Workshops by Thiagi, 2000.

Ukens, Lorraine L. *All Together Now!* San Francisco: Jossey-Bass/Pfeiffer, 1999.

West, Edie. *The Big Book of Icebreakers.* New York: McGraw-Hill, 1999.

Info-lines

Buckner, Marilyn. "Simulation and Role Play." No. 8412 (revised 1999).

Preziosi, Robert. "Icebreakers." No. 8911 (revised 1999).

Sharpe, Cat, ed. "10 Great Games and How to Use Them." No. 8411 (revised 1999).

Job Aid

Adapt-and-Play Guidelines

Use this step-by-step guide to adapt, play, and debrief a game that incorporates your own training objectives.

Step 1: Select Game

Adaptability	Topic and audience Number of players Training facilities	**Playability**	Fun to play User-friendly rules Fits allotted time

Step 2: Develop Game Content

Outcomes	Learning outcomes Demonstrated behaviors	**Input**	Information to be covered Question format

Step 3: Resource Supplies

Training	Prepared lecture Handouts or readings Overheads/visuals	**Audiovisual**	Flipchart, overhead projector Powerpoint or other software Video or audio recorder
Supplies	Paper and pencils Felt-tipped markers Masking tape, pins Index cards Dictionary/other resources	**Game Props**	Timer, noisemaker Game cards, game sheets Name cards or badges Ticket and prizes Accessories (dice, pawns, and so forth)

Step 4: Room Logistics

Players	Set up tables and chairs. Set out game materials.	**Instructor**	Set out handouts and references. Check out audiovisuals.

Step 5: Game Preliminaries

Set-Up	Form and seat teams (as required); distribute game materials. Introduce game: objective(s), rules of play, and time of play.

Step 6: Game Play

Start Play	Present game situation(s). Players take appropriate action. Alternate play.
End Play	Call time at end of round or game. Tally score. Announce winners (optional).

Step 7: Closure/Debriefing Questions

What?	What did you experience? How do you feel? What happened?
So What?	What learning happened? What one major idea or concept did you learn?
Now What?	How does this relate to real life? What can you take back to the work site?

Simulation and Role Play

Issue 8412

Simulation and Role Play

CONTRIBUTING AUTHOR

Marilyn Buckner, Ph.D.
National Training Systems, Inc.
P.O. Box 8436
Atlanta, GA 31106
Tel.: 404.875.1953
Fax: 404.875.0947

Editorial Staff for 8412

Editor
Madelyn R. Callahan

Revised 1999

Editor
Cat Sharpe

Contributing Editor
Ann Bruen

Production Design
Anne Morgan

Learning by Playing

We begin learning by pretending. Play is an essential learning experience in our development, for in our childhood imaginations, the real world exists for us with all its possibilities, but none of its risks. As adults, too, we learn well by incorporating the tools of these early learning experiences. Simulation and role play enable us to create a manageable version of our world where we can practice behaviors and correct our mistakes. Creating models of real-life situations prepares us to function more effectively in the real world.

A *simulation* is an intensive, interactive experience in which the content and roles assumed by participants are designed to reflect what people encounter in specific environments. In essence, a simulation is a simplified and contrived situation that contains enough illusion of reality to induce real-world-like responses by those participating in the exercise.

While simulations often have rules "for play," possess room for alternative strategic tactics, and can be fun, they are not, by definition, games. While games generally focus on one intent (that of winning), simulations stress the complex, real-life situations and array of goals that organizations attempt to implement on a daily basis. In addition, the simulated environment should offer opportunities for action and reflection that are not always inherent in a "pure play" environment.

In role playing, participants act out a particular situation or problem before the rest of the group. These activities can help accomplish a wide variety of training objectives, ranging from providing information to changing attitudes. For example, participants can work out handling a complaining customer or practice effective sales techniques.

As organizations respond to rapidly changing economic and technological environments, the need for effective time- and cost-efficient training becomes critical. This issue of *Info-line* will explain how to maximize the benefits of simulation with special attention to simulation games and role play.

Simulation

Simulations are not a new idea (see *A Brief History of Simulations* on the next page). The simulation (experiential learning method) creates an environment that requires participants to be involved in some type of personally meaningful activity, leading to a real sense of personal accomplishment or failure for the results obtained.

An understanding of how people learn is essential to the development of proper simulations. Employers tend to ask employees and potential employees for information that falls only within certain parameters—the "knowledge" category. They do this 80 to 90 percent of the time. While these kinds of questions are not bad, per se, using the same method for garnering our answers can be. Utilizing a higher order of questions requires more "brain power" and, therefore, a more elaborate and comprehensive mode of operational thought.

Luckily, there exist a variety of documented learning models that involve a number of avenues by which to pursue the quest for better employee and organization performance. One model suggests four states that are necessary for effecting behavioral, attitudinal, and knowledge change: concrete experience; observation and reflection; formation of abstract concepts and generalizations; and testing implications of concepts in new situations. Others suggest that learning should be integrative, focusing on learning from differences in content, point of view, and style.

Perhaps one of the best-known models is presented in detail in *Bloom's Taxonomy* (see sidebar for details). Bloom's Taxonomy requires participants to become involved in activities that enable them to apply prior knowledge and theory to the learning experience. When considering a simulation for company use, examine how each of Bloom's components fits with *your* objectives.

A Brief History of Simulations

Simulations have been used for education and development since ancient times. Wei-Hai originated the first war game simulations in China about 3000 BC. These games bore a vague similarity to the early 17th-century warfare game, chess. Soon these parlor exercises became "serious," as observed in the development of other elaborate war games in Germany during the 17th and 18th centuries.

Further development of these games took place during modern times, when many military officers trained with war games in the 1930s and 1940s came home to use their military training in managing civilian businesses. Some of the business game/war game evolution can be traced to the 1950s, when a number of games were developed for organizations to use when they needed to provide training in decision making without the risk of delegating real responsibilities to novices.

Based on a new theory of education, which revolved around the learner instead of the instructor, the successes of war games and operations research techniques, and the development of high-speed computers, propelled the business gaming movement into the nation's business schools and corporate training and development operations. Today, numerous business games are in existence, and thousands of business executives have played them.

Adapted from "The Role of Management Games and Simulations in Education and Research," by Bernard Keys and Joseph Wolfe, Journal of Management, *volume 16, number 2 (1990).*

Simulations are based on the premise that effective training requires a balance of three essential factors:

Content: the dissemination of new ideas, principles, or concepts.

Experience: the opportunity to apply content in an experiential environment.

Feedback: on actions taken and the relationship between performance and the subsequent result.

The two most important steps to take before designing or implementing any simulation are:

1. Review your objectives (identify organization issues that need addressing).

2. Determine group needs.

Once you have reviewed your organization's issues and expectations, set your goals and give some thought to how you are going to achieve them. Before undertaking the time (which varies) and the expense (which also varies) to implement any simulation, however, you also should be aware of the following: Do you need to train better managers? Link organizational goals? Are your employees team-oriented? And, are all teams consciously aware that they are on the same side—making the most of the organization? For further ideas about linking goals within the organization, see the sidebar *Integrating Leadership Skills.*

Remember, there are variations within the audience. Simulations need to be tailored to your participants: Are they executive, middle management, or supervisory? Those models of behaviors promoting improved performance within *each organizational level* should be fully examined prior to making a simulation choice. What problem-solving and interpersonal behavior techniques are required for different job titles? For example, an improvement in executive performance (where the focus is more on organizational issues) may require a distinctly different simulation than one that is targeting a group of managers (whose jobs tend to focus on managing groups). Still another simulation would be appropriate for a group of supervisors, whose focus is most likely on individual issues.

The decision regarding what simulation to use should also be based on the whole picture of the current organization. What methods have been used before to improve or fix the current state of the organization? Have executive interviews taken place, asking what they would like their employees to do differently? Sometimes organizations will use a focus group to identify target individuals and ask them directly what skills they think they need to learn and how the learning experience should be positioned. Others have used more quantitative methods such as training needs analysis to gather data on specific issues. For further information on these topics, see the following *Info-line*s: No. 8502, "Be a Better Needs Analyst"; No. 9401, "Needs Assessment by Focus Group"; No. 9408, "Strategic Needs Analysis"; No. 9611, "Conducting a Mini Needs Assessment"; and No. 9713, "The Role of the Performance Needs Analyst."

Timing

Many of the popular simulations take two or three days to complete. In this fast-paced society, not many organizations have that kind of time to spare. The challenge for those designing a simulation is to find ways to collapse the learning experience into a more feasible time frame—perhaps, one or one-and-a-half days.

The Culture of Simulations

As one might imagine, not every simulation is suited to every organization. Often enough, however, a simulation can (and should be) adaptable to a variety of corporate climates and types of industry. Nonetheless, this does not necessarily translate when one is moving from one hemisphere to another, or even between different corporate cultures within the same country.

The rules of business conduct are not immutable. What is appropriate in Austin, Texas, may be deemed entirely inappropriate in Hokkaido, Japan.

Bloom's Taxonomy

In 1956, Benjamin Bloom headed a group of educational psychologists who developed a classification of levels of intellectual behavior important in learning. When you are choosing or designing simulations for your organization, take into account the following question categories as defined by Bloom:

Knowledge:
- remembering
- memorizing
- recognizing
- recalling identification
- recall of information (who, what, when, where, how?)

Comprehension:
- interpreting
- translating from one medium to another
- describing in one's own words
- organization and selection of facts and ideas

Application:
- problem solving
- applying information to produce some result
- use of facts, rules, and principles (How is…an example of…? How is…related to…? Why is…significant?)

Analysis:
- subdividing something to show how it is put together
- finding the underlying structure of a communication
- identifying motives

Synthesis (putting together):
- putting many parts together to make a new whole
- a professional activity referred to as design
- an open-ended process with more than one correct answer
- engineering design of a new product or process

Evaluation (judging):
- making a judgment about a solution, design, report, material
- may involve internal (best models) or external (environmental, legal, economic, sociological) criteria
- selection among designs for implementation
- evaluation of old systems for upgrade

Integrating Leadership Skills

Research shows that executive programs appear to be leading the trend in the use of simulations. Therefore, the introduction of leadership change skills, a primary goal of a leadership simulation, can serve to reinforce all other organizational goals. Here is a list of subgoals to consider when you want to link and integrate leadership skills with other goals within the organization:

● To increase insight into individual development plans for training, promotions.

● To diagnose and develop leadership abilities.

● To develop strategy behaviors not currently present in the organization (for example, teams, process redesign).

● To increase knowledge of the key success factors of a business, and how these relate to the environment.

● To reveal the characteristics of an organization's existing culture for greater understanding, or to change it.

● To introduce new managers to the dynamics of the management process.

● To illustrate concepts such as agenda setting, networking, and influencing upward.

● To understand and appreciate the benefits of teamwork and collaboration in the problem-solving process.

● To understand the linkages between performance and organizational outcomes.

● To diagnose the skills of managers.

● To learn how to think more strategically.

What one does, wears, or says may be fine in advertising, but entirely misconstrued in the more structured world of banking. In simulations, much like the real world, people behave according to their cultures and values. Since each simulation is a little "world" composed at will, consider carefully the culture you are dealing with before choosing your simulation.

Designing Simulations

When designing your simulation, first select and define your themes and goals. Then begin the design process by choosing techniques, identifying your scoring and feedback procedures, and finally, defining your debrief process (see the *Designing Simulations Model* opposite).

Choosing a Simulation

The choice of a simulation involves clearly defining one's goals. Determine the key issues within the organization. What is the context? Is there a major cultural change? A total organizational transformation needed in order to become a smoothly run organization? A need to learn a new skill? Does the organization want to introduce new leadership behaviors for a new culture and, therefore, make the leadership goals more participative? Or should the leadership model be limited to that of a strategic planning focus?

Decide if the simulation should be assessment oriented—that is, focused on giving feedback to the employees on their leadership skills. Or should it be more developmental in its approach, focusing on teaching the skills in a risk-free environment? Remember to link the simulation to a 360-degree feedback process so that employees can validate their skills sets against another objective source of feedback. (For more information, see *Info-line* No. 9508, "How to Build and Use a 360-Degree Feedback System.")

Finally, decide which model to use—a situational leadership model or a change leadership model. The situational leadership model concentrates heavily on the supervisory skills of balancing task and relationship behaviors, while on the whole, the change leadership model focuses more on the organization and change within it.

Useful Techniques

There are a number of commonly used techniques to choose from, depending on the goals you have established for your simulation.

■ *In-Basket Exercises*
Similar to what can be found on every manager's desk, the in-basket holds massive amounts of information identifying problems or decisions that need to be made.

■ *Role Play Situations*
In contrast to the in-baskets, which attempt to uncover analytical and decision-making skills, role plays are most effective for illustrating participants' interpersonal skills. They are particularly useful in leadership simulations.

■ *Small Group Discussions*
Key to complex simulation design, this technique enables group members to learn from what they have just experienced. The simulation can include such areas as analyzing strategic, financial, and marketing situations, or discussing the restructuring of the organization.

■ *The "Wildcard"*
These are random events thrown into the simulation to see how people will react and respond to an "abnormal" state of affairs. A wildcard can be anything from a sudden loss of capital, normally counted upon, to a seemingly sudden threat of a hostile takeover or loss of a key employee.

Designing Simulations Model

Here are specific steps you should follow when designing your simulations.

Selection/Defining		**Designing**		
1 **What**	**2** **How/Process**	**3** **Techniques**	**4** **Score/Feedback**	**5** **Debrief**
• Themes/Issues • Context • Audience	• Goals • Learnings • Theory/Models	• In-Baskets • Role Plays • Discussions • Physical Activity • Cases (One vs. Mini) • Computer	• Reports • Presentations • Self-Evaluations • Observers	• Who • What • How • Amount

Copyright ©1996 Marilyn Buckner and Lynn Slavenski.

Scoring and Feedback Procedures

If you are using an assessment approach to simulation design, choose some method of testing to provide feedback. This method of scoring is simplest when judging financial or quantitative models, in which you can ask multiple-choice questions. When dealing with qualitative or leadership simulations, however, use a scoring of possible right answers, similar to the grading of essays by a college professor. When using presentations, have other teams score their content and delivery. The important thing is to have individuals self-score by giving them "typical" right answers and having them compare their own answers. This provides them with a checklist of events, which they can use when returning to their workplace.

If you are using a purely developmental approach to simulation design, you probably would not need a scoring component, and a debrief discussion would suffice.

Debriefing

Debriefing the participants of a simulation helps reinforce the original goals and can ensure that participants focus on implementing their new knowledge in a variety of real-life situations. Furthermore, the debrief provides trainers with a measurement of their effectiveness in teaching these new concepts, thereby offering opportunities for future improvement in the design, practice, and outcome of simulation implementation.

As debriefing may very well be one of the most important components of a successful simulation, a multistage approach is recommended, with each stage identified by a specific question. While there are several effective approaches you can take (ranging from asking participants to discuss their experiences with one another, to administering a carefully construction questionnaire), the main component of the debrief will consist of the following key questions:

- What happened?
- Why did it happen?
- How will you apply this in the future?

When considering the "how" of the debrief, decide whether it will be more effective or convenient to perform it in small or large groups. If your simulation is of a fairly complex nature, is delivered to a large group, or has used more than one facilitator, then the small group approach may be best.

Review both the content of the simulation and its outcomes. Were the rules of the simulation explained well enough that the participants "got" its meaning? For example, if your simulation was supposed to serve the purpose of team building, did its design fully promote that aspect, or was it so competitive that the participants became overwhelmed with the need to win?

The "how" component of the debrief can and should consist of a variety of approaches. While the final outcome of the simulated environment itself may seem of extreme importance to the participants (whose focus may have been more on competition amongst themselves than on the teamwork that needs to occur for an organization to run at optimum efficiency), the facilitator's role should encourage participants to review the simulation as an entire, ongoing process, rather than a series of discrete events occurring in a vacuum. Participants should be coached to reflect on *how* outcomes occurred, examining the roles they play in determining those outcomes.

Consider carefully how much time to devote to the debrief. Often, it is one of the most neglected aspects of the process. Remember that whatever the amount of time you choose to spend, the action or reflection process of the simulation is absolutely essential.

Drawbacks

One obvious shortcoming of using a simulation is that although a good simulation is similar to, it is not the same as, reality. Like all knowledge, the simulation model is culture conditioned and contextual, so the value depends on the context in which it is used. One must be ever-vigilant in using the simulation *critically*, not as a pure representation of reality. The experience of a simulation may be best used as inspiration for the *critical examination* of one's own business. A simulation is only as good as the thought and follow-up devoted to it.

The amount of resources required to conduct simulations is another possible drawback. They take longer and demand more of participants than other teaching techniques. The potentially positive outcomes of utilizing simulations can far outweigh their possible drawbacks, however, as long as those who are implementing the simulation approach it in an organized and well-considered manner.

Multimedia Simulations

Noting that content, experience, and feedback are essential components of successful simulations, and that they must occur in a relatively specific milieu, many multimedia producers are creating programs that mirror a simulation for accessing the abundant, sophisticated (but sometimes hidden) business intelligence. Although most simulations are delivered via CD-ROM, Internet delivery or some combination of CD-ROMs and the Internet or intranet are becoming popular. For an overview of the organizational and learner benefits of these kinds of simulations, see *Benefits of Multimedia Training* at right.

Benefits of Multimedia Training

For the Organization

Reduces training delivery time by 30 to 50 percent.

Increases productivity through cross-training, efficient retraining, less time away from job.

Reduces training costs; once break-even point is reached, training is free.

Ensures every trainee reaches a level of mastery.

Reduces the need for a dedicated training facility.

Requires fewer trainers and subject matter experts.

Delivers standardized, consistent instruction.

Relates directly to job skills and performance through customized course materials.

For the Learner

Reduces learning time up to 50 percent.

Increases retention by 25 to 50 percent.

Evaluates existing knowledge to avoid unnecessary training.

Provides individualized, self-paced instruction.

Allows flexible time, place, and privacy for training.

Provides unlimited practice and remediation.

Delivers consistent, nonjudgmental instruction.

Relates directly to job skills and performance through customized course materials.

Courtesy of Electronic Learning Facilitators, Inc., as printed in Training & Development, *August 1998.*

Successful Simulations

Here are 10 secrets for creating successful training simulations. They represent lessons learned from hard-fought struggles to understand the elusive, often perverse human dynamics at work in simulation training. Taken in sequence, they can supply relatively safe passage through the tricky terrain of simulation design.

1. Don't Confuse Replication with Simulation.

The temptation in designing a simulation is to make a small-scale replica of some full-blown reality. But in "soft skills" training, the job of the designer is to look past the details to the essence of reality.

2. Choose the Right Subject to Simulate.

Some subjects lend themselves better to simulation training than others. A topic is more apt to be suitable for simulation if it embodies at least one of the following characteristics:

- Seeing the world through others people's eyes. The simulation can illuminate the threat posed by a competitor.

- Performing tasks simultaneously. In the real world, skills are often needed in clumps; a simulation can create an environment in which several tasks are completed at the same time.

- Performing under pressure. Simulations can create environments full of genuine but nonthreatening pressure, affording trainees opportunities to practice their skills under duress.

- Developing systems thinking. A simulation can put people inside a system, whereby they see firsthand how change to one component affects the others.

- Recognizing cognitive dissonance. Holding contradictory attitudes or beliefs without being aware of it is known as *cognitive dissonance*. Simulations can reveal these contradictions.

3. Develop a Design Plan.

In preparing to design a simulation, you must make two key planning decisions: design it alone (or use a design team); or employ a structured creative process (fly by the seat of your pants). Whatever you decide, you will need to fill the following positions:

- Principal designer, who has firsthand knowledge of training simulations (and, for a team, the commitment to lead).

- Subject matter expert, who has a thorough understanding of the subject to be simulated.

- Administrator, who sets and maintains the design schedule, oversees acquisition or production of materials, and schedules tests.

- Client or representative, who provides a reality check as the project develops (in an oversight capacity only).

A well-defined creative program should make use of these suggestions: avoid premature closure of ideas; get outside a problem and look at it from different angles; and give your subconscious a chance to work on the problem.

4. Ensure Trainees Take Responsibility for Actions.

Whenever trainees disavow responsibility for their behavior during the simulation, their motivation to learn from the experience evaporates. When you design your simulation, watch out for these guaranteed responsibility evaders:

- Pretending. Design all roles in simulation so trainees must be themselves.

- Using competition for its own sake. If competition is not a factor in the real-world situation you are simulating, leave it out.

- Giving inappropriate value to chance. Limit chance to events that actually occur randomly in the real world.

5. Use Symbols to Deal with Emotional Ideas.

Occasionally a simulation focuses on an emotionally charged issue that threatens to overpower the learning experience. Avoid participants' assuming stereotypical roles by assigning each group names that represent an abstract concept—for example, Circles, Squares, and Triangles, with the Squares having power over the other groups.

6. Don't Play Games with Trainees.

If the odds are going to be stacked in favor of one group, have the facilitator reveal that at the start, so that trainees don't feel manipulated. Do not trivialize the experience by using cute names like the "Yell and Holler Telephone Company" or "Caught in the Act Security Services."

7. Use Nontrainees to Add Realism.

When appropriate, using people who have no stake in the outcome of the simulation can add real-world authenticity to the training experience.

8. Develop an Appropriate Assessment Model.

Quantitative models for assessing trainee performance may be appropriate for quantitative simulations—those dealing with financial or other formulaic disciplines—but for most qualitative simulations they are not suitable.

9. Alpha Test Your Simulation.

Alpha testing is a design technique for evaluating the basic assumptions of the simulation, its overall structure, and the logic of its progression. If problems surface, be prepared to reinvent the whole simulation if necessary.

10. Set Your Own Standards for Success.

When you spell out the purpose and goals of your simulation at the beginning of the design process, you are defining standards by which to judge its ultimate success. Don't lose sight of those standards as your project nears completion.

Adapted from "10 Secrets of Successful Simulations," by R. Garry Shirts, Training, *October 1992.*

When deciding whether or not to use multimedia simulations, trainers need to address the following issues:

Content: Does the material lend itself to media presentation; does it need frequent revision?

Audience: Where are the learners; how well do they read; are they comfortable with computers?

Environment: Is there access to computers; what kind of computers; are they part of a local area network?

Implementation: Will learners have time to study; how will progress be measured and recorded; is there enough hardware available?

Multimedia products attempt to simulate a variety of real-world situations so convincingly that trainees make the same choices they would in actual situations. They also experience the real-world consequences of their decisions, through the use of unexpected emails, phone calls, organizational charts, memos, and actual interactions with persons represented in videos. A multimedia approach alone, however, is limited in simulating interpersonal situations that occur in a business climate. The nuances of human interaction skills and sensitivities are impossible to render adequately with video alone. Therefore, although multimedia simulations are useful in many areas, they lack the group interactions that live simulations offer.

Role Plays

Role play activities can help you accomplish a wide variety of training objectives. To get your point across with impact, make the right choices in selecting and carrying out the role play.

Always start with ideal physical surroundings. Choose a room that is large enough to accommodate multiple role playing comfortably (single role plays work well in any size room). The room should measure at least 25, but no more than 50 square feet per person. Avoid a room with stationary seating, like some classrooms or an auditorium. You will need an open space with movable furniture.

Avoid noisy locations that are open to distraction. No one should be able to enter the room, observe through the windows, or eavesdrop on the sessions. Restrict telephone or visitor interruptions. Try to find a location with adjacent breakout rooms, or use available partitions, blackboards, or large plants for privacy.

You can use role plays to accomplish many training goals, such as:

● maximize participation and stimulate thinking

● promote learning through imitation, observation, feedback, analysis, and conceptualization

● inform and train participants, evaluate their performance, and improve their skills

● test and practice new behaviors participants can use in their jobs

● develop skills for implementing solutions and decisions

● develop interpersonal and practical skills in areas such as counseling, interviewing, customer relations, effective selling, and conflict management

● experience and understand a variety of problem situations from others' points of view and learn how to empathize with persons being discriminated against

● generate feedback that will give participants insight into their behavior, help them understand how others view them, and encourage them to be sensitive to others

Types of Role Plays

The trainer has a variety of role-play techniques to choose from.

■ *Single Role Plays*

Volunteer players act out one role at a time before the group. For example, one participant plays a customer relations manager and another plays the role of complaining customer. The manager must demonstrate the most effective way of easing the customer's anger and handling their complaint.

Single role plays have the advantage of allowing the group to share the experience and, under the direction of the trainer, analyze different facets of human behavior and problem solving. But only one person is able to practice skills, and players may be embarrassed to perform in front of the group. Poor performance may invite negative criticism that can be difficult for the trainer to handle. Thus, single role plays should be used only after multiple role plays, or when the group has become comfortable and members trust one another.

■ *Role Rotation*

Volunteers take turns playing the same role. Using the example above, one person plays the role of the customer relations manager and another the angry customer. After one player finishes handling the complaint problem, the other takes over the role of manager and demonstrates his or her approach to the problem.

Because the role passes from one participant to another, players are not embarrassed as in single role plays. Role rotation also provides the advantage of a range of problem-solving techniques and promotes further analysis and discussion. In a large group, however, it can be too time consuming and runs the risk of losing the training focus.

■ *Multiple Role Plays*

Small teams perform role plays simultaneously. Everyone has a chance to participate in a non-threatening format that reduces anxiety and embarrassment (see *Curing the Spotlight Syndrome* at right). Teams generate a broad variety of ideas and conclusions from the same data, and then discuss their outcomes, providing a variety of approaches to problem solving.

Multiple role plays have some disadvantages, however. Processing discussions may be limited; teams may be interested in discussing their individual outcomes but not those of other teams whom they have not observed. In addition, teams may be distracted by the other activity, and trainers may have scheduling difficulties because teams will begin and conclude enactments at varying times.

■ *Spontaneous Role Plays*

Without a planned structure or script, players improvise problem situations, agreeing on what to portray and assisting each other in developing roles and the situation as the exercise progresses. In this instance, trainers have more interaction with their players and help them develop feeling and insight during the enactment, but they must be skilled directors and work well with improvisations.

Deep involvement in the role play and analysis help trainees better understand the underlying reasons for various behaviors, but the involvement of only a few players leaves the rest of the group in the role of observers. In addition, players may feel anxious about performing in front of the group.

Other Scenarios

A number of additional role-play situations can be used effectively.

Soliloquy. A role player is given a script and describes his or her character in detail while the group observes. Players discuss their feelings and obtain support and useful feedback from the group.

Curing the Spotlight Syndrome

Anxiety can inhibit learning for the shy individual forced to the center of attention in a role play. Here are some ways to eliminate stage fright.

■ *Before*

Choose a quite, private setting for your role play activity. Introduce the activity by informing the group that each person will be playing a role during the session. Follow this with a comprehensive orientation of the activity that includes specific purposes, methods, and feedback guidelines. Explain that the role-playing environment is safe, without real-world consequences for mistakes.

■ *During*

Establish a supportive atmosphere that will encourage participation; use multiple role plays before single or rotational role plays. Allow participants to develop their own experiences for the role plays and processing guidelines. Choose role plays that could produce favorable experiences on the *first* try. Never start by appointing participants; ask for volunteers. Don't use role players who will be inhibited by each other's presence, for example, a boss and subordinate. If possible, rehearse, so the acting will be appropriate and natural.

■ *After*

Read aloud the rules for conducting discussion of single role plays. Establish feedback guidelines to ensure that comments will emphasize the positive aspects of the performance. Use *nondirective* or open-ended discussion methods that let trainees determine the course of the discussion and give them more opportunities to participate.

■ *Tips*

Use role plays late in the program when trainees are more comfortable with one another and more confident about taking risks. Use role play planning sheets before beginning the activity and self-evaluation sheets after it ends.

Reversal. Two role players switch roles and take on each other's characters. This method is useful for helping players understand another's point of view, and for illustrating how each character is perceived by the other and how that perception affects behavior.

Doubling. This is a variation of the soliloquy, in which one player responds to the other as their "inner voice," conscience, or auxiliary ego, articulating those silent thoughts and feelings the other cannot express without difficulty. This method is useful for helping players focus and clarify issues.

Mirror. One player reflects or mirrors another's role. This scenario can be used to engage players who resist demonstrating their ideas and helps them communicate without negative feedback.

Empty Chair. A player speaks openly to an empty chair that represents a person with whom he or she is experiencing communication problems. This technique gives trainees practice in overcoming difficulties addressing the person without worrying about their reaction.

Designing Role Plays

Design your role plays in three parts: preparation, enactment, and analysis. **Prepare** trainees by explaining role play objectives and reading role descriptions. Start **enactments** without dramatic buildup, and focus on learning desired skills and behaviors. **Analyze** participants' success with applying the new behaviors, not their acting ability. Permit trainees to demonstrate their alternative interpretations of roles.

Begin by writing simple role plays, using short sentences and a job-related vocabulary; then build up to complex ones. Define clear purposes and training objectives through the use of surveys, interviews, and questionnaires regarding training needs. Identify goals and problems related to these objectives, and design component roles and situations accordingly. Prepare instructions well in advance so that you can test them to ensure that participants will understand what they are to do and why. Design a discussion format of key issues.

Design Tips

● To ensure involvement, ask participants to discuss their problems handling specific situations and include these concerns in the role play scripts.

● Choose problems around which you can build a conflict situation easily, and focus on behaviors that require only two or three characters.

● Define role play characters by giving each one a name, age, personality, reputation, job title, strengths, weaknesses, and a perspective on the problem.

● Use gender-neutral names, so that any male or female participant can play the roles.

● Make the role play flexible. Characters and situations must not be so defined that players feel locked into the activity and unable to exercise their creativity.

● Don't pose too many conflicts, or problems that are beyond the players' control.

● Write cases that invite creative solutions; participants should be able to handle the problem in a variety of ways.

How to Conduct Role Plays

Arrange chairs in a circle so trainees can see one another easily. Solicit volunteers to play roles and describe the situation to the rest of the group. Distribute written role descriptions clearly explaining the characters' identity, feelings, motives, and situations, and allow sufficient time for players to adjust to their roles. Tell participants what to focus on and explain that they are portraying their *characters'* emotions, not their own.

Begin by stating the identity of the characters and briefly describing the initial actions. Intervene during a single role play only when the actor is having difficulty with the burden of illustrating the desired skill. Never intervene in multiple role play. In this case, role players and observers learn by finding their own solutions.

Enactment Tips

● Choose players who have the appropriate experience and technical backgrounds for their roles.

● To ensure productive learning experiences, control players' sidetracking, overacting, or irrelevant behaviors.

● Discourage participants from portraying their personal problems, and avoid using situations that may embarrass players.

● Be prepared to handle emotional problems or difficulties that may affect participants.

● If you are planning to videotape role plays, obtain consent from the group beforehand. Use a fixed camera to avoid distracting and inhibiting the players.

● Consult with players only in *private* showings of the tape, permitting them to critique their performances before the group analysis.

Follow up role plays with analysis so players can learn how others perceive their solutions to problems. Focus analysis on training objectives—for example, sharpening decision-making skills or communication skills. Have the players discuss their behaviors, reasons for acting as they did, and feelings about other role players' behaviors. Use printed sheets for observation, listing questions regarding verbal responses, nonverbal behavior, and players' interpretations of one another's behaviors and expressions. Following are some tips to help you:

● Never rush through a follow-up discussion.

● Aim to have trainees understand that there can be a variety of solutions to a problem.

● Have the individual or groups of players explain the reasons for their outcomes, and then open up a group discussion.

● Use a set of prepared questions that focus on behavioral issues or skills development—stressing techniques for effective performance—and ask participants how they can apply what they have learned to their jobs.

● Summarize the learning in printed handouts or present it orally.

Putting It All Together

Remember that simulations and role plays don't just happen. They are versatile teaching tools applicable to a variety of educational objectives, but they must be planned and carried out with care. Used properly, they can bring realism to concepts that have been learned in a more formal manner. Moreover, they can be a good technique for encouraging class camaraderie, measuring participant understanding, and stimulating trainees' interest in further inquiry.

References & Resources

Articles

Alexander, George, and Ron Lawrence. "Creating a Process Improvement Situation." *Journal for Quality and Participation,* October/November 1996, pp. 18-24.

Balli, Sandra J. "Oh No… Not Role Play Again!" *Training & Development,* February 1995, pp. 14-15.

Eline, Leanne. "A Virtual Reality Check for Manufacturers." *Technical Training,* January/February 1998, pp. 10-14.

Garhart, Casey. "Simulations: How Real Is Real Enough?" *Journal of Interactive Instruction Development,* Fall 1991, pp. 15-18.

Keys, Bernard, and Joseph Wolfe. "The Role of Management Games and Simulations in Education and Research." *Journal of Management,* volume 16, number 2 (1990), pp. 307-336.

Lierman, Bruce. "How to Develop a Training Simulation." *Training & Development,* February 1994, pp. 50-52.

Mattoon, Joseph S. "Modeling and Simulation: A Rationale for Implementing New Training Technologies." *Educational Technology,* July/August 1996, pp. 17-26.

McAteer, Peter F. "Simulations: Learning Tools for the 1990s." *Training & Development,* October 1991, pp. 19-22.

McBride, Mary, and Mike Uretsky. "Global Strategy: Making It Happen Through Simulation." *National Productivity Review,* Spring 1991, pp. 245-252.

Morag, Meir. "Free-Play Simulation in CBT." *Technical & Skills Training,* October 1995, pp. 20-23.

Parzinger, Thomas M. "A Valuable Training and Development Tool." *Bankers Magazine,* May/June 1992, pp. 75-80.

Reintzell, John F. "When Training Saves Lives." *Training & Development,* January 1997, pp. 41-42.

Salopek, Jennifer J. "Workstation Meets Playstation." *Training & Development,* August 1998, pp. 26-35.

Shirts, R. Garry. "10 Secrets of Successful Simulations." *Training,* October 1992, pp. 79-83.

Slack, Kim. "Training for the Real Thing." *Training & Development,* May 1993, pp. 79-89.

Smith, Vernita C. "Live It, Learn It." *Human Resource Executive,* June 1997, pp. 38-41.

Solomon, Charlene M. "Simulation Training Builds Teams Through Experience." *Personnel Journal,* June 1993, pp. 100-108.

Storts, Carol. "The Case for Industrial Simulation." *Technical & Skills Training,* November/December 1996, pp. 20-23.

Wager, Walter W., et al. "Simulations: Selection and Development." *Performance Improvement Quarterly,* volume 5, number 2 (1992), pp. 47-64.

Wook, Choi. "Designing Effective Scenarios for Computer-Based Instructional Simulations: Classification of Essential Features." *Educational Technology,* September/October 1997, pp. 13-21.

References & Resources

Books

Eitington, J. *The Winning Trainer.* Houston: Gulf, 1984.

Fripp, John. *Learning Through Simulations.* London: McGraw-Hill, 1993.

Jones, Ken. *Simulations: A Handbook for Teachers and Trainers.* London: Kogan Page, 1995.

Laird, D. "Tips on Using Role Plays." In *The Training & Development Sourcebook,* edited by L.S. Baird, et al. Amherst, MA: HRD Press, 1983.

Randall, J.S. "Methods of Teaching." In *The Training & Development Sourcebook,* edited by L.S. Baird, et al. Amherst, MA: HRD Press, 1983.

Shaw, M.E., et al. *Role Playing: A Practical Manual for Group Facilitators.* San Diego: University Associates, 1980.

Info-lines

Austin, Mary. "Needs Assessment by Focus Group." No. 9401 (revised 1998).

Callahan, Madelyn R., ed. "Be a Better Needs Analyst." No. 8502 (revised 1998).

Gupta, Kavita. "Conducting a Mini Needs Assessment." No. 9611 (revised 1999).

Kirrane, Diane. "The Role of the Performance Needs Analyst." No. 9713.

Shaver, Warren J. "How to Build and Use a 360-Degree Feedback System." No. 9508 (revised 1998).

Sparhawk, Sally. "Strategic Needs Analysis." No. 9408 (revised 1999).

Job Aid

Selecting a Simulation

The fit of a simulation to your organization is key. The following checklist can help you in finding the simulation that is right for you.

☐ The type of business context (for example, manufacturing, services, global or domestic, government, public or private sector).

☐ The organizational structure (for example, functional, product or matrix, team-based, decentralized, or cross-functional).

☐ Turbulent versus stable environment.

☐ The number of corporate versus divisional problem situations.

☐ The amount of individual versus group actions required.

☐ How much and what type of feedback required.

☐ The type of culture the participants have come from (for example, authority-based versus group consensus-based cultures).

☐ The mixture of individuals from different hierarchical levels.

☐ The amount of reading participants are required to prepare.

☐ The need for an "assessment of skills" approach without prior information versus a "development" approach, which provides information before the simulation to increase success in the exercise.

☐ Decide how important "playful" versus "serious" is.

☐ Length of time available.

☐ Decide if "physical-handling or movement" simulations are needed versus "knowledge based."

Coaching and Feedback

Issue 9006

Coaching and Feedback

AUTHOR

Barbara Darraugh

Revised 1997

Editor
Cat Sharpe

Associate Editor
Patrick McHugh

Designer
Steven M. Blackwood

Coaching and Feedback

The coaching process is central to performance management. Coaching refers to the managerial activity that creates, by communication alone, the climate, environment, and context that empowers individuals and teams to generate results. The root meaning of the verb "to coach" is "to convey a valued person from where he or she is to where he or she wants to be." The coach's job is to do this through encouragement and knowledge, rather than punishment and threats.

Both coaching and management have a common goal—the achievement of something through the actions of others. Both depend on the quality of communication between supervisors and employees. This issue of *Info-line* covers the coaching process and its most important component, feedback.

What Is Coaching?

Nancy Austin and Tom Peters in *A Passion for Excellence* define coaching as "face-to-face leadership that pulls together people with diverse backgrounds, talents, experiences, and interests; encourages them to step up to responsibility and continued achievement, and treats them as full-scale partners and contributors." It is the process used by managers to empower individual employees to put forth their best efforts, that is, to reach the limits of their abilities.

Good coaches share several characteristics. They are usually soft-spoken, articulate, humble, charming, witty, respectful of their team members or employees, direct, and dedicated to the project, company, or sport, and to its employees or players. They are task oriented—they focus on what it takes to achieve the best results or "win" the next game rather than what went wrong with the last. Most important, although they expect the best from their subordinates or players, good coaches don't punish employees or players for their errors.

These kinds of coaches also share some common practices:

■ *Clarity*
They are clear about the purpose of the activity. In order to produce the best work, the coach deals with the full spectrum of human concerns, issues, and possibilities.

■ *Ethics*
Coaches are ethical. They respect rules and procedures, but don't limit their thinking to what's allowed by the rules or procedures. Although all processes are governed by rules and procedures, those rules and procedures evolve over time.

■ *Commitment*
They are committed not just to the activity but to their employees and maintain a personal stake in the success and well being of each worker. They are also committed to preparation and practice.

■ *Accept No Limitations*
They do not recognize that there are limits to the performance of either an individual, team, or an organization.

■ *Continuous Communicators*
They are in continuous communication with their employees and other constituents—owners, the public, and their competition.

■ *Accept Responsibility*
They are personally responsible for the outcome of their activity, without robbing the workers or team members of their responsibility.

■ *Honesty*
They are honest, direct, and model the qualities they demand of their workers.

■ *Big Picture Awareness*
They are aware of the overall team picture and what is occurring in all aspects of the activity that has an impact on the team.

■ *Uncompromising*
They are uncompromising in their attention to detail.

■ *Learners and Teachers*
They are learners as well as teachers and coaches. Coaches recognize that they can learn from their players.

■ *Optimistic and Dependable*
They do what they say they will do and don't dwell on past failures.

Composite Coach

In addition to job-related knowledge, Donald Kirkpatrick writes in *How to Improve Performance Through Appraisal and Coaching*, a good coach also has the following skills and abilities:

- recruiting players and staff of assistants
- establishing goals and objectives
- planning and organization
- communication
- motivating each person as an individual
- teaching
- correcting and criticizing without causing resentment
- making decisions
- listening
- discipline
- measuring performance and progress toward goals
- finding the best way, which isn't always the coach's way
- operating effectively under stress

The ideal coach, according to Kirkpatrick, also has the following personal qualities:

- enthusiasm and dedication
- self-control

- patience
- impartiality
- integrity and honesty
- friendliness
- self-confidence
- humility
- perseverance
- genuine concern for players
- warmth
- optimism
- resourcefulness
- vision
- forcefulness
- consistency
- being part of the team
- open-mindedness
- willingness to accept criticism
- sense of humor
- flexibility
- love of the sport
- accepting success and failure as part of the game
- strong sense of moral values

In a business context, coaching is a comprehensive and distinctive way of relating to others. It provides supervisors with a way to develop themselves and others, produces results solely through communication, and is driven by commitment of both the manager and his or her subordinates to the goal.

Coaching in the workplace means that supervisors and their employees form a team or partnership. This team or partnership shares common interests:

- The supervisor and his or her employees gain if the team or partnership is a success.

- Both of their livelihoods depend on the effort's success.

- Both have to use resources efficiently.

- Both have to take risks in order to survive or prosper.

Coaching Skills and Behaviors

Successful coaches exhibit certain behaviors. In general, coaches support their employee's needs, create choices, seek commitment, and provide avenues of self-expression. Coaches achieve a critical balance between being supportive and caring and being clear and direct about what is expected of the employee. Coaching behaviors fall into three basic categories.

Supporting Behaviors

This behavior demonstrates caring, concern, and acceptance and leads to reduced tension and more open communications. The most significant supporting behaviors include the supervisor's:

- collaboration on solutions to problem areas

- help and assistance, where needed

- concern about the worker's needs and objectives

- empathy

- expression of the employee's value and his or her work contribution, including encouragement and recognition

- acceptance of responsibility

- allowing time for the employee to vent his or her feelings

Initiating Behaviors

These behaviors encourage the employee to discuss the work situation. A supervisor's initiating behaviors include:

- providing feedback and analysis of issues and concerns

- clarifying his or her goals, expectations, and requirements

- planning solutions and changes

- gaining employee commitment to solutions and changes

- outlining consequences of the employee's actions

Non-Supporting Behaviors

Supervisors exhibit non-supporting behavior when they are aggressive or exercise their power. They come across as being adversarial and hostile. Non-supporting behaviors include:

- doubt, anger, accusations

- threats, discipline, referral to higher levels of authority

- demonstrations of frustration

- one-way communications

- unwillingness to help

Selected Skills

Coaching is the "day-to-day, *hands-on* process of helping employees recognize opportunities to improve their performance and capabilities," write Charles D. Horth, Harry E. Wilkerson, and Robert Benfari in "The Manager's Role as Coach and Mentor." Horth, Wilkerson, and Benfari identify four areas in which coaches require considerable skill:

Observational Skills
The coach should be able to spot opportunities for an employee to expand his or her capabilities and improve performance. Once these opportunities are recognized, the coach should relate them to the employee.

Analytical Skills
Two types of analytical skills are called for: the ability to define opportunities for an employee to expand his or her capabilities and the ability to determine when coaching is required to improve performance.

Interviewing Skills
Coaches need to be able to ask the right questions and elicit the "right" responses. Skillful coaches use the following three methods:

1. Open-ended questions. These encourage the employee to think about the problem, to think about things he or she may not have considered previously to achieve an insight or to draw a conclusion.

2. Closed questions. These guide a discussion into a specific topic or area, or garner specific information when a discussion is too general.

3. Reflective questions. These restate in question form something the employee has said. They are used to prevent any misunderstandings.

Feedback Skills
How the supervisor presents his or her observations can cause the employee to become defensive, angry, or intimidated, or open to discussion about how to improve a difficult situation.

- no concern or disregard and indifference to an employee's needs and objectives

- creation of adverse circumstances—timing or circumstances surrounding discussion, leading to feelings of surprise, exposure, or frustration on the employee's part

Business Coaches

Coaching in a business setting usually is focused on improving performance. The manager needs to get the best effort and performance from his or her staff and should be trying to get the best effort and performance from each of his or her subordinates. Coaching, in the sense used here, means taking responsibility for a subordinate's output, behavior, and professional development. The manager and the subordinate become a team striving to get the best performance possible from each individual.

Traditionally, managers have treated the results or symptoms of poor performance rather than the cause. For example, a manager tries to gain results—improve an employee's performance—by offering a cash incentive in the form of either a bonus or a raise. The reason for the employee's non-performance may not be a lack of motivation, but a lack of knowledge. By offering this "carrot," the supervisor, despite his or her good intentions, may only frustrate the employee further. Determining the cause of poor performance is the most important aspect of coaching.

Roles for the Coach

Just as coaching is one of the roles that managers play, coaching itself comprises roles. Austin and Peters note that mentoring, counseling, and confronting are all parts of coaching. These are not distinct roles—there is a certain amount of overlap in that coaching is involved in training workers, usually in one-on-one situations.

Mentoring

This is the process by which an employee learns the culture of the organization. A more experienced, higher level manager decides to be an advocate for a new manager or employee who is perceived to have "star" potential. The mentor's job is to prepare the "star" for promotion or increased responsibility, to fine-tune already good skills or performance, broaden the prospect's exposure to other parts of the company, and to alert the manager's peers to a promising performer. The training given under the "mentoring" label is often political. A good mentor displays the following characteristics:

- treats all individuals as equals

- keeps an eye open for opportunities for his or her people to learn new jobs and accept new responsibilities

- makes corporate culture explicit and understandable and assists subordinates in understanding their power and limits

- discusses individual career plans and goals within the context of recent accomplishments

- is not threatened by the subordinate's exceptional ability or skill

- wants his or her subordinates to succeed

Coaching Tips

Steven J. Stowell, co-founder of the Center for Management and Organization Effectiveness, conducted a study of 26 coaches in a nationwide service organization to determine important coaching behaviors. The following are among his conclusions:

- Coaching sessions require 35 to 45 minutes and should focus on only one or two issues.

- Coaches can use as much as 60 percent of session time and not be dominating or over-controlling.

- Coaches should plan, prepare, and rehearse the coaching session.

- Employees who were hired by the coach are more likely to be successfully coached than those who were in place when the coach assumed his or her position.

- Employees were more than twice as willing to engage in coaching sessions than the coaches.

- Employees would rather discuss task- or job-related issues, while the coaches studied preferred to talk about the employee's personal style, skills, and communications style.

- Employees who the leader feels need coaching the most, are often the least interested in being coached.

For more information on mentoring, refer to *Info-line* No. 0004, "Mentoring."

Coaching

Coaching differs from mentoring in that it is the ability to gain optimal performance from all employees where as mentoring usually concentrates on just one individual. A further differentiation is that coaching encourages people to contribute and participate, while mentoring begins when an individual's outstanding characteristics begin to speak for themselves. Coaching is aimed at increasing an already satisfactory employee's performance by the regular communication by the boss as to specific advice on what to do and how to do it. Coaching is appropriate when a supervisor wants to do any of the following:

- develop teamwork
- encourage people to work to their limits
- express confidence and support
- provide recognition, credit, or reassurance
- celebrate team or individual accomplishment

For additional information on teams and motivation, see *Info-line*s No. 9108, "How to Motivate Employees"; No. 8701, "Team Building at its Best"; and No. 9212, "How to Build a Successful Team."

Counseling

Counseling tends to be problem oriented. An employee may come to the supervisor looking for advice on how to resolve a particular personal issue or performance problem. The supervisor may simply listen and outline options. The training given under the "counseling" label is often personal observations or a wider view than the employee may be able to develop on his or her own. Counseling is appropriate when an employee:

- is not performing as well as usual

- does not improve performance after educating and coaching

- asks for help to solve a personal problem

- is unsure about what to do next

- experiences failure or disappointment, especially after being given an increase in responsibility or a promotion

Confronting

Confronting is also problem oriented, but it is a step or two beyond counseling. This usually arises when the problem discussed during counseling sessions is not resolved to the supervisor's satisfaction. In confronting, the supervisor discusses with the employee the immediate results of continued poor performance and is usually disciplinary. Confronting is appropriate when any of the following occur:

- An employee can't or won't correct problem performance after counseling and ensuring that expected performance levels are understood.

- The employee is disrupting the team's performance or contributing to others' decisions to transfer or leave the company.

- The employee is unhappy or unable to do his or her job.

- The employee needs to know the consequences of continued poor performance.

Analyzing Performance Problems

The aim of the performance management process is to achieve optimal results. The aim of coaching is to ensure that each employee is putting forth his or her best efforts to achieve results. This process has two steps: analyzing performance problems and the discussion with the employee. These steps often overlap.

Supervisors need to be familiar enough with the employee's job to be able to pinpoint potential problems early in the performance management process. This is easier if standards have been preset and agreed upon by both the supervisor and the employee.

The Importance of Listening

Coaching is not just giving an employee a status report on his or her performance level. A good coach is also a good listener. He or she listens to pick up on key points that may need further explanation or probing. Supervisors should listen carefully and be careful to understand everything that is being said as well as what is *not* being said.

Arthur X. Deegan in *Coaching: A Management Skill for Improving Individual Performance* lists seven different listening responses that may encourage employees to continue talking. These responses show that the supervisor is attentive, interested, and willing to hear more.

Nodding. A gentle nod indicates that the supervisor has heard what was being said, grasped it, and is ready for the next part.

Casual remark. A small word or two—"I see," "That's interesting," or "Really"—also shows that the listener has heard what was said and is ready for more.

The pause. A silence of up to 30 seconds may encourage the speaker to continue his or her discourse. A pause without the supervisor's look of encouragement, however, may become awkward and make the subordinate feel ill at ease.

The echo. Repeating the subordinate's last two or three words will show him or her that the supervisor has been listening and signals that he or she is ready to hear more. Overuse of this technique, however, may cause the employee to feel he or she is being mimicked.

The mirror. This technique calls for paraphrasing the employee's discussion and should be done only during a natural pause in the conversation.

Hearing what is not said. Supervisors sometimes need a sixth sense to find out just what is on the subordinate's mind. These "unspokens" are often as important or more so than what the employee actually says. Supervisors need to develop the ability to listen for less-than-full commitment and interpret from what is said what the employee actually means.

During the analysis stage, the supervisor identifies the problem—the lack of achievement of a particular agreed-upon standard. This problem usually is the result of a particular behavior. For example, an employee is usually late with his or her weekly report. The supervisor must identify what is causing this chronic lateness. What is the employee doing wrong or failing to do right that is causing

the result? There are several areas the coach should examine.

■ **Role/Person Match**

Re-examine whether the person is right for the job.

■ **Task Clarity**

The employee needs to know what is expected of him or her in order to accomplish the task. "You can't expect a player to make the right moves if that player doesn't know what 'right moves' means!"

■ **Task Priority**

The employee needs to know those areas of his or her job that are most important. Supervisors telegraph their priorities by the questions they ask, what they worry about, get excited about, request reports on, use as the basis for promotions, or talk about in meetings.

■ **Competence**

Performance problems can be caused by a skill deficiency. Supervisors need to separate skill deficiency from "will deficiency." Could the employee do it if his or her life depended on it?

■ **Obstacles**

There may be real or imagined barriers that interfere with good performance. A printer, for example, cannot maintain high quality in his or her press runs if the press machinery needs maintenance.

■ **Reward for Failure**

Employees may perceive that they receive more reward for poor or average service—even if it is negative attention—than for good performance.

■ **Performance Feedback**

Employees need clear, rapid input on what and how they are doing. As former Dallas Cowboys coach Tom Landry said, "Find ways for players to measure what they can do, to measure what they can have confidence in—and what price they pay for success."

■ **Valid Outcomes**

Part of the coach's job is to find out what motivates employees. Rewards for excellent performance need to be based on what the employee values, rather than what his or her supervisor thinks would be a good reward.

During this data-collection stage, the supervisor may discover that the employee is away from his

Coaching Analysis: What Is Influencing Unsatisfactory Performance?

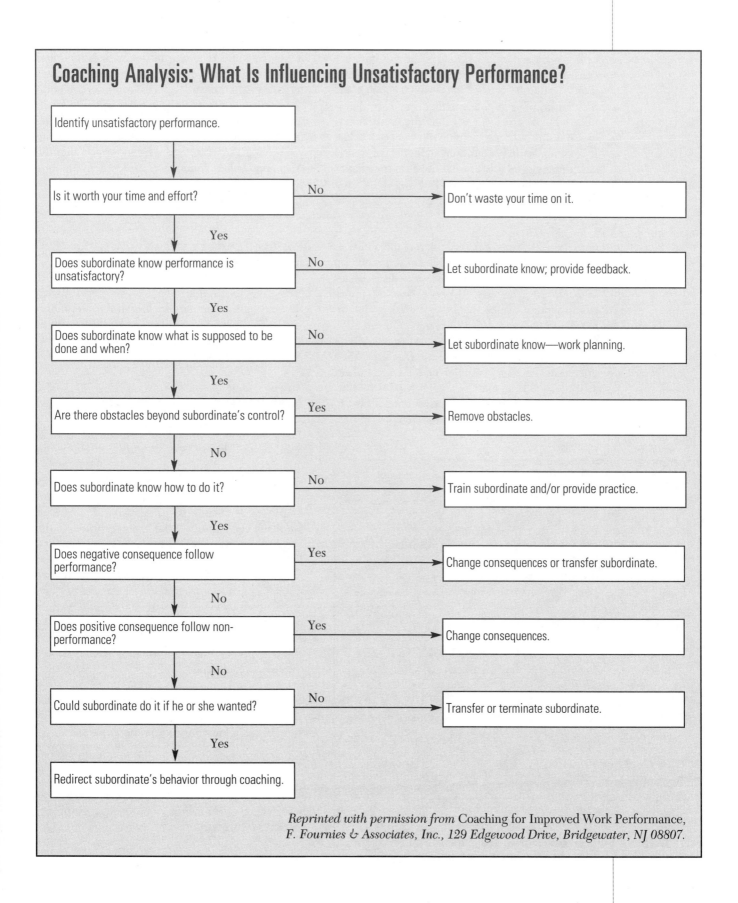

Identify unsatisfactory performance.

↓

Is it worth your time and effort? — No → Don't waste your time on it.

↓ Yes

Does subordinate know performance is unsatisfactory? — No → Let subordinate know; provide feedback.

↓ Yes

Does subordinate know what is supposed to be done and when? — No → Let subordinate know—work planning.

↓ Yes

Are there obstacles beyond subordinate's control? — Yes → Remove obstacles.

↓ No

Does subordinate know how to do it? — No → Train subordinate and/or provide practice.

↓ Yes

Does negative consequence follow performance? — Yes → Change consequences or transfer subordinate.

↓ No

Does positive consequence follow non-performance? — Yes → Change consequences.

↓ No

Could subordinate do it if he or she wanted? — No → Transfer or terminate subordinate.

↓ Yes

Redirect subordinate's behavior through coaching.

Reprinted with permission from Coaching for Improved Work Performance, *F. Fournies & Associates, Inc., 129 Edgewood Drive, Bridgewater, NJ 08807.*

or her work station a lot, that he or she spends a considerable amount of time on less important items, or that he or she takes extended lunch and rest breaks. The supervisor then needs to determine why the employee is exhibiting these behaviors and this often means interviewing the worker. It is extremely important that supervisors listen in a non-judgmental way to what the employee has to say. For additional reading on listening skills, refer to *Info-line* No. 8806, "Learning to Listen, Listening to Learn."

One "trick" of successful coaching is the ability to correct mistakes without causing resentment. In other words, successful coaches provide feedback in a "de-fused" manner. Through coaching, unsatisfactory performance is corrected while maintaining the employee's sense of dignity and integrity. One error should not call into question everything the employee has done or will do. One error does not make the person stupid, clumsy, or bad. An attitude, while it may be difficult to live with, should be tolerated if the person contributes to the best of his or her ability to the task.

Feedback Skills

Feedback, like most supervisory skills, is an acquired behavior. Doug Steward, in *The Power of People Skills*, provides the following suggestions for improving a supervisor's feedback skills:

Give feedback directly. Employees who receive a boss's praise through a third party often regard the praise suspiciously and, therefore, don't act on it. As a result, the employee may become insecure and distrustful.

Deliver feedback immediately. Give feedback as soon as possible after the event. Don't save feedback—whether good or bad—for the performance appraisal interview.

Be specific. Vague or generalized feedback never leads to improved performance.

Give feedback honestly. Feedback should only be given concerning behavior that the employee has some control over. Remember that employees can "see through" superficial or condescending feedback.

Distribute feedback equally. The Leave Alone, Zap You (LAZY) model of feedback is ineffective. Under this model, employees receive no feedback until they do something wrong.

Feedback

The giving and receiving of feedback is the heart of coaching. Since coaches view their subordinates as partners in the work effort, clear, effective communication is essential. This often requires a balanced discussion of the work situation in which the supervisor provides understanding all the while preserving the employee's freedom and dignity. This approach is generally considered a "supportive" approach.

There are two types of feedback:

Positive feedback indicates that performance meets or exceeds the supervisor's expectations.

Negative feedback indicates that performance does not meet expectations. Constructive criticism is designed to bring below-par performance up to standard without alienating the employee or creating other performance problems.

Positive Praise

Many supervisors operate under the "no news is good news" theory. Unless an employee hears otherwise, he or she is supposed to assume that everything is going well. Unfortunately, this approach is rarely successful. Even when an employee is doing exceptionally well, a lack of feedback can foster a "who cares" attitude in the employee toward his or her job. A supervisor's failure to praise or otherwise reward behavior that deserves praise will eventually result in the employee's failure to perform at satisfactory levels. An employee deserves some recognition when he or she does any of the following:

- exceeds his or her performance standards by a noticeable degree

- assists other workers in meeting their standards

- volunteers for a difficult or unpopular job

- when he or she has been consistently good over a long period of time

- offers suggestions on ways to improve procedures or product quality

- makes an effort to improve

Effective praise, when communicated sincerely and clearly, acknowledges the employee's commitment and effort. It also reflects the supervisor's and upper management's appreciation. To be truly effective, praise should be given as soon after the exceptional performance as possible.

Constructive Criticism

Negative feedback or criticizing an employee when his or her performance is not up to standards is often an unpleasant and dissatisfying experience for both the supervisor and employee. Unless handled well, negative feedback can make an employee hostile, angry, and generally non-cooperative. Constructive criticism attempts to correct problem behavior without alienating the employee.

Use the following guidelines for constructive criticism:

1. Make sure it is motivated by an honest attempt to help both the employee and the organization. Constructive criticism is not an attempt to hurt, punish, or humiliate the employee.

2. Ensure that is it based on dialogue, not monologue. Talk with the employee, not at the employee. He or she often has more information about the factors affecting his or her job than the supervisor does.

3. Conduct it at a time and place when and where the employee is prepared to receive it. Setting the stage for criticism will increase the chances of its acceptance.

4. Make sure it results in a consensus about the problem. One outcome of feedback is gaining the employee's agreement that a problem exists and on possible solutions.

5. Focus on behavior and performance, not personalities. Feedback is more effective when it focuses on what the employee did, rather than on who he or she is.

6. Offer specific suggestions for improvement. The employee should leave the session knowing what he or she needs to do to improve his or her performance.

7. Conclude with a specific agreement. The supervisor and the employee should agree on what will change, when it will change, and the consequences of not changing.

After the coaching session, the supervisor must show his or her interest in the employee by following up the discussion. Check back with the worker to see whether the problem behavior has stopped, and praise the employee for his or her improved performance.

The Ten Commandments of Feedback

Excellent feedback preserves an individual's dignity and integrity while allowing for improvement in his or her behavior. Bob Wood and Andrew Scott in "The Gentle Art of Feedback" offer the following ten suggestions for giving feedback.

1. Offer feedback on observed behavior, not on any perceived attitudes.

2. Offer a description of what you saw and how you felt, rather than a judgment.

3. Focus on behavior that can be changed.

4. Choose those aspects of job performance that are most important and limit comments to those.

5. Ask questions rather than make statements.

6. Set the ground rules in advance.

7. Comment on the things that an employee did well, as well as areas for improvement.

8. Relate all your feedback to specific items of behavior; don't make statements about general feelings or impressions.

9. Observe personal limits; don't give too much feedback at once.

10. Before offering any feedback, consider its value to the employee.

References & Resources

Articles

Banning, Larry K. "Executive Counsel." *Human Resource Executive,* January 1997, pp. 46-49.

Bivens, Becky. "Coaching for Results." *Journal for Quality & Participation,* June 1996, pp. 50-53.

Campbell, Robert B., and Lynne Moses Garfinkel. "Strategies for Success in Measuring Performance." *HRMagazine,* June 1996, pp. 98-104.

Capozzoli, Thomas. "Developing Productive Employees." *Supervision,* October 1993, pp. 16-17.

Caudron, Shari. "Hire A Coach?" *Industry Week,* October 21, 1996, pp. 87-91.

Corcoran, Kevin J. "The Power of Sales Coaching." *Training & Development,* December 1994, pp. 28-32.

Darling, Marilyn J. "Coaching People Through Difficult Times." *HRMagazine,* November 1994, pp. 70-73.

Fowler, Alan. "How to Provide Effective Feedback." *People Management,* July 11, 1996, pp. 44-45.

Frankel, Louis P., and Karen L. Otazo. "Employee Coaching: The Way to Gain Commitment, Not Just Compliance." *Employment Relations Today,* Autumn 1992, pp. 311-320.

Graham, Steven, et al. "Manager Coaching Skills: What Makes a Good Coach?" *Performance Improvement Quarterly,* volume 7, number 2, (1994), pp. 81-94.

Gunn, Erik. "Mentoring: The Democratic Version." *Training,* August 1995, pp. 64-67.

Hequet, Marc. "Giving Good Feedback." *Training,* September 1994, pp. 72-77.

"How to Provide Effective Feedback." *People Management,* July 11, 1996, pp. 44-45.

Howell, Kate, and Esther Cameron. "The Benefits of an Outsider's Opinion." *People Management,* August 8, 1996, pp. 28-30.

Kennedy, Marilyn Moats. "Good Coach, Bad Coach." *Across the Board,* September 1994, pp. 11-12.

Koonce, Richard. "One on One." *Training & Development,* February 1994, pp. 34-40.

Lawson, Karen. "First You Train, Then You Coach." *Bottomline,* May/June 1992, pp. 34-35.

Leeds, Dorothy. "Training One-on-One." *Training & Development,* September 1996, pp. 42-44.

Longenecker, Clinten O., and Gary Pinkel. "Coaching to Win at Work." *Manage,* February 1997, pp. 19-21.

Lucas, Robert William. "Performance Coaching: Now and for the Future." *HR Focus,* January 1994, p. 13.

Ludeman, Kate. "To Fill the Feedback Void." *Training & Development,* August 1995, pp. 38-41.

Madzar, Svjetlana. "Feedback Seeking Behavior: A Review of the Literature and Implications for HRD Practitioners." *Human Resource Development Quarterly,* Winter 1995, pp. 337-349.

Marchetti, Michele. "Pepsi's New Generation of Employee Feedback." *Sales & Marketing Management,* August 1996, pp. 38-39.

Marsh, Linda. "Good Manager: Good Coach? — What is Needed for Effective Coaching?" *Industrial & Commercial Training,* volume 24, number 9, (1992), pp. 3-8.

Martocchio, Joseph J., and James Dulebohn. "Performance Feedback Effects in Training: The Role of Perceived Controllability." *Personnel Psychology,* Summer 1994, pp. 357-373.

References & Resources

McDermott, Lynda. "Wanted: Chief Executive Coach." *Training & Development,* May 1996, pp. 67-70.

Monoky, John F. "Mastering the Coaching Call." *Industrial Distribution,* June 1996, p. 112.

Mullins, Brenda, and Bill Mullins. "Coaching Winners." *Canadian Insurance,* January 1994, p. 34.

Nakache, Patricia. "Can You Handle the Truth About Your Career?" *Fortune,* July 1997, p. 208.

Rancourt, Karen. "Real-time Coaching Boosts Performance." *Training & Development,* April 1995, pp. 53-56.

Rosenberg, DeAnne. "Coaching Without Criticizing." *Executive Excellence,* August 1992, pp. 14-15.

Tyler, Kathryn. "Careful Criticism Brings Better Performance." *HR Magazine,* April 1997, pp. 57-62.

Waldroop, James, and Timothy Butler. "The Executive as Coach." *Harvard Business Review,* November/December 1996, pp. 111-117.

Witherspoon, Robert, et al. "Coaching as a Collaboration." *Training & Development,* March 1996, pp. 14-16.

Zemke, Ron. "The Corporate Coach." *Training,* December 1996, pp. 24-28.

Books

Finnerty, Madeline F., and Robert L. Craig, eds. *The ASTD Training and Development Handbook: A Guide to Human Resource Development.* New York: McGraw-Hill, 1996.

Fournies, Ferdinand F. *Coaching for Improved Work Performance.* New York: Van Nostrand Reinhold, 1978.

Kinlaw, Dennis C. *The ASTD Trainer's Sourcebook: Coaching.* New York: McGraw-Hill, 1996.

Maurer, Rick. *Feedback Toolkit: 16 Tools for Better Communication in the Workplace.* Portland, OR: Productivity Press, 1994.

Parry, Scott B. *From Managing to Empowering: An Action Guide to Developing Winning Facilitation Skills.* White Plains, NY: Quality Resources, 1994.

Peters, Tom, and Nancy Austin. *A Passion for Excellence.* New York: Random House, 1984.

Shula, Don, and Ken Blanchard. *Everyone's a Coach: You Can Inspire Anyone to be a Winner.* New York: HarperBusiness, 1995.

Sussman, Lyle, et al. *Constructive Feedback.* Homewood, IL: Dow Jones-Irwin, 1984.

Whitmore, John. *Coaching for Performance: A Practical Guide to Growing Your Own Skills.* San Diego: Pfeiffer, 1994.

Info-lines

Butruille, Susan, ed. "Basic Training for Trainers." No. 8808 (revised 1998).

Callahan, Madelyn R., ed. "10 Great Games and How to Use Them." No. 8411 (revised 1999).

Cohen, Stephen L. "Build a Strong Assessment Center." No. 8512.

Darraugh, Barbara, ed. "How to Facilitate." No. 9406 (revised 1999).

———. "How to Motivate Employees." No. 9108 (revised 1997).

———. "Negotiating Skills." No. 9001.

Eline, Leanne. "How to Prepare and Use Effective Visual Aids." No. 8410 (revised 1997).

Job Aid

Coaching Checklist

Ferdinand Fournies in *Coaching for Improved Work Performance* details the following coaching steps:

1. Get agreement that a problem exists and on what the problem is.
2. Discuss solutions.
3. Agree to a plan of action.
4. Follow up on plan implementation.
5. Praise improvements or schedule more coaching.

Use the following checklist and areas for comments to guide you to more effective coaching:

☐ **Identify the problem.** Good coaching begins with separating the behavior from the person, and that, in turn, means identifying the cause rather than the effect. In some cases, it means listening to the employee to discover what obstacles stand in his or her way to optimum performance.

_____

☐ **Does the worker know that the problem exists?** Sometimes, performance problems exist because the individual worker or workers *think* their performance is acceptable. Another possibility is that, although the worker may know that he or she is not performing as expected, the deficiency itself is considered acceptable. These perceptions often result from too little feedback.

_____

☐ **Does the worker know what the supervisor's expectations are?** One reason workers don't perform up to a supervisor's expectations is that he or she does not know what those expectations are and, consequently, does not realize that a problem exists.

_____

☐ **Does the worker know how to meet the supervisor's expectations?** Even when a worker knows what the supervisor's expectations are, he or she may not know what he or she is supposed to do and when to do it.

_____

☐ **Are there obstacles outside the worker's control that are affecting the worker's performance?** Outside factors can have a direct effect on a worker's performance. Among these factors are equipment failure, late or incorrect reports or data, conflicting instructions, too many bosses, lack of materials or supplies.

_____

☐ **Does negative consequence follow good performance?** Unsatisfactory performance may occur because good performance is punished. This may be hard to recognize, and supervisors often have to take the worker's word for it. An example of a negative consequence is the secretary who has to accept another secretary's work because he or she finished his or her own tasks early.

_____

☐ **Does positive consequence follow poor performance?** Similar to the preceding item, the secretary who has part of his or her work taken away is getting rewarded for not getting his or her work accomplished.

_____

☐ **Could the worker perform to standards if he or she wanted to?** If the answer to this question is "no," the employee should be terminated or transferred.

_____

   The material appearing on this page is not covered by copyright and may be reproduced at will.